BUFFALO SOLDIERS

AFRICAN AMERICAN TROOPS IN THE US FORCES 1866–1945

OSPREY
PUBLISHING

BUFFALO SOLDIERS

AFRICAN AMERICAN TROOPS IN THE US FORCES 1866–1945

RON FIELD & ALEXANDER BIELAKOWSKI

First published in Great Britain in 2008 by Osprey Publishing,
Midland House, West Way, Botley, Oxford OX2 0PH, United Kingdom.
443 Park Avenue South, New York, NY 10016, USA.
Email: info@ospreypublishing.com

Previously published as Ron Field, Elite 107: *Buffalo Soldiers 1866–91*;
Ron Field, Elite 134: *Buffalo Soldiers 1892–1918*; and Alexander Bielakowski,
Elite 158: *African American Troops in World War II*.

A CIP catalog record for this book is available from the British Library

ISBN: 978 1 84603 343 8

Page layout by Myriam Bell Design, France
Index by Alan Thatcher
Typeset in Bembo and AT Quay Sans
Originated by United Graphic Pte Ltd., Singapore
Printed in China through Worldprint

08 09 10 11 12   10 9 8 7 6 5 4 3 2 1

For a catalog of all books published by Osprey please contact:

NORTH AMERICA
Osprey Direct, c/o Random House Distribution Center
400 Hahn Road, Westminster, MD 21157, USA
E-mail: uscustomerservice@ospreypublishing.com

ALL OTHER REGIONS
Osprey Direct, The Book Service Ltd, Distribution Centre, Colchester Road,
Frating Green, Colchester, Essex, CO7 7DW, UK
E-mail: customerservice@ospreypublishing.com

Osprey Publishing is supporting the Woodland Trust, the UK's leading woodland conservation charity,
by funding the dedication of trees.

www.ospreypublishing.com

Front cover: Left to right, top to bottom: Two troopers of the 9th Cavalry, late 19th century; African American
soldiers read letters on Saipan, 1944; AA crew Navy Cross winners, 1945; 15th NY National Guard, 1917

Editor's Note
The measurements in this book are provided in imperial only. For exact conversion to metric equivalents note:
feet to meters = multiply feet x 0.3058
yards to meters = multiply yards x 0.9114
miles to kilometers = multiply miles x 1.6093
pounds to kilograms = multiply pounds x 0.453

CONTENTS

Introduction – A birth of freedom   6
RON FIELD

Chronology   14

PART I: New Frontiers – Buffalo Soldiers 1866–91   20
RON FIELD

PART II: Buffalo Soldiers 1892–1941   90
RON FIELD

PART III: African American Troops in World War II   156
ALEXANDER BIELAKOWSKI

Conclusion – Integration during the Cold War   216
RON FIELD

Bibliography   221

Index   226

INTRODUCTION – A BIRTH OF FREEDOM

The success of the struggle for civil rights in America owes much to the courage and bravery of the African American soldier. During the years of Civil War from 1861 through 1865, when the American people stood at the crossroads of settling the issue of slavery, the black freedman and "contraband" (see below) proudly adopted the blue Union uniform and fought bravely at Island Mound, Port Hudson, and Battery Wagner. During the Indian Wars, when they earned the respect of the Native American, the "buffalo soldiers" of the Regular Army continued to serve with distinction in the hot deserts of the Southwest and the sub-zero snows of Dakota Territory. When the United States finally espoused a colonial empire and invaded Cuba in 1898, the black cavalry trooper was in the vanguard with Teddy Roosevelt's Rough Riders as they captured San Juan Hill. In 1917, they again shouldered arms and volunteered for service in their thousands during the Great War, although the few that saw combat were mostly attached to French divisions. In the face of continual prejudice and segregation during World War II, the black GI fought alongside the white GI in the Ardennes Forest during the Battle of the Bulge in 1944. When the Cold War finally erupted into open warfare in Korea in 1950, the black infantryman was among the first to stem the communist tide at Pusan. At every trial of arms facing the United States from 1861 through 1953, the African American soldier used his military prowess to gain deserved equality with his white comrade and, in so doing, eventually helped to achieve integration and full civil rights in America.

★ ★ ★

From the outset of the Civil War in 1861 until the Emancipation Proclamation of January 1, 1863, President Abraham Lincoln's administration

enforced an official policy prohibiting the enlistment of African Americans for military service. As a result, blacks were employed as laborers digging trenches and building fortifications for the Union army. They were also put to work on captured plantations to pick and process cotton in order to help with the Northern war effort. Many more were sent north to work in mills and factories, and on farms. However, several independent military organizations of African American troops were raised in 1862. By the fall of that year, the 1st, 2nd, and 3rd Louisiana Native Guard, and the 1st Louisiana Heavy Artillery (African Descent), had been formed in New Orleans, Louisiana. The 1st Kansas Colored Infantry, organized by Senator James H. Lane, participated in the action at Island Mound, Missouri, on October 27–29, 1862, and three companies of the 1st South Carolina Infantry (African Descent), formed at Port Royal, South Carolina, by Major-General David Hunter, were on coastal expeditions by November 1862.

As early as May 1861, some Army commanders challenged the policies of the Lincoln administration that prohibited interference with slave owners and their property, and instead employed fugitive slaves in support of federal military efforts. Major-General Benjamin Butler, commander of Fortress Monroe, Virginia, refused to return three fugitive slaves from a Confederate labor battalion to their owner. General Butler reasoned that since the owner considered them to be his property, and had taken up arms against the United States, this property was contraband of war. As such, these slaves were liable to confiscation and could be employed by the US military in its effort to suppress the rebellion. Coined by Butler, the term "contraband" became popular in the North, and eventually contrabands formed the nucleus of the United States Colored Troops.

The first official authorization to employ African Americans in federal service was the Second Confiscation and Militia Act of July 17, 1862. This permitted the president to "employ as many persons of African descent as he may deem necessary and proper for the suppression of this rebellion, and for this purpose he may organize and use them in such manner as he may judge best for the public welfare." As a result, blacks were used in a variety of capacities. In the trans-Mississippi West, they saw some combat, while in the Department of Tennessee and in the Deep South they were mainly assigned fatigue work. In the East, they served in both a combat and fatigue capacity.

Meanwhile, Lincoln did not officially authorize the use of blacks in combat until the issuance of the Emancipation Proclamation on January 1, 1863. Later that month, the governors of Rhode Island, Massachusetts, and Connecticut received permission to raise regiments of African American soldiers. Due to a lack of experience in organizing large numbers of black troops in the US Army, and resistance to arming them among some officers, early recruitment remained controversial and politically very sensitive. In order to expand recruitment of slave men in the Union-occupied South, Secretary of War Edwin M. Stanton dispatched General Daniel Ullmann to Louisiana, assigned General Edward A. Wild to North Carolina, and sent Adjutant-General Lorenzo Thomas to the upper Mississippi Valley. These officers were given broad authority for organizing regiments. They were to explain the administration's policy regarding African American soldiers and recruit white volunteers to raise and command them.

General Ullmann was charged with raising a black brigade in the Gulf region. This unit evolved from the Louisiana Native Guard into the Corps d'Afrique, which contained at its maximum by 1865 one regiment of cavalry, one of heavy artillery, five of engineers, and 25 of infantry. General Wild inaugurated black recruitment in the Union's tidewater North Carolina foothold and formed the 1st North Carolina Colored Volunteers, which expanded into the "African Brigade," composed of one regiment of heavy artillery and three of infantry by 1864.

The 4th US Colored Troops fought in the Richmond–Petersburg Campaign in 1864 and in Sherman's Carolinas Campaign in 1865. It lost a total of 292 men during its service, including three officers and 102 enlisted men killed or mortally wounded, and one officer and 186 enlisted men dead from disease. Retained in service at the end of the Civil War, this regiment was finally mustered out on May 4, 1866, by which time it was stationed at Fort Lincoln, northeast of Washington DC. Members of Company E, 4th USCT, pose for the camera together for the last time on November 17, 1865. (Library of Congress, LC-B817-7890)

The endeavors of General Thomas were particularly successful, and on May 22, 1863, the Bureau of Colored Troops was established to coordinate and organize regiments from all parts of the country. Created under War Department General Order No. 143, the bureau was responsible for handling "all matters relating to the organization of Colored Troops." The bureau was directly under the authority of the Adjutant-General's Office, and its procedures and rules were specific and strict. All African American regiments were now designated United States Colored Troops (USCT). In total, the USCT consisted of six regiments of cavalry; 12 of heavy artillery, plus one of light artillery and one independent battery; 141 of infantry, plus two pioneer companies and two brigade bands. Although they also served under the Bureau of Colored Troops, African American regiments that retained their state names consisted of the 54th and 55th Massachusetts Infantries (Colored), 5th Massachusetts Cavalry (Colored), 29th Connecticut Infantry (Colored), 6th and 7th Louisiana Infantries (African Descent), and 3rd Tennessee Infantry (African Descent). (Note: hereafter, for the sake of brevity, the suffix "Colored" borne by all African American units will usually be omitted.)

The bond forged between comrades is obvious in this quarter plate tintype of two unidentified African American soldiers proudly wearing the blue uniform with "eagle" buttons. (Library of Congress, LC-USZ62-132208)

Although Secretary of War Stanton wanted all officers of such units to be white, that policy was modified to allow African American chaplains and surgeons. By the end of the war, in addition to these appointments, there were 87 African American officers. Major Martin R. Delaney of the 104th USCT and Major Francis E. Dumas of the 74th USCT (formerly the 2nd Louisiana Native Guards) attained the highest rank among these officers.

A total of 178,892 African Americans served in the ranks of the USCT, under nearly 6,000 white officers and 87 black officers. Of the states in rebellion, Louisiana is credited with supplying the most volunteers at 24,052 ex-slaves and freedmen. Of the northern states, Pennsylvania provided the most at 8,612 freemen. The USCT fought in 39 major engagements and over 400 lesser ones. Sixteen African

American soldiers eventually received the Medal of Honor as a result of their service during the Civil War. As in other units, the death toll from disease was very high in the USCT. Deaths from disease and battle totaled approximately 37,000.

Formed unofficially at Fort Scott, Kansas, in August 1862, elements of the 1st Kansas Colored Infantry, commanded by Captain R. G. Ward, were the first African Americans to engage in combat with Confederate forces. Confronted by about 800 guerrilla cavalry near Island Mound in Bates County, Missouri, the black infantry were involved in skirmishing for three days during October 27–29, 1862. According to the after–battle report of Captain Ward, when a detachment of the 1st Kansas was charged by the Confederates: "I never saw a braver sight than that handful of brave men fighting 117 men who were all around and in amongst them. Not one surrendered or gave up a weapon." The Southern troops were eventually driven off with 18 killed and about 60 wounded, at the expense of eight dead and ten wounded in the ranks of the 1st Kansas, who were referred to by their captain as "heroes all, who deserve the lasting gratitude of all the friends of the cause and race."

Organized from members of the former Confederate Native Guards Regiment and composed exclusively of freemen of New Orleans, the 1st Louisiana Native Guard was mustered into federal service on September 27, 1862, and initially performed fatigue duty chopping wood, gathering supplies,

Eventually published as an engraving in *Harper's Weekly* on May 19, 1866, this drawing by Alfred Waud shows African American soldiers with their wives and families, having been mustered out at Little Rock, Arkansas. (Library of Congress, LC-USZC4-13286)

and digging earthworks. From January to May 1863, it also guarded the railway depots between Algiers (now part of New Orleans) and Brashear City (now called Morgan City). In mid 1863, this regiment, along with the 3rd Louisiana Native Guard, had an opportunity for combat and participated in the first assault of the Siege of Port Hudson on May 27, as well as the second assault on June 14. Both attacks were uncoordinated and the defenders easily turned them back, causing heavy Northern casualties. However, Andre Cailloux, a 43-year-old "free man of color" from New Orleans and captain of Company E, 1st Louisiana Native Guard, died heroically in the first assault. Although his body was left on the field of battle until the surrender of Port Hudson on July 9, 1863, Cailloux received a hero's funeral in New Orleans on July 29, and his death became a rallying cry for the recruitment of African American soldiers.

Equipped and trained at New Bedford, Massachusetts, the 54th Massachusetts was commanded by Colonel Robert Gould Shaw, the son of a Boston abolitionist, and included two sons of Frederick Douglass in its ranks. Eventually sent into the firing line on the South Carolina coast, this regiment also sought to prove that black soldiers could fight as well as white troops. Eight days after a combined Union army and navy action had captured the south end of Morris Island in Charleston Harbor on July 10, 1863, 624 officers and men of the 54th were ordered to lead an advance across a stretch of sandy beach to attack the Confederate strongpoint at Battery Wagner. With the capture of this fort, the port of Charleston, South Carolina, could be taken by Northern forces.

If the 54th Massachusetts had faltered in the face of the enemy cannon facing them across the open beach, the Union might have refused to put further black troops into battle. The brave attack of the 54th, however, supported by other troops, reached the Confederate earthworks under heavy gunfire, and one member of the regiment displayed extreme courage.

Twenty-three-year-old Sergeant William H. Carney reported that "the shot – grape, canister and hand grenades – came in showers, and the columns were leveled." The color-bearers of the four flags carried by the regiment were all killed or wounded during this action. Though wounded and covered in blood himself, Sergeant Carney picked up the national flag of his regiment and dragged it from the battlefield. For his bravery under fire, he became the first African American soldier to be awarded the Congressional Medal of Honor. Colonel Shaw and 41 other officers and men died and 61 others were wounded in the attack.

Although Battery Wagner remained uncaptured until July 15, 1863, the bravery displayed by the 54th Massachusetts further convinced the Lincoln Administration of the value of using black troops in a combat role during the

Civil War. A force of approximately 1,500 Confederate troops under Major-General Nathan Bedford Forrest stormed and captured a Union-built redoubt in Fort Pillow, Tennessee, on April 12, 1864. This post was defended by an African American garrison consisting of a detachment of the 2nd US Colored Light Artillery, commanded by Lieutenant Alexander Hunter, and a battalion of the 6th US Colored Heavy Artillery, under Major Lionel F. Booth, plus a white battalion of the 13th Tennessee Cavalry (Unionist) led by Major William F. Bradford. Of a 600-strong garrison, a total of approximately 264 men were killed or presumed dead, of which 182 were blacks. Many of the latter tried to surrender, but were shot in the head at point blank range. Often called the "Fort Pillow Massacre," it became one of the greatest atrocity stories of the Civil War. When charged with ruthless killing after the war, Forrest argued that the black soldiers were trying to escape. Racial animosity on the part of some men under his command, however, was an undeniable reason for the outcome.

The Confederacy used slaves unofficially as a labor force to build field fortifications from the beginning of the war. With a growing shortage of white soldiers, the use of blacks as a fighting force was seriously considered by some Confederate generals by 1863, but the idea was rejected in case it caused slave insurrection. On February 17, 1864, the government passed a law ordering all free blacks between the ages of 18 and 50 either to work in a military hospital or weapons factory, or to build field fortifications. Finally, with the Confederacy close to defeat in 1865, General Robert E. Lee, commander of the Confederate army, requested that blacks be armed to defend the South. On March 13, 1865, a desperate Confederate government tried to enlist 300,000 African Americans to be formed into all-black regiments and battalions. Several of the units formed at this time did see some combat during the last days of the Civil War. For example, as the Confederate army abandoned Richmond on April 3 of that year, elements of a black battalion organized by Majors James W. Pegram and Thomas P. Turner, and consisting of "persons of color, free and slave," went along with the wagon train headed south. A Southern soldier recalled: "I saw a wagon train guarded by Confederate negro soldiers. When within about one hundred yards of and in the rear of the wagon train, I observed some Union cavalry a short distance away on elevated ground forming to charge and the negro soldiers forming to meet the attack, which was met successfully… The cavalry charged again, and the negro soldiers surrendered."

The Civil War ended in April 1865, but the service of African American soldiers in the US forces did not. Although the numbers of African Americans in uniform dropped dramatically with the immediate end of hostilities, their Civil War record was only the beginning of a proud military history.

CHRONOLOGY

1861–65 AMERICAN CIVIL WAR

1862	July 17	Second Confiscation and Militia Act
	October 27–29	Island Mound, Missouri
1863	January 1	Emancipation Proclamation issued
	May 22	Bureau of Colored Troops established
	May 27 & June 14	Siege of Port Hudson
	July 10	Assault on Battery Wagner
1864	April 12	Fort Pillow massacre
1865	March 13	Confederacy arms slaves
1866	July 28	Act of Congress creates six Regular Army black regiments

1867–73 CAMPAIGN ON THE CENTRAL PLAINS

1867	August 2	Saline River
	August 21	Prairie Dog Creek
	September 15	Big Sandy Creek
1868	September 23–27	Arickaree Fork of the Republican River
	October 18	Beaver Creek
1871	May	10th Cavalry participates in arrest of Kiowa chiefs
1873	January	Arrest of Comancheros

1867–75 CAMPAIGN ON THE SOUTHERN PLAINS

1867	December 5	Eagle Springs
	December 26	Old Fort Lancaster
1868	September 14	Horse Head Hills
1869	June 7	Pecos River
1870	May 20	Kickapoo Springs

| 1872 | April | Howard's Well |
| | September 29 | North Fork of Red River |

1874–75 Red River War

1874	August 22	Anadarko
	October 24	Elk Creek
	November 8	McClellan Creek
1875	April 6	Cheyenne Agency

1875–81 CAMPAIGN IN WEST TEXAS

1875–77 Staked Plains and in the Texas "Panhandle"

| 1877 | July 10–August 14 | Nolan's "lost patrol" |

1876–90 NEW MEXICO, ARIZONA, & COLORADO

| 1877 | January 24 | Florida Mountains |

1876–78 Colfax County War in New Mexico

| 1877 | December 19 | San Elizario |

1877–78 Lincoln County War in New Mexico

| 1878 | July 19 | Lincoln |

1879 Ute Campaign in Colorado

| | October 1–5 | Milk Creek Canyon |

1879–81 Victorio Campaign in New Mexico

1879	September 18	Las Animas Canyon
1880	April 8	Hembrillo Canyon
	May 14	Old Fort Tularosa

	August 6	Rattlesnake Canyon
	September 1	Agua Chiquita Canyon
1881	August 12	Carrizo Canyon

1885–86 Geronimo Campaign in Arizona & Mexico

| 1886 | May 3 | Sierra Piñito |
| 1889 | May 11 | Cedar Springs |

1880–91 DAKOTA TERRITORY

1890–91 Wounded Knee Campaign

| 1890 | December 30 | Drexel Mission |

1894 COXEY'S REBELLION

1898 SPANISH-AMERICAN WAR

	June 24	Las Guásimas
	June 30	Tayabacoa
	July 1	San Juan Hill, El Caney, Kettle Hill
	July 25	Yauco

1899–1902 PHILIPPINE INSURRECTION

1899	October 6	Arayat
	November 18	O'Donnell
	December 7	Naguilian
1900	January 5	Camansi
	January 6–7	Iba
	July 4	Manacling
	December 17	Tagbac

| 1906 | July 24 | Tabon-Tabon |

1914–17 MEXICAN BORDER OPERATIONS

| | November 3–4 | Agua Prieta |
| | Dec 1914–Jan 1915 | Naco |

1916 Punitive Expedition

	April 1	Aguas Calientes
	April 12	Santa Cruz de Villegas
	June 21	Carrizal

1917–18 WORLD WAR I

1917	April 6	US declares war on Germany
	May 18	Selective Service Act
	June 15	Black officers begin training at Fort Des Moines
	November 29	All-black 92nd Infantry Division formed
1918	July 18–August 18	Butte de Mesnil
	August 30	Frapelle
	September 21	Binarsville
	September 26	Maison-en-Champagne
	September 28	Hill 188, Champagne Marne Sector
	September 29	Ardeuil & Sechault
	October 1	Monthois

1919–41 THE INTER-WAR YEARS

1920	June 4	Army Reorganization Act
1927		24th Infantry resurrected
1931		10th Cavalry squadrons separated
1939		47th and 48th Quartermaster Regiments formed

1940	August 1	1st Chemical Decontamination Company organized
	September 16	Selective Training and Service Act banned racial discrimination in conscription
	October	9th Cavalry assigned to 4th Brigade, 2nd Cavalry Division, first integrated division in US Army
1941	February 10	366th Infantry Regiment reactivated – it is the first all-black Regular Army unit officered only by African Americans
	March 19	99th Pursuit Squadron (Tuskegee Airmen) activated
	June 1	758th Tank Battalion activated
	June 25	Executive Order 8802, which prevents racial discrimination by corporations with US government defense contracts

1941–45 WORLD WAR II

1941	December 8	24th Infantry prepares for overseas deployment
	January	Benjamin O. Davis Sr, becomes first African American general officer in US history
1942	May 15	93rd Infantry Division reactivated
	June	99th Fighter Squadron enters combat in Mediterranean; USMC ordered to admit African Americans into its ranks
	October	US Navy creates first segregated construction battalions
	October 15	92nd Infantry Division reactivated
1943	February 25	2nd Cavalry Division reactivated
	June	African Americans integrate into the crew of a single Coast Guard cutter
	December 30	555th Parachute Infantry Company activated
1944	January	332nd Fighter Group deploys to Italy

	January–March	93rd Infantry Division deploys to Guadalcanal
	March–April	25th Infantry performs combat duties on Bougainville
	April	USS *Mason*, crewed entirely by African Americans, undergoes its shakedown cruise
	September 15	African American units land as part of 1st Marine Division on Peleliu
	October 10	761st Tank Battalion deploys to Normandy, the first African American armored unit in combat
	Dec 1944–Jan 1945	Battle of the Bulge
1945	March–June	2,000 African Americans are involved in the battle for Okinawa

1945–54 COLD WAR SERVICE

1946	February 27	Navy begins integration via Circular Letter 48-46
	June	Tuskegee Army Airfield closes
1947	October 29	*To Secure These Rights* published
1948	July 26	Executive Order 9981 signed by Truman
1950	January 16	Army begins integration via Special Regulations No. 600-629-1
	June 25	Korean War begins
	June 29	UN forces arrive in Korea
1951	July 26	US Army announces the integration of its Far East Command
1954	October 30	Last racially segregated unit in the US armed forces abolished

PART I

NEW FRONTIERS – BUFFALO SOLDIERS 1866–91

INTRODUCTION	22
ORGANIZATION	24
CAMPAIGNING ON THE CENTRAL PLAINS, 1867–73	32
CAMPAIGNING ON THE SOUTHERN PLAINS, 1867–75	42
CAMPAIGNING IN WEST TEXAS, 1875–81	55
CAMPAIGNING IN NEW MEXICO, ARIZONA, & COLORADO, 1876–90	59
DAKOTA TERRITORY, 1880–91	76
UNIFORMS	82
ARMS & EQUIPAGE	86

OPPOSITE
This young unidentified corporal, possibly of the 24th Infantry, wears an 1884-pattern blouse and 1872-pattern forage cap. He holds an M1873 Springfield rifle. (Herb Peck Jr collection)

INTRODUCTION

The African American soldier played a decisive role in the US Army on the Western Frontier during the period 1867 through 1891. Authorized by Congress in July 1866, the black soldiers of this period were organized into two cavalry and four infantry regiments, which were commanded by white officers, but whose enlisted personnel were African American. The mounted regiments were the 9th and 10th Cavalry, and the foot regiments were the 38th, 39th, 40th, and 41st Infantry (later consolidated into 24th and 25th Infantry). All were quickly nicknamed the "buffalo soldiers" by their Cheyenne and Comanche enemies. Until the early 1890s these troops constituted approximately 20 percent of all regular forces on active duty in the American West. By 1891, they had participated in approximately 130 actions against hostile Indians in Kansas, Indian Territory, Texas, New Mexico, Arizona, and Dakota Territory, as well as in Mexico. Twenty-two members of the various black regiments were awarded the Congressional Medal of Honor for extreme bravery and courage under fire. Countless others received commendations. Besides their battle record, they performed the everyday task of protecting settlers, travelers, and workers alike. They built roads and erected forts, plus put up thousands of miles of telegraph poles, all of which brought civilization to the American frontier.

A correspondent of the *Army & Navy Journal* left one of the best testimonials to the qualities of the buffalo soldiers. On campaign with the 9th Cavalry in New Mexico in 1881, he recalled:

> On the march, or in camp, they are cheerful and obedient. Their horses are well cared for, and in two companies I have seen but one man lounging in his saddle, and he had more white than black blood in his veins; no falling out of ranks, or watering at different times. If ordered on detached or dangerous

service, they never shirk it, and will ride hours without sleep, and apparently unfatigued. They do not appear to sleep, and in camp seem to be awake all night. If washed out, as I saw one company, they will change their camp in the middle of the night, laughing and cracking jokes. There is every evidence to show they will and do fight well. Their own as well as other officers and citizens who have fought with them, attest this fact.

This infantry sergeant wears service chevrons on his lower sleeves and has 1880-pattern, ¾in sterling silver, "Laidley" marksman's buttons on his collar. His belt and belt plate are part of the Model 1874 Palmer Brace system, minus the braces, which were abandoned after several years of field trials. (Herb Peck Jr Collection)

ORGANIZATION

In recognition of the contribution these "men of color" made to the Union victory, an Act of Congress, dated July 28, 1866, authorized the creation of six black Regular Army regiments as part of the additions to the "military peace establishment of the United States." General Philip Sheridan, commander of the Department of the Gulf, was authorized to raise the 9th Cavalry. A recruiting office was established in New Orleans, Louisiana, and later that year, a second office was opened in Louisville, Kentucky. This regiment was placed under Colonel Edward Hatch, who had commanded a division of Union cavalry during the Civil War and played a decisive role in the Union victory at Nashville in December 1864.

The organization of the 10th Cavalry began on September 21, 1866, at Fort Leavenworth, Kansas, and Benjamin H. Grierson was awarded the colonelcy of this regiment. A commander of Illinois cavalry in Tennessee, Louisiana, and Mississippi during the Civil War, Grierson earned a reputation as a fearlessly efficient officer when he led a 600-mile mounted raid into rebel territory in 1863. The 10th Cavalry took over a year to organize, but by July 1867 eight companies of enlisted men had been recruited within the Departments of Missouri, Arkansas, and the Platte.

These black cavalry regiments were organized on the general plan of white units, with the exception of one important feature. Each had a white regimental chaplain attached, whose duty included the instruction of the black enlisted men in reading and writing. Until that time, Army chaplains were not assigned to specific regiments. Furthermore, both the 9th and the 10th Cavalry were designated two veterinary surgeons each, whereas the white cavalry regiments had only one.

Regarding the foot soldiers, the 38th Infantry, commanded by Colonel William B. Hazen, was assembled at Jefferson Barracks, Missouri, during 1866

and marched across the plains to New Mexico. The 39th Infantry, under Colonel Joseph A. Mower, began recruiting at Alexandria, Louisiana. The 40th Infantry, under Colonel Nelson A. Miles, was organized in Washington DC, while recruits were gathered for the 41st Infantry in Louisiana, Alabama, and Ohio.

As part of the consolidation of the Army via General Orders No. 16, the reorganization of the four black infantry regiments began on March 10, 1869. The 39th Infantry, based in North Carolina, proceeded to New Orleans where it was amalgamated with the 40th Infantry to become the 25th Infantry, under the command of Colonel Mower, with headquarters at Jackson Barracks. On June 8, 1870, this regiment was assigned to posts throughout the Texas frontier. Meanwhile, the 38th Infantry was transferred to Fort McKavitt, Texas, where it was consolidated with the 41st Infantry to become the 24th Infantry, under Colonel Ranald S. Mackenzie. The 24th Infantry was to serve continuously in the heat and hostility of the Texas frontier until 1888, longer than any other infantry regiment of the Army.

"Captain Dodge's colored troopers to the rescue." This engraving, based on a drawing by Frederic Remington, depicts the moment when Captain Francis Dodge and 35 troopers of Company D, 9th Cavalry, arrived at Milk Creek on October 2, 1879, to relieve the command of Major T. T. Thornburgh, which had been attacked by Ute Indians for about four days. (Anne S. K. Brown Military Collection, Brown University Library)

ENLISTMENT

The period of enlistment for cavalry was five years, while the infantry served three years, with recruits for all regiments receiving $13 a month, plus "room, board, and clothing." Many of those who joined these new units had served in all-black regiments during the Civil War. Others were newly freed slaves or free blacks from the North. Almost 40 percent of those recruited into the 9th Cavalry had prior military service, mainly with the 116th US Colored Troops, stationed at Ringgold Barracks, Texas, in 1865. Although farmers

Relationships between the buffalo soldiers and white civilians were often strained. This Remington drawing depicts the shoot-out at San Angelo, Texas, following the murder of a member of the 10th Cavalry in 1881. (From Remington, *Done in the Open* [New York: P. F. Collier & Son, 1898, 1902])

and laborers constituted most of the remainder, about 10 percent were artisans or domestic servants. Recruiting officers of the 10th Cavalry were instructed to enlist "colored men sufficiently educated to fill the positions of noncommissioned officers [NCOs], clerks and mechanics," plus other "superior men" who would be a "credit to the regiment."

Regarding the original white officers appointed to the black regiments, all were required to have experienced two years' active field service in the Civil War with the rank of captain or above. Two-thirds of these were drawn from the volunteer regiments, while the remaining third were expected to have seen Regular Army service. Appointment to a black regiment was not popular, despite possibilities for greater rank and more rapid promotion.

The need for replacements for the black regiments was constant throughout the frontier wars, especially with such a short term of service in the infantry regiments. Some of the reorganized companies of the 24th Infantry were almost non-existent by 1870. According to a report in the *Army & Navy Journal*, Company E, stationed at Fort Griffin, Texas, lost by expiration of service 26 men in January and February, 29 men in March and April, and 33 men in April, leaving on June 1, 1870, "but one man in the company." By October of that year, the unit was the smallest infantry regiment in the Army, with only 431 officers and men on its roster. The 25th Infantry was not much better off with a complement of 482. At the same time, a concerted effort was made to replenish the ranks of the cavalry regiments. The same journal reported that all "disposable colored cavalry recruits" were being collected at the Carlisle Barracks in Pennsylvania, and at Fort Leavenworth in Kansas, to be sent to the 9th and 10th Cavalry.

BLACK OFFICERS

Although Army regulations did not prevent the commissioning of black officers or the promotion of black NCOs as commissioned officers, not a single African American rose through the ranks of the buffalo soldiers to hold such a rank between 1866 and 1895. Between the years 1870 and 1889, only 22 blacks received appointments to the US Military Academy at West Point. Twelve of these managed to pass the entrance examination but only three succeeded in surviving four years of discrimination and social ostracism to graduate from the academy: Henry O. Flipper, John H. Alexander, and Charles H. Young graduated in 1877, 1887, and 1889 respectively.

Henry Flipper was assigned to the 10th Cavalry at Fort Sill, Oklahoma, where he supervised the construction of a drainage system that prevented

Originally published in *Progress*, a weekly journal produced in Philadelphia by John W. Forney, the letters of Captain Nicholas Nolan offered rare support for Lieutenant Henry Flipper, the first African American officer cadet to graduate from West Point.

Fort Elliott, Texas, September 4th, 1879

... Now, my dear Price, in the Class of '77 Lieutenant Henry O. Flipper graduated in the Halves, and by so doing, had the privilege of selecting the arm of the service he preferred. He selected the 10th Cavalry, and was assigned to Company A of that regiment, commanded by the representative Paddy of the regiment [a reference to himself]. Mr. Flipper reported to me at Fort Sill on my arrival from Fort Concho, and I immediately extended to him the hand of fellowship. I have ever since been intimately associated with him, and have found him to be all that West Point turns out. It appears that the lady of some officer, who, I presume, never smelt powder, has written from this post to some Northern papers, commenting on myself and family for receiving and entertaining Mr. Flipper. This, evidently, is done on account of his color, and no allowance is made for his grand attainments. The only thing that I regret is that I do not know the husband of the lady, in order to hold him responsible for her action in this matter. I am pleased that Mr. Flipper is an officer of my company, and I am satisfied that he does not consider that all Irishmen are opposed to his race, but are willing to take the hand of all who have been oppressed like themselves...

– "The Color Line," *Army & Navy Journal* (October 11, 1879) 176

The first African American to graduate from West Point, Henry O. Flipper was assigned to the 10th Cavalry as a second lieutenant from 1877 until 1881, when he was wrongfully dismissed from service. (Courtesy of US House of Representatives, NARA)

the spread of malaria at the post. "Flipper's Ditch" is a national historic landmark today. Fighting in the Warm Springs Apache campaign in 1880, he commanded the couriers who brought word of the renegade Victorio's arrival at Eagle Springs, Texas, from Mexico, riding 98 miles in 22 hours.

As well as fighting Apaches, Flipper went on to serve as a signal officer and quartermaster at several other posts, before being wrongfully accused of embezzling money from commissary funds while serving as Acting Commissary of Subsistence at Fort Davis, Texas, in 1881. He denied the charge, claiming that he had been set up by his fellow officers, who hated him because he was black. A court-martial found him not guilty of embezzlement, but convicted him of conduct unbecoming an officer. Thus he was dismissed from the Army and spent many years trying unsuccessfully to clear his name. Henry Flipper died without vindication in 1940, but in 1976 the US Army granted him an honorable discharge, following which a review board stated that he had been singled out because of his race. President Bill Clinton issued him a full pardon in 1999.

Both Alexander and Young were assigned to the 9th Cavalry. The former was attached to Troop M, stationed at Fort Washakie, Wyoming, in March 1888, and subsequently served in Nebraska and Dakota Territory. He was detailed as professor at the Department of Military Science and Tactics at Wilberforce University, in Xenia, Ohio. This institute became the first black college authorized to grant commissions to college students. Lieutenant Alexander continued to serve in this position until his death from a heart attack in March 1894.

Charles Young graduated from West Point in 1889 and remained on active duty for 33 years. He became the highest-ranking black officer during World War I, and the first black officer to hold the rank of colonel. His service included assignments as military attaché to Haiti and Liberia. He was the second officer to hold the position of Professor of Military Science and Tactics at Wilberforce University. His command and staff assignments had carried him to Haiti, the Philippines, and the Republic of Liberia. In January 1922 Colonel Young died, and was buried in Arlington National Cemetery.

DISCRIMINATION

Inevitably, the black regulars were the victims of racial prejudice and discrimination. In 1867 a dispute developed between Colonel Grierson and Colonel William Hoffman, the commanding officer at Fort Leavenworth, when the 10th Cavalry was ordered to establish camp in a swampy area about 1 mile south of the permanent barracks. These two officers subsequently

Garrison life, 1873–80

This parade ground scene depicts the uniforms adopted as part of the new uniform regulations for the US Army prescribed during the period 1873–80. The 10th Cavalry trumpeter (1) is distinguished by the herringbone pattern trim on the chest of his yellow-faced basque, or short-skirted jacket. His Prussian-style, "duck-billed" helmet is bound with patent leather. The 1in seam stripes on his reinforced trousers indicate that he was also a bandsman. Attached to his waist belt is an M1858 Light Cavalry saber. The sergeant's (2) arms and equipment consist of a black buff leather waist belt with 1872-pattern Dyer pouch attached to the back; leather saber straps secured through two brass slings to his waist belt; and a black buff leather carbine sling to which is attached a Model 1872 Springfield carbine. The enlisted man of the 24th Infantry (3) wears the sky-blue faced coat. His dark-blue cloth 1872-pattern cap is also

piped with sky-blue trim, and has a white pompon mounted in a yellow metal ball and socket device. He carries an M1870 .50cal Springfield rifle musket. The enlisted man of the 25th Infantry (4) wears an 1874-pattern, five-button blouse and 1872-pattern forage cap with 1875-pattern crossed rifles insignia. He holds an M1873 Springfield rifle with fixed bayonet. His equipment consists of the 1874-pattern Palmer brace system with Type II McKeever cartridge boxes.

(Richard Hook © Osprey Publishing)

Colonel Edward Hatch ably commanded the 9th Cavalry from 1867 until his death following an accident while driving a buckboard in 1889. (Library of Congress, USZ62-78224)

engaged in a heated argument on the parade ground in front of the assembled command when Hoffman ordered Grierson not to form his men too close to the white troops. As a result, Grierson completed his regimental organization at Leavenworth as quickly as possible and sent his companies on to Fort Riley for further training.

Worse still were the disputes that sometimes occurred among the enlisted men. On January 20, 1869, a "small row" broke out at Fort Wallace, Kansas, between the troopers of the 10th Cavalry and the white soldiers of the 5th Infantry. This resulted in "three colored men being placed *hors de combat.*" According to a rather unsympathetic correspondent at the post, "One was wounded in the left arm, which was amputated by Dr. [J. A.] Fitz Gerald in artistic style. The other two were wounded in the legs, and it is a question whether they do not lose a leg apiece."

The buffalo soldiers were also wrongly accused of spreading disease. During the summer of 1866, a medical officer at Jefferson Barracks, Missouri, began an unfounded rumor that recruits of the 38th Infantry, being raised at that post, were responsible for beginning "a most disastrous outbreak of cholera on the high, dry plains of western Kansas." In fact, the barracks was stricken nearly one month after the buffalo soldiers had departed for Fort Harker, and the disease was most likely spread by civilians, either migrants from the wagon trains or workers on the railroad construction gangs.

Occasionally, the buffalo soldiers were the victims of cruelty from their own officers. During December 1872 and January 1873, Captain J. Lee Humfreville, Company K, 9th Cavalry, inflicted a number of cruelties on the men under his command while on detached service performing escort duty. Seven troopers were handcuffed and forced to march from Fort Richardson to Fort Clark, Texas (a distance of about 400 miles), tied to the back of an Army wagon. At the end of each day's march, the same men remained manacled and were required to carry a log weighing about 25lb up and down in front of a sentinel. On another occasion, Captain Humfreville punched Private Jerry Williams, who was being restrained by two NCOs. The officer next ordered Williams to be hung from a tree, following which he hit him over the head with a club. He also ordered Private Malachi G. Pope to be thrown into a stream during very cold weather and refused to allow any of these men to light camp fires at night time. On December 4, 1873, Captain Humfreville faced a court-martial and was dismissed from the service.

The buffalo soldiers continually encountered prejudice among the civilians they were garrisoned on the frontier to protect. One of the worst trouble spots was Fort Concho in Texas, where elements of the 10th Cavalry served alongside the white 16th Infantry during the late 1870s. Troopers visiting the nearby town of San Angelo were regularly exposed to insults and harassment from the local residents. On several occasions in 1878 and 1879 the soldiers demonstrated their willingness to retaliate by shooting up town saloons and business premises where they had been threatened or refused service. The worst incident occurred following the murder of Private William Watkins by a white sheep rancher in 1881. When news reached the fort, about 70 soldiers, black and white, converged on the town. According to the report of Colonel Grierson: "A good many shots were fired in the vicinity of the Hotel, but fortunately only one person [was] slightly wounded."

In the face of common adversity, the white troops developed a great respect for the buffalo soldiers toward the end of the Indian Wars. In April 1891, a member of the garrison at Fort Custer, in Montana, wrote: 'The colored troops of the 25th Infantry … get along extremely well with their white comrades of the 1st Cavalry, and the color line is exceedingly dim. So may it ever be. Men who wear the same uniform, eat the same rations, draw the same pay and fight for the same country, can ill afford to let the color of the skin form the cause of estrangement."

A FEMALE BUFFALO SOLDIER

In the absence of a thorough physical examination, Cathay Williams, the only black female to become a buffalo soldier, enlisted in Company A, 38th Infantry, on November 15, 1867. Born into slavery near Independence, Missouri, Williams was freed by Union forces during the Civil War, and served as a cook and laundress for the 8th Indiana Infantry from 1862 until the end of the conflict. Being tall and powerfully built, and calling herself "William Cathay," she easily fooled the recruiting officer of the 38th Infantry, who was anxious to secure volunteers to fill the ranks of his regiment. Her company arrived at Fort Cummings, New Mexico, on October 1, 1867, and for the next two years she helped protect miners and immigrants from Indian attack. When interviewed later in life, she recalled: "I carried my musket and did guard and other duties while in the Army, but finally I got tired and wanted to get off. I played sick, complained of pains in my side, and rheumatism in my knees. The post surgeon found out I was a woman and I got my discharge." She finally left the Army on October 14, 1868.

CAMPAIGNING ON THE CENTRAL PLAINS, 1867–73

The first black Regular Army soldiers to see action on the Great Plains belonged to the 38th Infantry. By June 1867 this regiment was recruited up to full strength and shortly afterwards was posted along the Smoky Hill River in Kansas as part of General Winfield Scott Hancock's campaign against the Cheyenne. Duties included escorting mail coaches, guarding relay stations, and protecting the construction gangs building the Kansas Pacific Railroad.

On June 26, 21-year-old Corporal David Turner and a detachment of Company K, 38th Infantry, assisted in the defense of supply wagons being escorted by elements of the 7th Cavalry. The black infantrymen had been assigned to guard a surveying party when the attack began. Realizing they

A Remington engraving depicting a detachment of Company K, 38th Infantry, helping the 7th Cavalry repel a Cheyenne attack at Fort Wallace in Kansas during June 1867. (Ron Field)

were needed on the firing line, they jumped into a wagon pulled by four mules and raced to reinforce the white troopers of Companies G and I, 7th Cavalry. Standing and firing from the wagon as they charged through the battle lines, the black soldiers joined in the three-hour fight and assisted in driving back about 300 Cheyenne led by Chief Roman Nose. According to Libby Custer, wife of the lieutenant-colonel of the 7th Cavalry: "When the skirmish-line was reached, the colored men leaped out and began firing again. No one had ordered them to leave their picket-station, but they were determined that no soldiering should be carried on in which their valor was not proved."

Shortly after this, seven companies of the 38th Infantry were ordered to New Mexico, where regimental headquarters was established at Fort Craig. This protected the central portion of the Camino Real, a trail that stretched from northern Mexico to Taos, New Mexico. Elements of the regiment were also posted at Forts Bayard, McRae, and Selden. Meanwhile, eight companies of the 41st Infantry were based along the Rio Grande River in Texas, with headquarters at the Ringgold Barracks. The remaining two infantry regiments were retained back east as part of the military occupation imposed on the defeated Southern states, with the 39th Infantry headquartered at Greenville, Louisiana, and the 40th Infantry on garrison duty in North and South Carolina.

In this photo by Alexander Gardner, a detachment of the 38th Infantry provides an escort atop a stagecoach in Kansas, c. 1867. The sergeant wears non-regulation leather gauntlets, while the enlisted men wear brass shoulder scales. (Kansas State Historical Society)

Small detachments of the 38th Infantry guarding surveying parties or stations along the railroad and wagon routes fought war parties, probably Cheyenne, in the summer of 1867. In the absence of a white officer, Sergeant S. Davis provided exemplary leadership, which was duly reported to his company commander:

Capt.

July 30th 1867

We had a very large fight last night and night before and it was [lucky] that we had a box of ammunition [with] us. None of the boys got killed. We killed 10 Indian Ponies that we found here this morning. We don't know whether we killed the riders or not. The sentinels like to got shot when they halted there but happened to lay down and they shot over and the balls went through the tents.

S. Davis
Sergt 38th U.S. Inf

– Letters Received, Department of the Missouri (1867) RG 393, NARA

SALINE RIVER, 1867

Meanwhile, the two cavalry regiments had reached their respective stations. The 9th Cavalry was headquartered with Companies A, B, E, and K at Camp Stockton, Texas. The remainder of the regiment was located at Forts Davis and Hudson and at Brownsville, Texas. The 10th Cavalry was posted in Kansas along the Smoky Hill River, with Companies I, K, L, and M headquartered at the stone-built Fort Riley, and the rest of the regiment spread throughout four other posts. The buffalo soldiers found Fort Riley in "very bad order," and spent much of their time cleaning and repairing the post.

The first fight between black cavalry troopers and Native Americans occurred on August 2, 1867, and involved Company F, 10th Cavalry, under the command of Captain George A. Armes. While trailing hostiles who had killed seven Union Pacific Railroad workers at Campbell's Camp, two officers and 34 men of this unit encountered about 75 Cheyenne by the Saline River, 40 miles northeast of Fort Hays. Armes ordered his command to dismount and fight on foot and later reported: "I kept my flankers well out, and advanced until I saw what was supposed to be a herd of buffalo, but close investigation discovered them to be Indians coming to the support of those around me.

I gave the command, 'To the left, march!' and started for the post." Under a blazing sun, the dismounted troopers held off their attackers during a running battle that lasted about six hours. With ammunition running low, they were pursued for about 15 miles until the Cheyenne finally gave up the chase as they neared Fort Hays. Captain Armes was wounded in the hip, while Sergeant William Christy, an ex-farmer from Pennsylvania, was shot through the head, and became the first black regular to be killed in action.

PRAIRIE DOG CREEK, 1867

On August 21, 1867, a force commanded by the same officer (sufficiently recovered from his wound), and consisting of 40 men of Company F, 10th Cavalry, and 95 men of the 18th Kansas Volunteer Cavalry, under Captain George Jennis, were scouting in several separate parties along the Saline River when the black unit was attacked by about 400 Cheyenne and Kiowa led by Chiefs Satanta and Roman Nose.

The black troopers fiercely held ground, but discovered they were completely surrounded and were ordered to dismount and herd their horses into a ravine. Captain Armes recorded: "The Indians fought me from 3 to 9 o'clock p.m. 'Satanta' in full army uniform on a beautiful grey horse, sounded the charge with his bugle at least a dozen times, whooping and yelling, and endeavoring to get his men to charge into the ravine, but only getting near enough to have at least twenty of his saddles emptied at a volley or a dozen or so ponies killed and wounded."

Eight troopers were wounded during the attack. At nightfall, Armes attempted to link up with other elements of his command. Finding his supply wagons guarded by 65 Kansas volunteers, he learned that Captain Jennis and 29 men were in a "helpless condition," having also been under attack since the previous evening. Sending out a relief force, they brought Jennis and his wounded in to safety.

Three black troopers pose for the camera of Will Soule, who accompanied the 10th Cavalry to Fort Sill in 1869. They appear to be wearing 1858-pattern sack coats shortened to the approximate length of the cavalry uniform jacket, while the sun reflects off the brass insignia fixed to the tops of their caps. Medicine Lodge Creek can be seen in the background. (US Army Artillery & Missile Center Museum, Fort Sill)

In the face of further attacks, Armes mounted about 20 black regulars and Kansan volunteers, and ordered a charge on the Indians. Galloping firstly toward Prairie Dog Creek, he then veered up hill toward the main body of warriors. Surprised by such decisive action, the Indians scattered but then rallied, having been reinforced by more braves. In danger of being encircled and cut off, Armes returned to his main force, after which the Indians withdrew. Losses for Armes on this occasion amounted to one soldier killed and scalped, and 11 wounded, while 14 Kansas volunteers and two guides were also wounded.

It was during these early actions that the nickname "buffalo soldiers" was acquired, although it is doubtful that the black troopers ever used the term themselves. Because of the African Americans' tight curly hair, which reminded the Indians of the woolly heads of the buffalo, the Cheyenne, Kiowa, and Comanche referred to their black opponents as "wild buffaloes." At first the Indians treated the black soldiers with contempt, but after a taste of their fighting qualities, they developed a great respect for those they continued to call "buffaloes" or "buffalo soldiers." Aware that the buffalo was an important animal to Native Americans, later generations of blacks accepted the name with pride and the buffalo symbol became a prominent feature of the regimental crest of the 10th Cavalry.

During March 1868, the headquarters of the 10th Cavalry was moved from Fort Riley to Fort Gibson in Indian Territory, following which Colonel Grierson assumed command of the District of the Indian Territory. Elements of the regiment were involved in the winter campaign of 1867–68 to stop hostile tribes from raiding border settlements in Texas and Kansas. On September 15, 1867, Company I under Captain George Washington Graham had been attacked by about 100 hostiles at Big Sandy Creek, Colorado. Fighting until dark, they lost ten horses killed or captured and killed seven Indians. A Civil War veteran, Graham had commanded a company of "galvanized Yankees" (Confederate prisoners-of-war recruited to serve on the Western frontier during the closing days of the Civil War) from North Carolina from 1863 through 1865, before his assignment to the 10th Cavalry. In 1870 he faced a court-martial and was cashiered for selling government property. During the next five years he became an outlaw, often finding himself on the receiving end of Army gunfire. He was eventually shot dead in October 1875.

RESCUE OF FORSYTH'S SCOUTS, 1868

On September 23, 1868, Captain Louis H. Carpenter and Company H, 10th Cavalry, nicknamed "Carpenter's Brunettes," were patrolling the Denver Road when couriers from Fort Wallace brought word that a company of civilian scouts under the command of Major George A. Forsyth was under attack on the Arickaree Fork of the Republican River. A field officer on detached service from the 10th Cavalry, Forsyth had received orders from General Philip Sheridan to "employ fifty first-class hardy frontiersmen" to be used as scouts against hostile Indians. Having pursued a Lakota and Cheyenne war party, these men were surrounded and forced to take refuge on a small island in the nearly dried-up bed of the Arickaree. There they dug in and made a stand. Shot in the head and leg, and with half his men either dead or wounded, Forsyth sent for help. After crawling through the Indian lines for several miles, two of his men finally brought word of their plight to Fort Wallace.

Leaving his supply wagons to catch up later, Captain Carpenter made all haste toward the Arickaree to relieve the beleaguered scouts. Company H arrived at the scene after the Indians had withdrawn, and the company commander's orderly, Private Reuben Waller, a former slave who had enlisted at Fort Leavenworth, Kansas, in 1867, recalled: "What a sight we saw – 30 wounded and dead men right in the middle of 50 dead horses, that had lain in the hot sun for ten days." While an Army surgeon attended to the wounded, Waller and the other buffalo soldiers began to feed the starving scouts with rations from their haversacks. "If the doctor had not arrived in time we would have killed them all by feeding them to death. The men were eating all we gave them, and it was plenty."

Several weeks after their return to Fort Wallace, some of the troopers of Company H took "French leave" and went to Pond Creek, 3 miles from the post. According to Waller: "When we got there we met the Beecher scouts, as they had been paid off. They sure treated us black soldiers right for what we had done for them." For his part in rescuing Forsyth's Scouts, Carpenter became the first officer in his regiment to be awarded the Congressional Medal of Honor, which was eventually issued to him on April 8, 1898.

Troopers of the 10th Cavalry built Fort Sill in 1869 using stone quarried nearby. Many of these buildings still surround the old post quadrangle today. (US Army Artillery & Missile Center Museum, Fort Sill)

Born into slavery on January 5, 1840, Reuben Waller served as a body servant for a Confederate cavalryman during the Civil War, and witnessed the Fort Pillow massacre and Lee's surrender at Appomattox Court House in 1865. Having developed "a great liking for the cavalry soldiers," he enlisted in the 10th Cavalry at Fort Leavenworth, Kansas, on July 16, 1867:

Well, we plunged right into the fights – Beaver Creek, Sand Creek, Cheyenne Wells, and many others. One great sensation was the rescue at Beecher Island, on the Arickare Creek, in Colorado, September, 1868. The Indians had surrounded General Forsyth and 50 brave men, and had killed and wounded 20 men, and had compelled the rest to live on dead horse flesh for nine days on a small island. Colonel L. H. Carpenter, with his Company H, 10th U.S. cavalry, was at Cheyenne Wells, Colo., 100 miles from Beecher Island. Jack Stillwell brought us word of the fix that Beecher was in and we entered the race for the island, and in 26 hours Colonel Carpenter and myself, as his hostler, rode into the rifle pits. And what a sight we saw – 30 wounded and dead men right in the middle of 50 dead horses, that had lain in the hot sun for ten days.

And these men had eaten the putrid flesh of those dead horses for eight days. The men were in a dying condition when Carpenter and myself dismounted and began to rescue them.

– Reuben Waller, "History of a Slave Written by Himself at the Age of 89," *The Beecher Island Annual: Ninety-Third Anniversary of the Battle of Beecher Island* (September 17, 18, 1868; Beecher Island, CO: The Beecher Island Battle Memorial Association, 1960) 86–89

BEAVER CREEK, 1868

On arrival at Fort Wallace, Carpenter reported having seen the tracks of a large party of Indians headed toward Beaver Creek. General Sheridan subsequently ordered seven companies of the 5th Cavalry, under Major William B. Royall, to pursue the hostiles. Major Eugene Carr, the senior field officer of this regiment, arrived at the fort several days later. As Carr was anxious to join the men of his regiment in anticipation of action, Captain Carpenter, commanding Companies H and I, 10th Cavalry, was ordered to escort him on this mission.

Unable to locate the 5th Cavalry, despite a 60-mile scout along Beaver Creek, Carr returned to Fort Wallace, leaving the bulk of Carpenter's men to continue the search. On October 18, 1868, Carpenter ordered Captain Graham to make one final attempt to find Royall's command. Accompanied by two buffalo soldiers, Graham had not gone more than 1,000 yards before being attacked by a large party of about 500 Sioux, Cheyenne, and Arapaho, led by a medicine man called Bullet Proof. Wearing buffalo robes cured, like that of their leader, in a "secret manner" with the horns left on, many of these Indians believed they were impervious to bullets.

As Graham and his men dashed back through a hail of bullets to the main camp, Carpenter reacted swiftly and moved his command to higher ground where he corralled the wagons in the form of a horseshoe. Company H was assigned to protect either flank, while Company I was detailed to cover the rear. The black troopers were ordered to dismount, tie their horses inside, and take up a defensive position behind the wagons. "A fire commenced from our seven-shooter Spencers which sounded like the fire of a line of infantry," recalled Captain Carpenter. "The Indians charged up around the wagons, firing rapidly and seriously wounded some of the men, but in a very short time they were driven back in wild disorder, leaving the ground covered with ponies, arms, and some bodies."

Disappointed that their robes had not protected them, the hostiles withdrew, leaving ten Indians dead and three buffalo soldiers wounded. Forming his wagons into a double column, with men and animals inside, Carpenter subsequently moved his command back to the riverside, where they camped again for the night. Setting out on their return march the next

The 9th Cavalry Band performing at Santa Fe Plaza, New Mexico, in July 1880. Music was often used to lift the morale of the trail-worn troopers, and during the 1870s the band toured the various posts manned by their unit. The regiment was so undermanned during 1877 that these musicians were mounted and exchanged their instruments for Springfield carbines in order to chase renegade Apaches. (Photo by Ben Wittick, courtesy of Museum of New Mexico, Neg. No. 50887)

day, they reached the safety of Fort Wallace on October 21, 1868. Six days later, General Sheridan published a general order complimenting the officers and men of the 10th Cavalry for their gallantry under fire at Beaver Creek.

THE PEACE COMMISSION, 1869

With the commencement of President Ulysses S. Grant's Peace Policy on March 4, 1869, the 10th Cavalry became part of an army of occupation.

During this period, the Plains tribes were brought into reservations managed predominantly by agents composed of members of the Society of Friends, or Quakers. Regarded as hostiles, the Indians who rejected reservation life kept the buffalo soldiers very busy.

During the summer of 1869, four companies of the 10th Cavalry established Camp Wichita at Medicine Lodge Creek in Indian Territory. By August of that year it was named Fort Sill. Members of the regiment were responsible for constructing this post, much of which was built from stone quarried nearby. A typical evening with the buffalo soldiers during this period was described by an *Army & Navy Journal* correspondent: "The monotony of the camp is relieved by the songs of the minstrel troupes in the different companies until taps blows, when all is still except the howling of the wolf or the bark of the coyote, relieved by the 'tum tum tum' of the rawhide drum in the Indian camp [nearby]."

From Fort Sill, the 10th Cavalry began to operate into northern Texas as well as Indian Territory. A detachment of the regiment escorted General Sherman when he inspected conditions in the Brazos River region following a Kiowa attack on a government wagon train on January 24, 1871. With a further massacre of a civilian wagon train on May 18, three companies of the regiment took part in the peaceful arrest of the Kiowa chiefs Satank, Eagle Heart, Big Tree, and Big Bow, after Satank admitted he had led the attack.

At the beginning of 1873, Colonel Grierson was ordered to St Louis as Superintendent of the Mounted Recruiting Service, and Lieutenant-Colonel John W. "Black Jack" Davidson commanded the 10th Cavalry, by then headquartered at Fort Gibson, in Indian Territory, until 1875.

During January 1873, Davidson received word that the Comancheros were selling whisky to the Southern Cheyenne and Arapaho. For generations, these New Mexico outlaws had traded liquor, arms, and ammunition to the Kiowas and Comanches on the Staked Plains, in return for livestock and other plunder of the Indian raids on Texas settlements. As a result, Lieutenant Richard H. Pratt and 20 troopers of Company D, 10th Cavalry, were ordered to set out from Camp Supply in sub-zero weather to bring back under arrest those responsible. Although a severe north wind turned their march into an ordeal, the same weather conditions kept the Comancheros in their cabins, enabling Pratt to round up 15 prisoners, plus their baggage, which contained "rot-gut-whisky, guns, ammo, clothing and foodstuffs." As they returned to Camp Supply, however, 13 buffalo soldiers developed severely frostbitten hands and feet, and were subsequently hospitalized. The Comancheros were fined only $10 and sentenced to a month in jail, following which they were back in business.

OPPOSITE
Sergeant E. D. Gibson, 10th Cavalry, wears an 1874-pattern blouse edged all around with yellow worsted braid, even though this was meant to be on the collar and cuffs only. As the chevrons indicating rank are absent from his upper sleeves, this photo was possibly taken prior to the issuance of General Order No. 21, which permitted such insignia to be added to the blouse as well as the dress jacket and overcoat. He holds an 1876-pattern campaign hat in his left hand. His sky-blue kersey trousers are embellished with 1in stripes commensurate with his rank, while his shirt, vest, and necktie are civilian private purchase. (The Frontier Army Museum, Fort Leavenworth)

CAMPAIGNING ON THE SOUTHERN PLAINS, 1867–75

The principal duty of the 9th Cavalry stationed on the Texas plains was to establish and protect the mail and stage route from San Antonio to El Paso, and to reinstate law and order in the country contiguous to the Rio Grande frontier, which had been disrupted by Mexicans as well as by Native Americans during the Civil War years. Elements of the regiment did not settle well at their new posting. On April 9, 1867, a "mutiny," or more properly a protest, broke out in the ranks of Companies A, E, and K at the regimental headquarters at San Pedro Springs, near San Antonio, as a result of the brutality of Lieutenant Edward Heyl. This officer had several of his men suspended from tree limbs by their wrists for failure to respond promptly to his orders. Before order could be restored, Lieutenant Seth Griffin, of Company A, received a mortal wound, while Lieutenant Fred Smith, of Company K, was forced to shoot two of his troopers.

To compound their problems, the 9th Cavalry were not well received by the local Texans, who felt they were being subjected to a particularly harsh form of post-war reconstruction by the federal government and saw the assignment of black soldiers as a deliberate attempt to humiliate them further.

EAGLE SPRINGS, 1867

Troopers of the 9th Cavalry first brushed with hostile Indians on October 1, 1867, when two men from Company D were ambushed and killed by Kickapoos while carrying mail to Fort Stockton. Two months later, on December 5, an NCO in Company F, 9th Cavalry, showed great courage in action. Sergeant Jacob B. Wilks was sent with a detail of 12 men to carry the mail to Fort Bliss, at El Paso. During such duty, each man usually carried a mail sack strapped to the cantle of his saddle. Attacked at Eagle Springs by about 100 Apaches, Wilks recalled:

> We were on an open plain without any protection whatever, but we dismounted, held our horses by the halter-reins, kept close together and withheld our fire until the Indians charged up within close range. Our rapid fire from long range guns wrought such havoc that in the evening they drew off, after killing one of our men… Contrary to orders, he mounted, dashed away calling us to follow him and charged right in among the Indians and was killed.

Scouting near the Pecos River, 1870

During January 1870, Captain Francis Dodge, commanding Company D, 9th Cavalry, and Company K, 24th Infantry, discovered a Mescalero Apache village near the Pecos River in Texas. Despite being detected, Captain Dodge ordered his men to attack and they surged so quickly on to the mesa top that the Indians were forced to leave their dead behind as they made their escape. Typical of the period, the buffalo soldiers still wear Civil War surplus clothing. The mounted corporal (1) wears an 1854-pattern, 12-button uniform jacket. Headgear consists of an 1858-pattern forage cap with stamped brass insignia. He holds an M1860 Light Cavalry saber and has an M1865 .50cal Spencer carbine. The infantrymen (2 & 3) carry the M1866 .50cal Springfield rifle musket, popularly known as the "Allin Conversion," or "Trapdoor" Springfield. The figure at right wears an 1858-pattern, four-button sack coat, while the soldier at left is stripped down to a non-regulation flannel undershirt. Their equipment includes the experimental M1866 cartridge boxes.

(Richard Hook © Osprey Publishing)

Heading out under cover of darkness, Wilks feared further ambush along the trail and struck out through the mountains for the Rio Grande below Fort Quitman, carrying the body of the dead trooper strapped to his horse. Encountering a mule train heavily laden with army supplies, he warned wagon-master Naile that hostile Apaches were nearby and advised him to corral his wagons. This had hardly been completed when the Indians appeared and a furious attack ensued. Successfully driven off, the hostiles crossed into Mexico. While re-hitching his teams and getting back on the trail, Naile informed the black NCO, "Sergeant, you just saved my train."

OLD FORT LANCASTER, 1867

The first significant fight in which troopers of the 9th Cavalry were involved occurred on December 26 of the same year, when a force of Kickapoos, Lipans, Mexicans, and some white American renegades, estimated at between 900 and 1,500 strong, attacked Company K, under Captain William Frohock, which was encamped by the ruins of Old Fort Lancaster some 75 miles east of Fort Stockton. Assaulted on two sides and threatened from a third, the soldiers were saved when their corralled horses stampeded through the lines of their assailants. "Had this stampede not occurred," recalled Captain Frohock, "it is doubtful if the defense against such overwhelming odds could have been successful." Once in possession of the army horses, the hostiles and their allies withdrew and formed a mile-wide line of battle. Refusing to accept the loss, Frohock deployed the bulk of his company as skirmishers, leaving the remainder to protect the camp. "I advanced upon their lines," he recollected, "which receiving our fire, broke and reformed to the rear, several times; always, however, keeping the horses behind them and themselves beyond the reach of our shots." The troopers kept up the chase for about 4 miles before running out of ammunition and yielding to the dark. After a vicious three-hour fight, 20 Indians lay dead and Privates Andrew Trimble, William Sharpe, and Eli Boyer, who guarded the cavalry horses, were missing, presumed dead, having been surprised, roped, and dragged away.

The presence of white men among the hostiles indicated that former Confederate soldiers were carrying on the war that had ended for most of the participants 32 months before, in 1865. Indeed, Captain Frohock noted that several of his men reported seeing among the foe "white men … who spoke English draped in Confederate uniforms." Despite the loss of the horses, the action at Fort Lancaster proved that the black troopers of the 9th Cavalry were combat effective and could hold their own even when greatly outnumbered.

In their next large-scale action, the 9th Cavalry scored a complete victory over the Native Americans. On September 14, 1868, a scouting detachment under Lieutenant Patrick Cusack, consisting of 60 NCOs and enlisted men from Companies C, F, and K, plus a party of Mexican guides, discovered about 200 hostile Lipan Apaches, under Chief Arsart, encamped near Horse Head Hills, about 80 miles southeast of Fort Davis, Texas. About 50 Indians were killed or wounded, two white captives were released, and 198 head of cattle were retrieved. Only one of the buffalo soldiers was wounded.

After the battle, Lieutenant Cusack gave his men a free rein in collecting souvenirs, which included scalps. Upon their return to Fort Davis, an observer noted that some of the black troopers were "rigged out" in "full Indian costume," with "most fantastic head-dresses" and their "faces painted in a comical style."

PECOS RIVER, 1869

The buffalo soldiers were not always so successful in action. On June 7, 1869, an expedition composed of detachments from Companies G, L, and M, 9th Cavalry, under immediate command of Captain John M. Bacon and accompanied by Colonel Mackenzie, 24th Infantry, commanding the Sub-District of the Pecos, tracked down about 100 hostile Lipan and Mescalero Apaches near the Pecos River in Texas. The troopers charged the Indians and drove them back, killing two. During a second charge, the hostiles fled, some escaping toward the mountains and the remainder down the river. Pursuit of the hostiles was maintained for about 80 miles throughout the next day, but the Indian tactic of crossing and re-crossing the river, and frequently changing mounts, enabled them to outrun the buffalo soldiers, whose horses became exhausted. Bacon's command returned to Fort Clark on June 25, having traveled 432 miles over the most barely accessible region of the state.

By the late 1880s, the band of the 9th Cavalry was wearing a modified 1884-pattern blouse with a row of five buttons added either side. Worsted aiguillettes were adopted for bandsmen in the mid 1880s. Note the "lyre" insignia on his cap, first authorized in October 1885. (Nebraska State Historical Society)

Similar engagements occurred during the fall of that year. On November 24, Captain Edward Heyl, commanding a scouting expedition composed of 20 enlisted men of Companies F and M, 9th Cavalry, discovered the trail of a small party of hostiles near the South Fork of the Llano River. During the surprise attack on the Indian camp, Captain Heyl killed a warrior at close quarters, following which he was severely wounded by an arrow in the left side.

KICKAPOO SPRINGS, 1870

A 19-year-old ex-slave turned sharecropper when he enlisted in Company F, 9th Cavalry, in 1866, Sergeant Emanuel Stance commanded a particularly successful 11-man scouting expedition out of Fort McKavett, Texas, on May 20, 1870. After riding about 14 miles, Stance encountered a band of Apaches making across the hills with a small herd of stolen horses. Forming his tiny command into line of battle, he ordered a charge. The startled Indians ran and the troopers captured nine horses.

The next day, on their return to the fort, Stance and his detachment observed a party of Apaches about to attack a small government wagon train near Kickapoo Springs. Once again he ordered a charge and four days later reported: "I set the Spencers to talking and whistling about their ears so lively that they broke in confusion and fled to the hills, leaving us their herd of five horses." Some of the Indians made one last stand, reappearing in the rear of the buffalo soldiers. Wheeling his command around, Stance ordered them to open fire, and later stated that after "a few volleys they left me to continue my march in peace." On July 9, 1870, just six weeks after the engagements with the Apaches, Emanuel Stance became the first enlisted buffalo soldier to be awarded the Medal of Honor.

HOWARD'S WELL, 1872

Typically, new recruits to the buffalo soldiers did not always acquit themselves well in action. During April 1872, the headquarters of the 9th Cavalry was transferred from Fort Stockton to Fort Clark, Texas. As Companies A and H rode to their new quarters, Captain John S. Loud, who was in overall command, sent a sergeant and two troopers ahead to secure forage for the horses. Approaching Howard's Well, a watering place en route, Loud's column spied a large band of Kiowa and Mexicans, led by Chief Big Bow, attacking and plundering a wagon train carrying ordnance and commissary supplies, also bound for Fort Stockton.

Traveling in a field ambulance at the head of the column, the wife of the commanding officer grabbed a carbine from the driver and began to blaze away at the hostiles. Soon joined by the black troopers, she drove the Indians off. As they approached the scene, Loud's command found the charred remains of 11 dead, among whom were women and children. They also found their sergeant and his detachment holed up behind a breastwork of forage. Although wounded, the three men had managed to hold off the Indians until relief arrived. After tending to the three survivors, Captain Loud ordered his African American troopers, many of whom were new recruits, to track down the hostiles and renegades. Loud reported:

> After following the trail some seven or eight miles, the cavalry came upon the Indians in force, on the summit of a steep and almost impassable bluff. Here a sharp fight occurred, in which, I regret to say, Lieutenant [Frederick R.] Vincent [Company H] fell while bravely leading and attempting to control his men … [and] Captain [Michael] Cooney [Company A] was painfully, though not seriously, injured by his horse falling and dragging him while moving at a rapid gait. He, however, remounted and retained his command. The men of his company behaved very well, but being in great part recruits, without experience in Indian fighting, which was the case in Company H to a still greater extent, squandered their ammunition, as sometimes even old troops not well under control will do with repeating or magazine arms.

First Lieutenant Frederick R. Vincent, Company H, 9th Cavalry, was mortally wounded while leading raw recruits into battle near Howard's Well, Texas, in 1872. His dying words were, "Tell them I was in the front." (Courtesy of Frohne's Historic Military)

Subjected to a fierce counterattack, Captain Cooney and his command were forced to withdraw. The subsequent battle report stated that Lieutenant Vincent did "not receive a necessarily fatal wound, but seeing that his new men required the stimulus of his example, he insisted upon being put on his horse, and placed himself at their head, when, from his exertions and consequent loss of blood, he soon fell exhausted and never recovered." In fact, Vincent had been wounded in both legs and both femoral arteries were severed, following which he bled to death. According to his comrades, his dying words were, "Tell them I was in the front. Goodbye."

NORTH FORK OF THE RED RIVER, 1872

On occasions, the black infantrymen were required to serve as mounted troops. On January 17, 1868, Lieutenant Bethel M. Custer, 38th Infantry, was ordered to pursue Indian cattle thieves with "all the troops able to mount mules." During the summer of 1872, Company I, 24th Infantry, commanded by Captain J.W. Clous, was provided with horses and assigned to an expedition led by Colonel Ranald S. MacKenzie, 4th Cavalry, against the Comancheros. The climax of this expedition was the surprise attack on the village of the Comanche band led by Mow-way, at the North Fork of the Red River, on September 29, 1872. Attacking in "columns-of-four," MacKenzie's force killed 23 braves and took 124 prisoners, mostly women and children. It also dealt the Comancheros' trade a crippling blow by proving that the Staked Plains was no longer an Indian sanctuary. Upon MacKenzie's recommendation, several officers and men under his command, including Captain Clous, were awarded the Medal of Honor. On March 12, 1873, Captain Clous and his black mounted infantrymen were ordered to report for duty to Colonel Hatch, 9th Cavalry, and became part of the force deployed between Fort McIntosh and the lower Rio Grande River to protect settlers from further incursions of Indians and Mexican thieves. Company E, 24th Infantry, was also mounted and serving with the 9th Cavalry by July 1874.

THE RED RIVER WAR, 1874–75

Both the 9th and the 10th Cavalry, and the 25th Infantry, became involved in a series of engagements fought in Indian Territory and the Texas "Panhandle" in 1874. Known as the Red River War, the fighting began on August 22 when a Nakoni Comanche chief called Big Red Food, influenced

This Remington engraving depicts a detail of the 10th Cavalry conducting a "scout" through the Sierra Bonitos, Arizona Territory, in 1888. Note the officer second in line is wearing a white summer helmet. (Anne S. K. Brown Military Collection, Brown University Library)

by the exhortations of a medicine man named Isa-tai, refused to enroll at the Wichita Agency, at Anadarko in Indian Territory. This post was garrisoned by Company I, 25th Infantry, under Captain Gaines Lawson.

Battle of Anadarko, 1874

Receiving word via courier of impending trouble, four companies of the 10th Cavalry at Fort Sill, under Lieutenant-Colonel Davidson, were ordered to the Agency to disarm and arrest the hostiles. Recently remounted and rearmed, and with ranks replenished, the black troopers advanced on the

In 1919, Sergeant John Casey wrote an account of hard winter campaigning with the 10th Cavalry in Indian Territory during 1873:

In a very short time, probably ten or twenty days, the regiment was moved out on campaign [from Fort Sill] in pursuit of Chief Lone Wolf and the Kiowa and Comanche Indians who had gone on the war path… In this campaign the regiment was for ten days snowed in without rations but one hardtack a meal and very little coffee because our supply train was lost in the snowstorm. For ten days they wandered across the plains and could not find our camp. In the meantime I was detailed under the lieutenant with twenty men from my company to go to the rescue of a band of buffalo hunters who were surrounded by a band of Indians and had asked for reinforcement and we were sent to relieve them. During this trip each man was only allowed to carry one blanket and his poncho and we had to drive our picket pins between the pommel and cantle of the saddle. In this way we had to sleep with our heads on our saddles and the horses kept us awake and uncovered most of the night. It was very cold and we nearly froze. After five days out we got orders to return to headquarters…

It rained and snowed continually all day and night and we had no overcoats only our ponchos. When we reached headquarters, about 12 o'clock at night, the snow was six or eight inches deep. In this we had to lay down to sleep with our clothes and blankets wringing wet and the weather continued very cold during the entire time we were there, which was ten days or more. In the meantime we were on half rations or less…We had to go one-half or a mile to cut down cottonwood trees and carry the limbs for the horses to eat. This was all the food they had during the whole ten days and we had to carry wood and build log heap fires in the rear of our horses, night and day, to keep them from freezing to death. We had no tents to sleep under only shelter tent halves.

—VA Pension File, SC 138442, John F. Casey, NARA

James Satchell and Samuel Pipton, Troop C, 9th Cavalry. Pipton has a post 1885-pattern sharpshooter's cross on his chest, plus what appears to be a skirmisher's medallion. Satchell's crossed sabers device may have been awarded for swordsmanship. They both carry the M1860 Light Cavalry saber. (The Frontier Army Museum, Fort Leavenworth)

nearby Comanche camp. There they came under fire from their rear as hostile Kiowas under Lone Wolf and Woman's Heart joined in the fray, enabling Big Red Food's band to escape. Both Sergeant Lewis Mack, of Company H, and Private Adam Cork, of Company E, were wounded, while several horses were hit. Davidson abruptly swerved his command into the tree-lined riverside, where the men dismounted and fought on foot.

Company L, under Captain Little, was next ordered to drive out the Kiowa, who had taken up position behind a commissary building and corral. Circling Little's right flank, the hostiles splashed across the river and rode off toward the settlement of some friendly Delaware Indians. Pursued by Company H commanded by Captain Carpenter, and cut off by Captain Lawson's black infantrymen who deployed toward the saw mill, they were charged and routed, but not before they had killed four civilians. Private William Branch, 25th Infantry, recalled: "We went in and fit 'em, and 'twer like fightin' a wasp's nest."

Davidson then regrouped his command, and led them swiftly back to the Wichita Agency, which he found threatened by a swarm of Comanche and Kiowa warriors who had climbed the nearby bluffs. After securing the Agency buildings, Davidson ordered Captain Charles D. Viele, with Company C, to drive the Indians off the bluffs. This was achieved by dusk. Under cover of night, the cavalry commander ordered the black troopers to dig trenches, while others were posted in the agency, the trader's store, and in a long line of buildings and large stacks of hay belonging to the settlement. About 300 Indians attempted to recapture the bluffs at dawn the next day, but were again driven off by Companies E, H, and L under Captain Carpenter. Foiled in their various attempts to destroy the Wichita

Agency, the hostiles set fire to the surrounding dry grass in hopes of burning the buildings down, but Captain Lawson and his infantrymen started counter-fires, and managed to save them. The 10th Cavalry sustained only four troopers wounded, and the 25th Infantry only one soldier wounded, during this action.

Elk Creek, 1874

Elements of both black cavalry regiments were among the troops that spent the next six months scouring the Staked Plains of the Texas Panhandle for about 1,200 Indians who had joined Big Red Food. On September 1, 1874, five companies of the 9th Cavalry and two of the 10th Cavalry, under

Skirmish at Elk Creek, 1874

On October 24, 1874, three companies of the 10th Cavalry, under Major George W. Schofield, surprised and captured a large Indian camp near Elk Creek on the Staked Plains in the Texas Panhandle. The plate depicts the "personal combat" that took place between Private Alfred Pinkston, Company M, 10th Cavalry, and a Comanche warrior. After a violent struggle, the Indian fell dead from a saber thrust. Pinkston wears the campaign uniform prescribed for cavalry in 1872. This consisted of a plaited blouse with yellow cavalry piping, and a black, folding hat. Neither of these items of clothing proved to be very popular with the troops. He also wears 1872-pattern sky-blue kersey trousers and 1872-pattern boots. He wields an M1860 Light Cavalry saber, and has an M1873 Springfield carbine attached to his carbine sling. His equipment consists of one of the 50 sets of 1872-pattern cavalry brace systems that his company was issued for trial purposes during July–September 1874. He is seated in an 1872 modification of the 1859 McClellan saddle, and his plain gray woolen saddle blanket is army issue.

(Richard Hook © Osprey Publishing)

Lieutenant-Colonel George P. Buell, headed west from Fort Griffin. A force under Lieutenant-Colonel Davidson, consisting of six companies of the 10th Cavalry and three companies of the 11th Infantry, plus a section of mountain howitzers, advanced westward from Fort Cobb on October 21. The role of both these forces was to drive the hostiles into the path of two other large army columns under Colonels Miles and Mackenzie advancing east across the Staked Plains. On October 24, three companies of Davidson's column, under Major Schofield, surprised and captured a large Comanche camp on Elk Creek. As a result of this action, Schofield captured 64 warriors, including Big Red Food, plus 250 women and children and the entire Comanche herd of 2,000 ponies.

McClellan Creek, 1874

On November 8, 1874, Colonel Davidson's column struck the trail of a large number of Cheyenne near the North Fork of McClellan Creek. In an effort to intercept these Indians, who had already clashed with another column under Colonel Nelson Miles, he ordered Captain Viele, 10th Cavalry, and 120 men with the strongest horses, plus 40 scouts, to pursue them as swiftly as possible. According to Davidson, his force sighted the Cheyenne and chased them from:

> ... the fork of McClellan's Creek to the Canadian [River], westward 96 miles, from whence the exhausted state of the stock [of horses] rendered a return necessary. The Indians were pursued so closely as to force them to abandon ponies and mules packed, and were engaged by the scouts on the second and third days, but could not be brought to a stand. On the morning of the 13th began a violent rain-storm, changing to sleet and snow, which lasted until the morning of the 19th, freezing to death nearly 100 animals, and freezing the feet of 26 men.

CHEYENNE AGENCY, 1875

The Red River War was over by the beginning of 1875 and the 10th Cavalry was transferred to West Texas. However, Companies D and M of the regiment remained in Indian Territory despite their depleted ranks, and became involved in dismounting, disarming, and imprisoning the ringleaders of the recent uprising. On April 6, 1875, while a small group of hostiles were being brought in to the Cheyenne Agency blacksmith to be shackled, a Cheyenne called Black Horse escaped and his escort fired after him, accidentally killing a reservation Indian. In response, the enraged Cheyenne opened fire with rifles and arrows, wounding two troopers of Company M, 10th Cavalry, under Captain A. S. B. Keyes. Fleeing to a nearby sand hill on the south side of the North Fork of the Canadian River, about 150 Cheyenne warriors dug in, in readiness for battle. Three companies of cavalry surrounded the Cheyenne position. Captain William Rafferty, with Company M, 6th Cavalry, was deployed to the east side of the sand hill, while the 60 men of Companies D and M, 10th Cavalry, took up positions to the west. Rafferty's white troopers dismounted and charged but were repulsed. Lieutenant-Colonel Thomas H. Neill, 6th Cavalry, arrived shortly after and ordered a mounted charge, but Captain Keyes and Captain S. T. Norvell, commanding Company D, 10th Cavalry, informed him that the sandy ground to their front was unsuitable for such an action. Neill

This first sergeant of Company B, 24th Infantry, wears the five-button blouse with exterior pockets adopted in late 1884. The crossed rifles insignia on his 1872-pattern forage cap was adopted via General Order No. 96 on November 19, 1875. (Herb Peck Jr Collection)

next ordered a Gatling gun to spray the Cheyenne position at 400 yards, following which a general assault on foot was begun.

According to Neill's after-battle report, the black troopers failed to join in and the attack failed, allowing the Indians to slip away under cover of darkness. However, according to Captain Norvell, the buffalo soldiers did attempt to advance, but were subjected to intense fire, not only from the Cheyenne, but from the Gatling gun in their rear, which came dangerously close to mowing some of them down. Some years later, Corporal Perry Hayman, of Company M, 10th Cavalry, recalled:

As the first set of fours crossed the river, the Indians opened upon us and Corporal George Berry was wounded. We charged them… While rolling around on the ground [after being ordered to take cover] my rifle got some sand in the breech. I had to take a stick to clean it out, and in so doing I got in full view of the Indians. It was here that I got shot in the right side. I laid down behind a stump, and again those Indians fired a number of shots, but none of them hit me… I stayed there until dark, and then I managed to crawl away.

When pursuit was ordered the following morning, Hayman crawled out of his tent and began to saddle his horse, but was ordered to the rear for treatment.

Captain Norvell's subsequent attempts to gain proper recognition for the buffalo soldiers at the Cheyenne Agency came to naught, despite the fact that his company sustained three men wounded, one of them mortally, while Keye's company had nine men wounded, three severely. Following this action, Companies D and M, 10th Cavalry, joined the rest of their regiment in West Texas, with headquarters at Fort Concho, while the 9th Cavalry was transferred to New Mexico.

While stationed at Fort Concho, the band of the 10th Cavalry played a valuable role in lifting the spirits of the buffalo soldiers. The wife of one of the officers recalled:

> … each member is a black man, except the leader, who is a German. To this man is due great credit. He has taught them the alphabet of music and can now compare them favorably with any band in the army. They certainly play well. While I write, soft tender notes from Schubert go wandering away into oblivion. When the troops return from their "summer tour" in the "field," the band (every man mounted on a white horse) goes out to escort them in, all in full uniform, their brass instruments glittering in the sun and their inspiring martial music echoing "over hill and dale."

CAMPAIGNING IN WEST TEXAS, 1875–81

ON THE STAKED PLAINS, 1875

In response to continued cattle raids and horse stealing, Lieutenant-Colonel William Shafter, 24th Infantry, was ordered to sweep the remaining Indians and Comancheros off the Staked Plains. On July 14, 1875, he led a four-month long expedition from Fort Concho that marked the first time the area had been thoroughly explored. The troops involved consisted of six companies of the 10th Cavalry, two companies of the 24th Infantry, one of the 25th Infantry, plus a group of Black-Seminole Indian Scouts. Determined to find and destroy the Indians on the Staked Plains, Shafter embarked on one of the most demanding marches ever made by the buffalo soldiers when his column set out from his supply camp on August 5, 1875. They trudged across 860 miles of waterless prairie in 52 days, arriving back at camp without success on September 25, having lost only 29 horses. Another scouting expedition led by Captain T. A. Baldwin covered 340 miles, including one march of 38 hours without water. These operations temporarily swept the Staked Plains clear of Indians, and led to the beginning of a general settlement of the region.

NOLAN'S "LOST PATROL," 1877

Two years later, in 1877, trouble developed again on the Staked Plains when a band of Kwahada Comanches began to attack hunting parties and newly settled white homesteaders. On July 10, in the midst of an arid summer, Captain Nicholas Nolan left Fort Concho with orders to find and punish the marauders. His command consisted of 60 troopers of Company A, 10th Cavalry, many of whom were raw recruits. Marching to the headwaters of the North Concho River, Nolan eventually turned north across the Colorado

River toward Bull Creek, 140 miles from Fort Concho, where he established a supply camp. At Bull Creek he encountered a party of 28 buffalo hunters, in company with the veteran Mexican–American guide José Tafoya, who were searching for Indian cattle thieves. Without a guide of his own, and grateful for reinforcements, Nolan was happy to join forces with Tafoya, who had scouted for the Army during earlier campaigns on the Staked Plains. Having scoured the area, the guide believed that the Indians were hiding at or near Double Lakes. Preferring to march at night to avoid the searing heat of the day, Nolan, with 40 troopers, set out for Double Lakes on the evening of July 19 in company with Tafoya and the buffalo hunters. He left a sergeant and 19 men to guard the supply camp. Reaching Double Lakes after riding for three days with little water, the patrol found no Indians, and spent the rest of the day digging holes in the dried up lake bed in order to find the little water that remained. Following this, and for the next eight days, the party staggered on behind Tafoya – more in search of water than of Indians, and finding neither. A routine Army scout was turning into disaster.

On the fifth day of this march, some of Nolan's new recruits were overcome with exhaustion and dehydration, and began to fall from their saddles. Detailing Sergeant William Umbles to stay with two of the weakest troopers, and instructing him to bring them into camp once they had rested, Nolan continued after Tafoya, who had ridden on ahead with a small group of the fittest civilians to look for water. With so many men unable to ride, Nolan was forced to make a "dry" bivouac that night, and was amazed to witness the mutinous Sergeant Umbles and the sick men ride by "within easy hailing distance" without halting. During the same night, the horses belonging to some of the buffalo hunters stampeded. Having lost his guide, Nolan decided to take his men back to Double Lakes where he knew they would find some water.

On the return march, Corporal Gilmore deserted after having been ordered to remain behind to look after another sick trooper. Lance Corporal Freemont and two enlisted men also deserted the command shortly after. Nolan arrived back at Double Lakes having been without water for 86 hours. During this last march the buffalo soldiers survived by drinking the blood of their dead horses and their own urine. Nolan's men straggled back into Double Lakes on July 30, and the next day help arrived in the form of Captain P. L. Lee, with Company G, 10th Cavalry, who had happened by on a scout from Fort Griffin. Lee accompanied Nolan back to his supply camp, where they rested further.

Meanwhile, Sergeant Umbles and Corporals Gilmore and Freemont had arrived back at Fort Concho to report falsely that Indians had attacked their unit, and that "two officers and twenty-six enlisted soldiers had been killed." The "Staked Plains Horror," as the *Galveston Daily News* called it, quickly grabbed the attention of the press across the nation. In response to the news from the deserters, a column under Lieutenant R. G. Smither was sent out to find Nolan. After medical aid and rest, the patrol finally arrived back at Fort Concho on August 14, 1877. Although most of Nolan's troopers had eventually straggled back into his supply camp, four men had died. Sergeant Umbles and Corporals Gilmore and Freemont were clapped in irons, court-martialed and dishonorably discharged.

ACROSS THE BORDER, 1876–77

Meanwhile, elements of the 10th Cavalry formed the only mounted troops assigned to protect the Rio Grande area. In the face of constant Indian raids across the river, and further trouble from Mexican bandits and revolutionaries who sought "refuge" on American soil, General E. O. C. Ord, commanding the Department of Texas, ordered Colonel Shafter at Fort Duncan to organize an expedition to attack a large Lipan and Kickapoo camp known to be in the vicinity of Saragossa, Mexico. Shafter's column consisted of three companies of the 10th Cavalry, detachments of the 24th and 25th Infantry, and a party of Black-Seminole scouts. After pushing southwest for five days, Shafter became concerned that he might be cut off by Mexican troops if his whole force advanced further. He therefore ordered Lieutenant George Evans, with 20 picked troopers, plus Lieutenant John L. Bullis, commanding the Seminole scouts, to march on to the village.

Evans and Bullis covered the remaining 110 miles in just 24 hours, and located the camp of 23 lodges about 5 miles from Saragossa. Attacking at dawn on July 30, 1876, they took the Indians completely by surprise and savage hand-to-hand fighting ensued. The Indians were swiftly put to flight, leaving 14 warriors dead. The lodges were burned and the strike force swiftly retraced its steps to the main command. Shafter promptly withdrew to the border, where the only man to be lost during the whole operation, Trooper Joseph Titus, Company B, 10th Cavalry, was drowned crossing back over the Rio Grande. Elements of the regiment conducted further successful expeditions into Mexico throughout the remainder of the year, and by August 1877 a total of 94 Mexican revolutionaries were captured north of the border.

On Campaign, 1872–91

As with all units of the Frontier Army, the buffalo soldiers looked very different from their parade ground appearance when on campaign. The 10th Cavalry sergeant (1), c. 1872, wears a civilian "fireman"-style shirt with plastron front, and crossed sabers crudely embroidered on each side of the falling collar. The only signs of his rank are the 1in seam stripes on his 1861-pattern sky-blue kersey trousers. He carries an M1865 trial Spencer repeating carbine and has a Remington .44cal New Model Army revolver tucked in his 1863-pattern black leather holster. The 9th Cavalry trooper (2), c. 1884, is dressed in an 1882-pattern shirt with yellow piping, an 1882-pattern campaign hat with "Brachers" Patent Ventilators and yellow cord. His colorful civilian neckerchief or bandana was standard, but non-regulation, campaign wear. His 1872-pattern sky-blue kersey trousers are reinforced with buckskin on seat and inner leg. Fastened by a yellow metal "H" plate, his blue woven 1881-pattern Mills belt has yellow painted selvages, or edging. He carries an M1873 Springfield "Trapdoor." The 25th Infantry enlisted man (3), c. 1890, wears clothing suitable for the harsh northern winters. His double-breasted buffalo-skin overcoat is worn over an 1884-pattern blouse. Headgear consists of an 1872-pattern forage cap with 1875-pattern crossed rifles insignia in front. He is armed with an M1873 Springfield rifle.

(Richard Hook © Osprey Publishing)

CAMPAIGNING IN NEW MEXICO, ARIZONA, & COLORADO, 1876–90

FLORIDA MOUNTAINS, 1876–77

The 9th Cavalry transferred to the District of New Mexico during the winter and spring of 1876–77. Scattered between nine forts and one camp, they began their campaign against the renegade Apaches led by Geronimo and Juh. The first clash between the buffalo soldiers and the Apaches took place in September 1876, when Captain Henry Carroll and 25 troopers of Company F, stationed at Fort Selden, encountered and attacked some renegades in the Florida Mountains, killing one warrior and wounding three.

A more dramatic action occurred on January 24, 1877, when a band of about 50 Chiricahuas attacked a detachment of the 6th Cavalry in Arizona and then headed east into an area patrolled by Company C, 9th Cavalry, based at Fort Bayard. Lieutenant Henry J. Wright, with six enlisted men and three Navajo scouts, set out to track down the renegades and force them back to their reservation. On the third day of the patrol, the Apaches were intercepted in the Florida Mountains, approximately 55 miles south of Silver City. Although greatly outnumbered, Lieutenant Wright and his men dismounted and approached the Apaches but, after a fruitless parley, the officer noticed that the Indians had quietly surrounded his patrol. He ordered his men to push their way through to their horses, but as they did so a deadly fight at close quarters broke out. Corporal Clinton Greaves fired his carbine until it was empty and then swung it like a club, knocking aside the Apaches and smashing a gap through the encircling warriors. While running for their mounts, the troopers were pinned down by the gunfire of other Apaches

The artist Remington
sketched this campfire
scene in Arizona
Territory in 1888 when
invited to take part in a
"scout" conducted by
the 10th Cavalry. (Anne
S. K. Brown Military
Collection, Brown
University Library)

The artist Remington sketched this campfire scene in Arizona Territory in 1888 when invited to take part in a "scout" conducted by the 10th Cavalry. (Anne S. K. Brown Military Collection, Brown University Library)

who had taken cover in surrounding rocks. Again Corporal Greaves reacted and raced for the horses while firing, fatally wounding two of the attackers. Rushing the mounts to his companions, Greaves enabled the cavalrymen to escape, taking 11 of the Indian horses with them. In the encounter, five of the Apaches were killed and not one of the cavalry patrol was seriously wounded.

Corporal Greaves was awarded the Medal of Honor, while three troopers and a Navajo scout received commendations for their part in the action.

CIVIL DISORDERS, 1876–78

During 1876–78, the 9th Cavalry became involved in several civil disorders. A dispute over a two million acre land grant in Colfax County, New Mexico, owned by the British-sponsored Maxwell Land Grant & Railway Company, involved the 9th Cavalry as a peacekeeping force during March 1876. Following several shootings and vigilante hangings, 30 troopers from Company L, under Captain France Moore, were ordered to Cimarron from Fort Union. There they were successfully assigned as detachments to escort law enforcement officers making arrests. Taking up quarters in a livery stable behind the St James Hotel, Moore instructed his men to stay away from the saloons. Needless to say, several ignored orders and were subsequently shot dead during an argument with some Texan cowboys. A few days later, another trooper robbed and killed two civilians. He was tried, found guilty, and hanged.

In mid December 1877, nine companies of the regiment were scraped together and ordered back to Texas, where rival factions were fighting over the rights to salt deposits at the foot of Guadalupe Peak, 100 miles east of El

Paso. Arriving at the nearby township of San Elizario with an advanced guard of 54 troopers and two howitzers, Colonel Hatch quickly assumed control and separated the warring factions with his trail-hardened buffalo soldiers.

The Lincoln County War, 1877–78

Elements of the 9th Cavalry next became involved in protecting life and property during the Lincoln County War. For many years Lincoln County, New Mexico, had enjoyed the unenviable reputation of having more thieves and murderers per square mile than any county in the American West. By 1878 a gang led by Alexander McSween, which included the likes of William Bonney, alias "Billy the Kid," was involved in a bloody conflict with the Murphy-Dolan faction. Situated a few miles north of the township of Lincoln was Fort Stanton, which was garrisoned by Companies F, H, and M, 9th Cavalry, under Lieutenant-Colonel N. A. M. Dudley. While carrying a note from Dudley to Sheriff George Peppin during July of that year, Private Berry Robinson of Company H fought his way single-handed through a small gang of outlaws, only to be fired on again when he entered Lincoln. Thrown from his horse as bullets kicked up dirt around him, the courier narrowly escaped death by scrambling for cover behind a hotel building.

Although half of his troopers were out scouting for renegade Indians in the Guadalupe and Sacramento mountains, Dudley was determined to restore law and order to Lincoln, which next experienced about four days' continual fighting. On July 19, 1878, he assembled a force consisting of 11 buffalo soldiers, 24 white infantrymen, one Gatling gun, and one 12-pounder brass mountain howitzer. Wearing full dress uniforms to create maximum impact, and supplied with 2,000 rounds of ammunition, this force rode into Lincoln as "neutrals" determined to protect the women and children of the

A troop of the 9th Cavalry parades in full dress sometime after the regimental headquarters was transferred to Fort McKinney, Wyoming, in 1885. (American Heritage Center, University of Wyoming)

community. Setting up camp in the middle of the town, Dudley pointed his howitzer at the building serving as headquarters for the McSween gang, and threatened to send a shell through it if his men were fired on again. Encouraged by support from the Army, Sheriff Peppin set fire to the McSween building and drove most of the occupants out. Billy the Kid and others fled, while Alexander McSween died in the blaze.

THE UTE CAMPAIGN, 1879

After years of white encroachment and mismanagement by Indian agencies, serious trouble broke out among the White River Utes on the border with New Mexico and Colorado during September 1879. In response, a mixed battalion of cavalry and infantry led by Major Thomas T. Thornburgh, 4th Infantry, left Fort Frederick Steele, Wyoming, for the scene of the outbreak, while Captain Francis Dodge, commanding Company D, 9th Cavalry, set out from an encampment on the Grand River. Thornburgh's column reached Milk Creek Canyon, Colorado, about 25 miles from the White River Agency, on September 29, but was ambushed and attacked by several hundred Utes. Forced to take up a defensive position behind a hastily prepared breastwork of dead animals and overturned wagons, Thornburgh was killed during the first few minutes of action, but his men held out for three days under the second-in-command, Captain J. Scott Payne. Realizing he was surrounded, Payne ordered his scout, J. P. Rankin, to fetch help. Meanwhile, Captain Dodge received word of their plight and rode hard for 23 hours to reach the beleaguered troopers at Milk Creek.

Facing dawn and another day of bitter fighting on October 1, Payne's force was greatly relieved to see Captain Dodge and his 35 black troopers galloping full pelt toward them out of the rising sun. A soldier in Payne's command recalled: "Cheer after cheer rent the air from our trenches when we

Photographed at Winfield, Kansas, in the studio of D. Rodocker, sometime after his regiment was assigned to Kansas and Indian Territory in 1881, Sergeant John Denny, Company B, 9th Cavalry, was awarded the Medal of Honor for helping to rescue a wounded comrade at Las Animas Canyon on September 18, 1879. (Christian Fleetwood Collection, Library of Congress)

ascertained who were coming. A lull in the firing enabled them to come in and shelter their horses as well as possible. They took [to] the fortifications quickly when the attack redoubled its fury. Had the heights been accessible, Captain Dodge would have charged them with his company, while we covered him from our rifle pits, but this was utterly impossible, the ascent being almost perpendicular." Another white trooper in the same command naively revealed his racial prejudice by commenting: "We forgot all about the danger of exposing ourselves and leaped up out of the pits to shake hands all around. Why, we took those darkies in right along with us in the pits. We let 'em sleep with us, and they took their knives and cut off slips of bacon from the same sides as we did."

Further attacks raged throughout the remainder of that day, during which Captain Dodge recorded: "Indians all around us and keep up a plaguing fire on our pit. All our animals are dead and we cannot communicate with the agency… The command is in good spirits, and we can hold out till succor

Also photographed by Rodocker at Winfield, Kansas, during the same period, this young trooper of Company B, 9th Cavalry, has 1885-pattern Blunt marksman's buttons attached either side of his collar. (Bob Kotchian Collection)

arrives." As night fell Sergeant Henry Johnson, Company D, 9th Cavalry, distinguished himself by leaving his fortified cover under heavy fire in order to offer encouragement to the men. Under cover of darkness on October 2, the same man showed extreme bravery when he fought his way to the nearby riverside, and returned with several pails filled with water to relieve the thirst of the wounded. On this occasion, Johnson is said to have commented: "Well, boss, I'se powerfully dry, and somebody's got to git water fo' me, or I'se got to git water fo' somebody!" As a result, Sergeant Johnson eventually received the Medal of Honor for courage under fire at Milk Creek.

After nearly a week, the siege of Milk Creek was lifted at dawn on October 5, 1879, when five companies of the 5th Cavalry, under Colonel Wesley Merritt, finally drove off the Utes. In a dispatch sent the same day, Merritt complimented the involvement of Captain Dodge and his buffalo soldiers, stating: "Too much praise cannot be given this gallant officer and his command for the very praiseworthy act in the reinforcement of Payne's command." The bravery of Company D, 9th Cavalry, was further acknowledged when "the colored citizens" of Denver, Colorado, gave a rousing reception in their honor as the troopers passed through that city en route to take up winter quarters on October 22, 1879. By the end of the year, the regimental band of the 9th Cavalry had added a new tune to its repertoire called "Captain Dodge's Relief."

THE VICTORIO CAMPAIGN, 1879–81

One of the most frustrating campaigns for the buffalo soldiers was the "Victorio War" of 1879–80. War chief of the Warm Springs Apaches, Victorio wished to remain at Ojo Caliente on the fringes of the Black Range, which was the ancestral home of his people. As a consequence, the black troopers became involved in hunting down the renegade and his band. In May 1879, Captain Charles D. Beyer, leading elements of Companies C and I, 9th Cavalry, first picked up the trail of Victorio, who responded by setting the underbrush and woodland afire in an attempt to thwart the soldiers. Beyer persisted and eventually caught up with the Apaches as they were building a breastwork on a rocky peak near the Continental Divide. During the ensuing firefight, Sergeant Thomas Boyne, of Company C, earned a Medal of Honor by rescuing Lieutenant Henry H. Wright, who was cut off when his horse was killed. Wright recalled: "I was engaged in bringing in a wounded man with a few men and was surprised by the Indians, my horse was killed and corralled by hostiles when Sergeant Thomas Boyne commanded a detachment sent to my assistance, flanked and gallantly charged the Indians driving them off."

On June 30, and several weeks after his encounter with Beyer, Victorio surrendered at the Mescalero Agency at Fort Stanton. But after refusing to be transported to the hated San Carlos Reservation in Arizona, he escaped on September 3, 1879. The next day he and his band attacked a nearby army camp, killing five black troopers of Company E, 9th Cavalry, and capturing all 50 of the horses belonging to this unit. As a result, the whole of the 9th and 10th Cavalry was eventually put in the field either to kill or capture the Apache leader. They did neither, although they did much to wear down the resilience of Victorio and his renegade warriors.

Las Animas Canyon, 1879

On September 18, 1879, Navajo scouts attached to a column led by Lieutenant-Colonel Dudley, composed of Companies A and B, 9th Cavalry, picked up the trail of Victorio in the canyons at the head of the Las Animas

River. Soon after, these troopers were caught in a three-way hail of bullets fired from the heights of Las Animas Canyon. Hastily dismounting, the troopers took cover behind rocks and boulders, where they remained completely pinned down. The gunfire was heard echoing and re-echoing down the canyon by the men of Companies C and G who were following behind. They rushed to the battle scene, only to be pinned down as well. All four companies eventually withdrew at nightfall, having sustained five troopers and three scouts killed.

Medals of Honor were awarded to three of the men involved in this engagement. After receiving orders to withdraw, Second Lieutenant Matthias W. Day, Company A, noticed two wounded troopers who were about to be left behind. He and Sergeant John Denny ran back under fire and assisted Private Alfred Freeland to safety. Lieutenant Day then went back alone to carry off Private Jeremiah Crump, who was more seriously wounded.

Elsewhere, Second Lieutenant Robert T. Emmet, Company G, was involved in a flanking attack on the Apaches when he and five troopers became cut off

These NCOs of the 9th Cavalry accompanied the body of Colonel Hatch to Fort Leavenworth for burial in 1889. Sergeant Nathan Fletcher, Company F (top right) was among those involved in the battle with Victorio at Hembrillo Canyon, New Mexico, in April 1880. Sergeant Robert Burley, Company G (seated, second from right), was among those who rode to the rescue. (Courtesy of Special Collections, US Military Academy, West Point) and surrounded. Realizing that the renegades were making for a position from which they could fire down on the retreating soldiers, Emmet ordered his men to hold their post until those down in the canyon bottom were out of danger. The officer then continued to hold the position while his party recovered its horses, enabling all six men finally to withdraw safely.

Following the failure at Las Animas, Lieutenant-Colonel Dudley was replaced in command of operations in southern New Mexico by Major Albert P. Morrow. On September 29–30, Morrow and detachments from Companies B, C, and G, 9th Cavalry, plus some Apache scouts, fought a running battle with Victorio's band along the Cuchillo Negro River, although the hostiles managed to elude capture. During the next month, the same officer chased Victorio across the border into Mexico, but again failed to capture or kill him, and eventually led his tattered command in to Fort Bayard, near the Mimbres River, where they rested and refitted. The success of Victorio in fending off the buffalo soldiers increased the ranks of his band to about 120 warriors as recruits joined him, especially from the Mescalero Reservation.

Hembrillo Canyon, 1880

With the return of Victorio to New Mexico in January 1880, Major Morrow again found himself pitted against an indefatigable foe. On February 23, Colonel Hatch came south and took personal command, ordering more of the 9th Cavalry into the field against the elusive Apache leader. He organized his force into three battalions, commanded by Major Morrow, Captain Ambrose Hooker, and Captain Henry Carroll respectively. Acting on advice that Victorio was encamped in Hembrillo Canyon in the San Andrés Mountains, Hatch planned a two-phase operation involving his battalions descending on the renegades from the north, east, and west. Meanwhile, Colonel Grierson received orders from General Sheridan to march from Texas with five companies of the 10th Cavalry. Hatch intended that this entire force should descend on the Mescalero Reservation after wiping out Victorio and his renegades.

Morrow set out from Fort Bayard on March 29 accompanied by Companies H, L, and M, plus a detachment of the 16th Infantry, and a few San Carlos Apache scouts. This column marched to Palomas, where it was joined by reinforcements from Arizona consisting of 85 troopers of the 6th Cavalry, commanded by Captain Curwen B. McClellan, and two companies of Indian scouts. This entire force next moved to Alemán Well on the Jornada del Muerto, near the western slopes of the San Andrés. Captain Carroll advanced westward from Fort Stanton with Companies A, D, F, and G, 9th Cavalry, while Captain Hooker headed south with Companies E, I, and K, 9th Cavalry, plus a small detachment of the 15th Infantry.

Unfortunately, Morrow's progress was delayed by a broken water pipe at Alemán Well, which caused his command to halt until the horses and men were properly watered. When his advanced party, under Captain McClellan, finally reached Hembrillo Canyon on April 8, they heard the sound of gunfire and found Carroll's command pinned down and surrounded. Realizing they were outnumbered, however, Victorio and his band melted away into the rocks, leaving eight soldiers wounded, including Captain Carroll.

Old Fort Tularosa, 1880

Following his success at Hembrillo Canyon, Victorio moved westward across the Rio Grande into the Mogollon Mountains, killing settlers and miners along

Old Fort Tularosa, 1880

At dusk on May 14, 1880, over 100 Warm Springs Apaches, led by the renegade chief Victorio, attacked Old Fort Tularosa, an abandoned Indian agency about 50 miles northwest of Ojo Caliente, in New Mexico. Inside the hastily repaired stockade, Sergeant George Jordan, commanding 25 troopers of Company K, 9th Cavalry, was all that stood between the local settlers and certain death. The plate shows the first clash of arms as the Apaches tried to rush the defenses. Sergeant Jordan and a squad of black troopers are dressed in a mixture of 1876-pattern, black wool campaign hats with "Brasher" spinner ventilator on each side of the crown, plus civilian brimmed hats. Despite the intense desert heat, Sergeant Jordan wears the 1874-pattern blouse with branch service trim removed, while others have stripped down to their shirt sleeves. They are armed with "Trapdoor" carbines and M1873 .45cal Colt Cavalry revolvers. Their equipment includes 1876-pattern, Type 3, tan canvas and leather "prairie belts" with revolver cartridge pouch and holster attached, plus Dyer ammunition pouches.

(Richard Hook © Osprey Publishing)

the way. Among the latter was James C. Cooney, brother of Captain Michael Cooney, commanding Company A, 9th Cavalry. Captain Cooney was subsequently presented with the sad task of burying his own brother. Meanwhile Colonel Hatch, with Hooker's battalion, pursued Victorio into Arizona, but the Apaches doubled back into New Mexico and headed toward Old Fort Tularosa, which consisted of a small community of squatters settled around an abandoned Indian agency about 50 miles northwest of Ojo Caliente.

Under orders to escort a train of provisions to Old Fort Tularosa and set up a supply base there for the regiment, Sergeant George Jordan, with 25 troopers of Company K, 9th Cavalry, was bedding down for an overnight stop at the Barlow and Sanderson Stage Station on May 13, when a lone rider galloped in yelling that Victorio and his band had been seen near the Old Fort. On foot, as their horses had long since been worn out, Jordan and his detachment marched through the night, arriving at their destination at dawn the next day to find that Victorio had not yet struck. Jordan set his men to work to repair and strengthen the old stockade surrounding the dilapidated agency buildings, inside which the local populace was gathered for safety.

More than 100 Apaches attacked at dusk on May 14, but the buffalo soldiers held their ground and drove the hostiles off. Jordan next dispatched ten of his troopers to prevent the mules and cattle from being stampeded. He later recalled: "Keeping under cover of the timber, the men quickly made their way to the herders and drove the Indians away, thus saving the men and stock... After it was all over the townspeople congratulated us for having repulsed ... more than 100 redskins." Victorio subsequently abandoned his attack and moved south into Mexico. In 1890, Sergeant Jordan received a Medal of Honor for the courage and leadership displayed at Old Fort Tularosa.

Rattlesnake Canyon, 1880

To keep the US Army guessing, Victorio next crossed the border into Texas in July 1880, where he encountered the 10th Cavalry. Learning from the experience of Hatch, Colonel Grierson decided not to attempt a long and fruitless pursuit of the Apaches, but determined to guard the mountain passes and water holes. Discovering that Victorio was headed toward Eagle Springs, Grierson lay in ambush at Tinaja de los Palmos, the only watering hole along the route, and surprised the Apaches, who nevertheless managed to fight their way out because the buffalo soldiers fired on one another in the dust and confusion of battle.

Grierson continued to monitor the movements of Victorio in his quest for water, and established another ambush in a canyon approaching

Called "A pull at the canteen," this engraving is based on a Remington sketch made while the artist was on a "scout" with the 10th Cavalry in the Sierra Bonitos in 1888. (Anne S. K. Brown Military Collection, Brown University Library)

Rattlesnake Springs on August 6, 1880. Captain Charles Viele was commanding Companies C and G, 10th Cavalry, as they waited for the Apaches to approach. In mid afternoon their vigil was rewarded as Victorio and his warriors rode toward them, unaware of the ambush. Seconds before the signal to fire was due to be given, Victorio sensed danger and halted his men. The buffalo soldiers opened fire, but the warriors swiftly withdrew out of range. Desperate for water and believing only a few soldiers lay in his path, Victorio attacked but was caught off guard and repulsed when Captain Carpenter, with Companies B and H, was ordered to counterattack. Meanwhile, a party of Victorio's warriors was beaten off in an attempt to cut off and attack Grierson's supply train, guarded by Company H, 24th Infantry, as it lumbered toward the spring. Victorio's warriors repeatedly charged the buffalo soldiers in an attempt to reach the water. Finally, as night fell, they fled into the Corissa Mountains with the troopers in furious pursuit, but the chase ended without further fighting on that occasion.

Five days later, the buffalo soldiers under Captains Carpenter and Nolan again picked up the trail of Victorio and his warriors. In the heat of the chase, the horses in Carpenter's company gave out, leaving Nolan's troopers to continue the pursuit. As had happened oft times before, Victorio's warriors crossed the Rio Grande River into Mexico before the US forces could catch them.

A combined operation involving both American and Mexican forces was finally mounted during September 1880. But on October 9, as these forces converged on Victorio and the remains of his band in the Tres Castillos Mountains, General Joaquin Terrazas informed Colonels Buell and Carr that the presence of American troops on Mexican soil was objectionable, and so they were withdrawn. Victorio was finally caught and killed by elements of the Mexican Army five days later.

Agua Chiquita Canyon, 1880

Despite the death of Victorio, troubles continued with the Apaches and the buffalo soldiers further distinguished themselves in combat. On September 1, 1880, Sergeant James Robinson and a detachment of nine troopers of Company G, 9th Cavalry, were attacked by hostiles while encamped at Agua Chiquita Canyon, New Mexico. Although outnumbered and with two men killed, Robinson ordered a charge and the Indians were driven off.

With most of their animals either dead or wounded, Private Alonzo Drake particularly distinguished himself by volunteering to ride for help on a wounded mule, bare back and alone, traveling 70 miles through hostile country to reach Fort Stanton in 21 hours. Along the way, he asked to borrow a saddle at a settlement near the Peñasco River, and was refused by a white farmer. On October 7, 1880, Sergeant Robinson and his detachment received a commendation from Colonel Hatch for their gallantry.

Carrizo Canyon, 1881

Several other members of the 9th Cavalry earned the coveted Medal of Honor during the continuation of the Indian campaign in 1881. On August

Photographed by assistant surgeon Edgar A. Mearns, a troop of the 10th Cavalry line up on the parade ground at Fort Verde in Arizona, c. 1886. These men would have been involved in the campaign against Geronimo. (Library of Congress, LC-USZ62-76430)

Sergeant Moses Williams and Private Augustus Walley, Company I, 9th Cavalry, both eventually received the Congressional Medal of Honor for bravery during the action against a small band of renegade Apaches led by Nana in the foothills of the Cuchillo Negro Mountains in August 1881:

War Department

41940 A.G.O.   Adjutant General's Office
Washington, November 23, 1896

Ordnance Sergeant Moses Williams
Fort Stevens, Oregon.
Thro. Headquarters Department of the Columbia,
Vancouver Barracks, Wash.

Sergeant:

I am instructed by the Assistant Secretary of War to transmit to you the accompanying medal of honor, awarded to you by direction of the President of the United States for most distinguished gallantry in action with hostile Apache Indians in the foot hills of the Cuchillo Negro Mountains, N.M., August 18, 1881, while serving as 1st Sergeant Troop "I" 9th Cavalry.

The remarks of the Assistant Secretary of War in making this award are as follows:

"This soldier rallied the detachment when his commanding officer was dismounted and unable to reach it; he skilfully conducted the right flank in a running fight for three or four hours; his keen-sightedness in discovering the Indians in hiding probably prevented the command from falling into a trap; and his coolness, bravery, and unflinching devotion to duty in standing by his commanding officer in an exposed position under a heavy fire from a large party of Indians was undoubtedly the means of saving the lives of at least three of his comrades."

Very respectfully,

Assistant Adjutant General.

– Adjutant-General Document File 41940, RG 94, NARA

Private Augustus Walley finally received his Medal of Honor on October 1, 1890.

Entitled "The brave conduct of Lieutenant Clark, of the Tenth (Colored) Cavalry, in rescuing, under fire, the wounded Corporal Scott," this engraving appeared on the front page of *Harper's Weekly* on August 21, 1886. According to Clark, Scott rode 40 miles "without a groan" following this action, stating that he had seen "forty men in one fight in a worse fix than he was." (Anne S. K. Brown Military Collection, Brown University Library)

12, Sergeant Thomas Shaw was part of a detachment of Company K in pursuit of a small renegade band led by Nana, one of Victorio's lieutenants. These Apaches had attacked a number of small settlements and ranches in southern New Mexico Territory. The out-numbered soldiers surprised the hostiles in Carrizo Canyon on the west side of the Mimbres Mountains. Sergeant Shaw was awarded the Medal of Honor for "extraordinary courage under fire" in preventing the Apaches from surrounding his command.

Four days later, during a firefight in the foothills of the Cuchillo Negro Mountains, Lieutenant George Burnett saved the life of an unhorsed trooper under fire. In the same action, Sergeant Moses Williams and Private Augustus Walley, of Company I, rescued three troopers in a similar predicament. On August 19, Sergeant Brent Woods, Company B, also saved the lives of several of his comrades, plus some civilians. All four men received the ultimate award for bravery.

THE GERONIMO CAMPAIGN, 1885–86

In the spring of 1885, the 10th Cavalry moved from Texas to the Department of Arizona, where they were needed in the campaign against Geronimo and his Chiricahua Apaches. When the column took up its march from Fort Davis and followed the route of the Southern Pacific Railroad, it comprised 11 troops plus the regimental band. At Camp Rice it was joined by Company I, and from that point to Bowie Station, Arizona, the whole regiment progressed together for the first time in its history. Headquarters was established at Whipple Barracks, while the remainder of the regiment was posted at Forts Apache, Verde, Thomas, and Grant.

The greater part of the 10th Cavalry was in the field during the whole of the Geronimo campaign of 1885–86, although the duty performed involved a dismal succession of inglorious days guarding water holes and mountain passes. One exception occurred in May 1886, when Company K, under Captain Thomas C. Lebo, pursued Geronimo's band into the Santa Cruz Valley after an Indian attack on a nearby ranch. Following a 200-mile chase, the buffalo soldiers brought their quarry to bay on the rocky slopes of the Sierra Piñito in Mexico, about 30 miles south of the border. As veterans of the Victorio campaign, the black troopers held firm as they were met with a wall of lead. Dismounting, they took cover, but one man was killed, while Corporal Edward Scott was severely wounded in both legs and lay exposed to enemy fire. Ignoring the hail of bullets, Lieutenant Powhattan Clarke rose from cover, made his way to his stricken comrade and carried him to safety. Lieutenant Clarke recalled: "I had some close calls while I was trying to pull the corporal from under fire and succeeded in getting him behind a bush and you can be sure it was a very new sensation to hear bullets whiz and strike within six inches of me and not be able to see anything."

Shortly after this, the enemy fire slackened and then ceased, as Geronimo escaped once more into the mountains. Lieutenant Clarke was later awarded the Medal of Honor for his bravery on May 3, 1886. In a letter to his mother, he stated: "Our troop has been highly complimented and the Captain is the hero of the hour. Do not tell me about the colored troops[,] there is not a troop in the U.S. Army that I would trust my life to as quickly as this K troop of ours."

After the surrender of Geronimo in August of the same year, a last remnant of his Apache band under Mangus continued to defy the government of the United States. On September 18, Captain Charles L. Cooper, commanding Troop H, 10th Cavalry, picked up the trail of Mangus in the White Mountains and pursued him over 40 miles of rough and rocky country. After a running fight, the Indians were cornered in the Black River Mountains and forced to surrender.

The 10th Cavalry and 24th Infantry continued to serve in Arizona throughout the remainder of the 1880s. In 1887, elements of both regiments were involved in the hunt for "The Apache Kid," a former Indian scout who went on the run following the murder of a fellow scout at the San Carlos Reservation. Despite a $5,000 reward for his recapture dead or alive, "The Kid" was never caught.

AMBUSH NEAR CEDAR SPRINGS, 1889

A regular duty for the buffalo soldiers involved guarding the army payroll as it was carried from post to post for distribution. In May 1889, paymaster Major Joseph W. Wham was under escort provided by eight enlisted men of the 24th Infantry and two troopers of the 10th Cavalry, when the party was ambushed on the trail between Fort Grant and Fort Thomas, near Cedar Springs Station, Arizona. A gang of outlaws placed a boulder in a narrow gorge through which the trail passed, and waited in the bluffs above. The soldiers were advancing toward the boulder blocking the road, when a signal shot was fired from the ledge of rocks about 50ft above to the right. A firefight ensued for about 30 minutes, during which eight of the enlisted men were wounded, two being shot twice. Succeeding in stealing $29,000, the bandits escaped into the mountains.

According to Paymaster Wham:

Corporal Isaiah Mays, Company B, 24th Infantry, was one of two men awarded the Medal of Honor for attempting to save the payroll at Cedar Springs in 1889. (Library of Congress)

Sergeant [Benjamin] Brown, though shot through the abdomen, did not quit the field until again wounded, this time through the arm. Private [Benjamin] Burge who was to my immediate right, received a bad wound in the hand, but gallantly held his post, resting his rifle on his forearm and continuing to

fire with much coolness until shot through the thigh and twice through the hat. Private [George] Arrington was shot through the shoulder while fighting from the same position. Private [Thornton] Hams, [James] Wheeler, and [Julius] Harrison were also wounded to my immediate left, while bravely doing their duty under a murderous cross fire. Private [Squire] Williams was shot through the leg near my ambulance at the first volley, but crawling behind cover continued the fire. Private [Hamilton] Lewis, my ambulance driver, was shot through the stomach, but the noble fellow was undaunted, and while the blood gushed from his terrible wound, he insisted that my clerk, W. F. Gibbon, should allow him to take the wounded Wheeler's gun ... and buckling on the belt heroically continued to fight until all present were wounded except myself and Corporal [Isaiah] Mays.

The latter soldier managed to walk and crawl about 2 miles to the Cottonwood Ranch and gave the alarm. Troops were called out from all the surrounding posts, plus a company of Apache scouts and a posse under US Marshall W. K. Meade. A local black woman who observed the attack was able to identify several of the bandits, including "Cyclone Bill," who were subsequently arrested and jailed. Sergeant Brown and Corporal Mays were both recommended for the Medal of Honor, which they received the following year.

Major Wham concluded his report of the attack by stating: "I was a soldier in [General] Grant's old regiment [21st Illinois], and during the entire Civil War it was justly proud of its record of 16 battles … but I never witnessed better courage or better fighting than shown by these colored soldiers, on May 11, 1889."

These gregarious members of the 25th Infantry were photographed in the snow at Fort Keogh, Montana, in 1890. Many of them wear buffalo coats, muskrat caps, and gauntlets. (Library of Congress)

DAKOTA TERRITORY, 1880–91

Following ten years of arduous service in Texas, during which time it garrisoned posts and sub-posts, guarded mails and public property, constructed over 1,000 miles of wagon roads and 300 miles of telegraph lines, and efficiently scouted a vast region of hostile mountains and plains, the 25th Infantry was transferred to Dakota Territory during the summer of 1880.

A local newspaper correspondent at Yankton described the scene when five companies of the regiment arrived via railroad and transferred to a riverboat:

> The lines were cast off, and amid the cheers of the occupants of the boat which were answered by the crowd on the shore, and the fine music of the regimental band, the *Peninah* steamed up the river, and the hundreds of spectators who had assembled on the banks of the river to witness the novelty of a regiment of colored troops, returned to town. The men of this regiment, during their short stay at Yankton, acted with the utmost decorum. There was no straggling or running up town after whisky, and there wasn't a drunken man among them. When the boat was loaded, it was not necessary to send out guards to hunt up stragglers. Every man was on hand and at the word of command marched aboard the boat. In regard to discipline and good conduct the colored troops have made a favorable impression.

Colonel George Andrews, with headquarters, the regimental band, and Companies B, F, G, and I, took up station at Fort Randall; Lieutenant-Colonel M. M. Blunt and Companies C and E at Fort Hale; and Companies A, D, H, and K at Fort Meade.

In June 1881, the 9th Cavalry was moved from New Mexico to Kansas and Indian Territory, where it remained until 1885. Most of these years were spent in garrison, although in 1884–85 elements of the regiment, plus a company of the 24th Infantry, became involved in policing and driving out illegal squatters, or "Boomers," who had established themselves in Oklahoma Territory, which was not open for settlement at that time.

In the summer of 1885, the 9th Cavalry was moved to the Department of the Platte, where it enjoyed a well-earned rest after the many scouts and campaigns of the preceding 18 years. Once again, the regiment mainly performed garrison duty until the Sioux uprising of 1890–91, during which it was the first in the field in November 1890, and the last to leave late in the following March after spending a severe winter under canvas.

African American regiments tended to serve long periods in the most remote locations on the Frontier. The 25th Infantry was no exception, and its companies were stationed at out-of-the-way posts in Texas for a decade from 1870 through 1880. Their commanding officer, Colonel George Andrews, eventually wrote to departmental headquarters pleading the case of his regiment:

Headquarters 25th Infantry
Department of Texas
San Antonio, Texas

Sir,

…I do not hesitate to state that the duties devolved upon the Regiment, during this long stay in one locality, have been onerous in the extreme… Speaking from memory (the records are not accessible to me at this time) the garrison of Fort Davis during the sixteen months ending with the year 1875 marched over 8000 miles, each company averaging over 108 miles per month, while scouting maps of over 1500 miles of country were made and forwarded.

Upon an examination of the Report of the Department Commander for 1879, I find that during the year the Infantry troops (not mounted) in the Department marched 4552 miles, of this distance the companies of my regiment marched 3700 miles, or over 81¼ per cent. I also find, that during the year, troops commanded by officers of Infantry, marched 6573½ miles, of this distance, 3121 miles, or 47⅜ per cent, were accomplished under the command of officers of my regiment…

– File 2169, AGO 1880, RG94, NARA

On May 17, 1880, the 25th Infantry started to leave Texas for Dakota Territory, having received orders to change stations with the 1st Infantry.

Some of the men of Company B, 25th Infantry, pose for the camera at Fort Snelling, Minnesota, in 1883. Kneeling at left is the musician, who is distinguished by the white herringbone braid across his chest. (US Army Signal Corps photo SC 83637)

WOUNDED KNEE, 1890–91

The Ghost Dance religion that spread throughout the western Plains tribes during the summer of 1890 led to nearly one fourth of the entire US Army being concentrated on or near the Indian reservations in northwestern Nebraska and southeastern Dakota. Stationed at Fort Robinson, Troops F, I, and K, 9th Cavalry, reached Pine Ridge by November 20, while Companies A and G were among the troops to reach the Rosebud Agency on the same day. Company D arrived at the latter location five days later. Other units involved at Pine Ridge included the 1st, 2nd, 5th, 6th, and 8th Cavalry, plus supporting foot soldiers including the 25th Infantry.

On December 18, 1890, a member of the 8th Infantry at the Rosebud observed: "Our cavalry has for soldiers negroes, and it is said that the two troops here are the best two of 'buffalo soldiers' in the service. Captains Cusack and Garrard take much pride in keeping these fellows up to the mark. They are good riders, are cheerful in the performance of their duty, and are good rifle shots."

Frightened by such a large military presence, the Indians panicked and left the reservations in droves. Matters went from bad to worse when Sitting Bull, spiritual leader of the Native Americans during the Little Bighorn campaign, was killed as the Indian police attempted to arrest him as a ringleader of the Ghost Dancers. Nonetheless, the soldiers managed to push most of them back on to the reservations, leaving only a small number of resisters to be rounded up.

During the same month, four companies of the 9th Cavalry, under Major Guy Henry, plus two Hotchkiss guns under Lieutenant J. L. Heyden, 1st Artillery, were assigned to scout the Badlands in search of Big Foot and his band, which was known to contain some of Sitting Bull's followers. Private Charles Creek recollected later: "You late [sic] out in the cold like a dog, not in a tent because the Indians gonna sneak up on you. It was so cold the spit froze when it left your mouth."

Henry's troopers were still out scouting on December 29 when a courier brought news of the slaughter of Big Foot's band at

A *Harper's Weekly* engraving entitled "Ejecting an Oklahoma Boomer." Following their transfer to Kansas in 1881, one of the duties of the 9th Cavalry was escorting "Boomers," or squatters, off Oklahoma Territory. (Anne S. K. Brown Military Collection, Brown University Library)

Wounded Knee Creek. In the face of a possible widespread Indian revolt, every soldier was needed at the reservations, and Henry arrived back at Pine Ridge with three of his companies at dawn the next day, having traveled 100 miles in about 24 hours. No sooner had his exhausted men unsaddled than word arrived that his train, still approaching the reservation with Company I as escort, was under attack. The Indian scouts with Henry's command refused to ride for help because their horses were "played out," and Corporal William O. Wilson, Troop I, 9th Cavalry, had volunteered to complete the dangerous mission, for which he later received a Medal of Honor. With the loss of one buffalo soldier killed, Henry's battalion beat off the Indians, who were led by Chief Two-Strike, and the wagons were brought safely in.

Drexel Mission, 1890

On December 30, 1890, the troops responsible for the massacre at Wounded Knee, consisting of eight companies of the 7th Cavalry commanded by Lieutenant-Colonel James W. Forsyth, responded to reports that Drexel mission at White Clay Creek, about 4 miles from Pine Ridge, was under

Corporal O. Wilson, Troop I, 9th Cavalry, eventually received a Medal of Honor for bravery near the Pine Ridge Agency on December 30, 1890. Several months later, in March 1891, he was on a charge for desertion, which was reduced to "absent without leave" after his letter to President Grover Cleveland dated May 30, 1891.

His recognition in battalion orders read:

Headquarters Battalion 9 Cav

Pine Ridge Agency, SD

Orders

No.1

On the morning of Dec 30th 1890 the wagon train of this command was attacked by hostile Indians. To obtain assistance it was necessary to send word to the Agency. The duty to be performed was one involving much risk as the Indians, knowing what was intended, would endeavour to intercept the messenger and overwhelmed by numbers certain death would follow.

Corporal Wm. O. Wilson, Troop I, 9 Cav, volunteered for the above duty, and though pursued by Indians succeeded. Such examples of soldier-like conduct were worthy of imitation, and reflect great credit not only upon Corpl Wilson but the 9th Cavalry. This order will be read to each troop.

Wilson's letter to the President stated:

I became under the influence of intoxication and while under and in that condition I absented myself from detachment and was absent about 9 hours that is from the time I [was] at the Agency and to the time I was arrested at Chardon Neb., on the evening of March 20th 1891 about 5 p.m. when I was about 23 miles from the Pine Ridge Agency. I had by hard riding become somewhat sober by this time. Then I began to realize what a rash step I had taken, and after I considered the matter over I had an idea that I would be looked for by Indian scouts and did not think that I would receive much mercy at their hands should they overtake me between there and Chardon.

So I concluded to go to Chardon Neb. and report to my detachment commander by telegram, which I did… I was arrested by a sheriff on an order of Lieut. Williams 6th Cavalry as a deserter, a crime that had never entered my mind… I am not a habitual drinker and was never intoxicated before. I would respectfully beg of the authority to give the facts a consideration.

Having been constantly on duty for about four months as acting Commissary Sergt. at Pine Ridge Agency, and Battalion 9th Cavalry in the field which was the most mental strain to which I had been subjected to in my life.

– NARA, M-929, roll 2

attack. Owing to a failure to post flank guards, Forsyth rode straight into an ambush, and found himself surrounded and pinned down by about 400 Indians led by Little Wound and Two-Strike.

Hearing the gunfire, Major Henry mounted up his exhausted buffalo soldiers and again led them into action. Reaching the entrance to the valley in which Forsyth was trapped, he deployed Captain Henry Wright, with Troops I and K, toward the east slope, while Captain John S. Loud and Troops D and F scaled the west slope. After some bitter fighting, the Indians were driven off and the men of the 7th Cavalry were rescued.

Drexel Mission, 1890

On December 30, 1890, a battalion of the 9th Cavalry, commanded by Major Guy Henry, rode to the rescue of Lieutenant-Colonel James W. Forsyth and eight troops of the 7th Cavalry, who had been ambushed and surrounded by about 400 Indians led by Chiefs Little Wound and Two-Strike near the Drexel Mission at White Clay Creek, in Dakota Territory. Using the element of surprise, the buffalo soldiers hacked their way through the hostiles to the relief of their white comrades. They are depicted charging through the snow wearing both 1883-pattern drab campaign hats and 1878-pattern muskrat caps. Some wear 1885-pattern muskrat mittens. Their 1884-pattern blouses have external pockets, while their 1882-pattern "sky-blue" kersey trousers have reinforced saddle pieces, and are tucked into 1872-pattern boots. One trooper wears an 1883-pattern canvas overcoat. They are armed with .45cal Colt revolvers

and Model 1885 Springfield carbines. Their equipment consists of tan woven carbine cartridge belts, to which are attached Forsyth modified 1881-pattern holsters. They are seated in 1885-pattern McClellan saddles and equipment.

(Richard Hook © Osprey Publishing)

UNIFORMS

Between 1866 and 1872, the peacetime US Army continued to wear the uniform prescribed in 1861. As a result, the African American infantry regiments were often photographed wearing 1851-pattern frock coats complete with brass shoulder scales, 1858-pattern forage caps, and even white dress gloves. Frock coats were sometimes replaced by four-button sack coats when on campaign, although some men modified the former garment by shortening the tails and altering the stand-up collar into the "falling" type.

As with all US Army units at this time, not all the uniforms originally issued to the black foot soldiers were acceptable. A Board of Survey was appointed to meet at the camp of the 39th Infantry, at Greenville, Louisiana, on January 5, 1867, to "investigate and report upon the condition of certain articles of clothing, camp and garrison equipage" received by Brevet Captain Charles H. Roberts, Acting Regimental Quartermaster, from Captain W. G. Hodge, Military Storekeeper, which were "alleged to be damaged."

At least one of the black infantry regiments may have been differently attired. In 1872, Cathay Williams, the woman who managed to enlist in the 38th Infantry, recalled: "The regiment I joined wore the Zouave uniform." This fact indicates that one of the black foot regiments was possibly issued with surplus Civil War Zouave clothing when first organized.

Mounted troops were no better off. According to a letter published in the *Army & Navy Journal* in October 1869, the clothing issued to the cavalry was of "so inferior a quality as to be intrinsically valueless. A month's wear necessitates a new outfit, if the soldier is to keep himself clean, as a soldier should. Even the very color of the clothing is not uniform. The pants in particular, have all the shades of which 'blue' is susceptible." The standard cavalry uniform for full dress consisted of the yellow-trimmed, 1854-pattern uniform jacket, the 1858-pattern cap, and sky-blue kersey trousers with saddle-piece reinforcement. When on campaign the jacket was replaced by the 1858-pattern, four-button sack coat.

Distribution of what is known as the 1872-pattern uniform was begun on July 1, 1873, and provided the buffalo soldiers, along with the rest of the US Army, with long-awaited new clothing. The issuance of old pattern clothing was officially stopped on December 19, 1879, and the Quartermaster General's annual report the following year stated: "The stock of old Army clothing left over at the close of the [civil] war has at length disappeared." The new cavalry uniform consisted of a Prussian-style, black cloth-covered helmet complete with brass fittings, yellow horsehair plume, and yellow worsted bands and cords. The short-skirted jacket, or basque, was piped and faced with yellow branch service trim. For full dress, the infantry received a jacket trimmed and piped with sky blue and a blue cloth cap trimmed with the same color, topped with a white pompon.

For campaign wear in 1872, all troops were prescribed a pleated blouse trimmed with branch service color, which was particularly unpopular. Headgear consisted of a low-crowned, chasseur-pattern forage cap, with insignia fastened to the front. The cavalry were also provided with a black, folding brimmed hat, which proved as unpopular as the pleated blouse. The latter item was replaced in 1874 by a plain, five-button blouse with cord trim in branch service color on collar and cuffs. In 1884, a plain blouse with three outside pockets was issued.

Regulations notwithstanding, the intermittent supply and a need to use up old-pattern clothing meant that a cavalry unit on campaign looked far from

This corporal of the 9th Cavalry was photographed at Pine Ridge in 1890. Proud of his .45cal Colt revolver, he has slid it around to the left side of his belt. He wears a non-regulation blanket on his pommel, underneath which is a horse cover. His wide-brimmed hat also appears to have been a private purchase. (Western History Department, Denver Public Library)

These two unidentified members of the 24th Infantry display examples of the surplus uniforms issued to the US Army after the Civil War. The first sergeant wears an 1851-pattern frock coat with the skirts removed, while the enlisted man at right has left his coat intact. His vest is non-regulation. (The Institute of Texan Cultures at UTSA, No. 68-1009a&b)

uniform in appearance – and the buffalo soldiers were no exception. A few days after riding to reinforce the besieged command at Milk Creek in October 1879, Company D, 9th Cavalry, was described thus: "Every shape of jacket, trousers, boot, and hat, of modern creation seemed represented in this troop, and under every dilapidated hat brim there was the honest, beaming darky visage, which the American is accustomed to associate with the brighter side of slavery life, rather than the dashing bravery which signalized the rescue on Milk River."

As a result of General Order No. 107 issued in 1872, US Army bands were required to wear the uniform of their regiment, but were permitted to adopt "such ornaments as they deem proper." In November 1879, the band of the 10th Cavalry ordered from military outfitters Baker & McKinney, of Grand Street, New York, a full dress uniform consisting of "the new [1872-pattern] regulation blue tunic, handsomely trimmed in yellow, black busby, with yellow feather on the side, baldrick and music box of yellow enameled leather, [and] gilt shoulder knots." The inclusion of the busby for musicians in 1872 suggests a much earlier date of introduction of this item to the US Army than was previously supposed.

In 1881, the infantry received new dress headgear consisting of a Prussian-style, black cloth-covered helmet with brass spike and fittings. The facing color of infantry was changed from sky blue to white in 1884. The 25th Infantry were issued with this new uniform following their transfer to Dakota Territory. An inspection report dated October 1, 1886, observed their "arms, belts and boxes, and the clothing (military dress) to be in excellent order."

Like most other US Army units, the buffalo soldiers were poorly supplied with winter clothing. Following the Red River War in the Texas Panhandle in 1874, John F. Casey, Company H, 10th Cavalry, stated: "It rained and

Garrison Life, 1882–91

The mounted 10th Cavalry trooper (1) wears an 1884-pattern, blouse with external pockets; 1882-pattern sky-blue kersey trousers; and an 1882-pattern enlisted man's helmet covered in off-white drill. His waist belt supports a Type II McKeever cartridge box; a pattern-1872 holster containing an M1873 .45cal Colt Cavalry revolver; and an M1860 Light Cavalry saber in a light metal scabbard. He is also armed with an M1885 Springfield carbine. The 24th Infantry corporal (2) wears the new full dress uniform with white facings prescribed for infantry via General Order No.120, issued on October 24, 1884. His Prussian-style, black felt-covered helmet was introduced in 1881. The bandsman of the 25th Infantry (3) is distinguished by the white herringbone braid across the chest, plus the white cord shoulder knots with aiguillette. The brown canvas uniform worn by the cavalry trooper on fatigue duty (4) was introduced in 1884. Fastened with six India rubber buttons, it has an outside pocket sewn on each breast. He also wears an 1883-pattern drab campaign hat.

(Richard Hook © Osprey Publishing)

snowed continually all day and night and we had no overcoats, only our ponchos." This is a reference to the rubber poncho issued to mounted troops. Company C, 10th Cavalry, under Lieutenant William Beck, was operating over the border near Mount Carmel, in Mexico, toward the end of November 1877 in bitterly cold weather "without great coats."

Although never officially adopted, buffalo skin coats were first purchased from commercial sources by the US Army in 1869. According to Sergeant Jacob Wilks, the troopers of the 9th Cavalry, after capturing the main Indian encampment at Tule Canyon on the Staked Plains during 1874, "found a vast amount of buffalo robes, of which each man made choice of the best."

ARMS & EQUIPAGE

Upon formation, the two black cavalry regiments were armed with M1860 .52cal, seven-shot Spencer carbines. The weapon of choice during the Civil War, it was capable of firing seven rimfire cartridges from its magazine in less than 30 seconds. This weapon was gradually replaced with the newer M1865 .50cal Spencer, with Stabler magazine cut-off device, which permitted manual reloading with a single cartridge while keeping the full magazine in reserve for emergencies. However, not all the buffalo soldiers received this improved weapon. During November 1869, the Spencers carried by Company G, 10th Cavalry, were condemned and the ordnance officer at the Leavenworth Arsenal was ordered to transfer to the commanding officer of that troop, then at Fort Dodge, Kansas, "seventy Sharpe's [sic] improved carbines," which were single-shot weapons. By September 1871, the 10th Cavalry had 845 Sharps carbines on its inventory.

In need of an Army-wide shoulder arm, the US military conducted cavalry trials during the period from 1871 through 1872 with four different types of M1870 carbine – the Remington, the Sharps, the Ward-Burton, and the Springfield. Popularly known as the "Allin Conversion" or "Trapdoor" Springfield, the latter weapon was loaded at the breech by means of a mechanism designed by Erskine S. Allin, Master Armorer of the Springfield Armory. This consisted of a rising breechblock hinged at the front, which was unlatched by a thumb piece to receive a copper-case cartridge.

In August 1871, Company L of the 9th Cavalry was issued with 27 each of these trial weapons, with orders to "give them a thorough trial, and promptly render monthly reports, on their merits, to the Chief of Ordnance, through the chief ordnance officer of the department." Finally, on May 20, 1873, the Springfield carbine was adopted as the standard shoulder arm for the US cavalry and would remain as such for the next 23 years. The 10th

The black infantry regiments were armed with the breech-loading Springfield "Trapdoor" rifle by 1873. Here is a detail showing the rising breech-block loading mechanism that gave the weapon its "Trapdoor" nickname. (Courtesy of the Ministry of Defence Pattern Room)

Cavalry was the first regiment to be completely rearmed with this weapon, which was issued during the first half of 1874. The 9th Cavalry received their Springfields during the second half of the same year.

Regarding side arms issued in 1866–67, the black cavalrymen carried either the M1860 Colt .44in Army revolver or the less popular Remington .44in New Model Army revolver, both of which were percussion. These were finally replaced, in 1874, by the breech-loading M1873 .45cal Colt Cavalry revolver, although elements of both cavalry regiments were also the first to trial the Smith and Wesson Model No. 3 revolver during 1875. Use of the latter weapon was much encouraged by Major George W. Schofield, 10th Cavalry, who was the brother of General John W. Schofield, who headed the Army board responsible for rearming the US Army during the early 1870s.

The four black infantry regiments were originally armed with the three-band M1866, .50cal "Trapdoor" Springfield rifle. About 25,000 muzzle-loading Springfields were converted to the "Allin" system after the Civil War. Following trials in 1872, the .45cal Model 1873 Springfield rifle was adopted and issued. This weapon was carried throughout the remaining years of the Indian Wars and underwent numerous minor changes culminating in the Model 1888 Springfield, which incorporated a unique bayonet that also served as a cleaning rod. The latter innovation was necessitated by financial and production considerations. A new smokeless repeating rifle was being considered for adoption by the US Army and, with the supply of Civil War bayonets exhausted, the M1888 "Trapdoor" with its combined bayonet and cleaning rod provided an economically viable substitute.

Experimental equipment was being trialed by all the black regiments throughout the Indian Wars. Photographed in 1892, this squad of Company F, 24th Infantry, at Fort Bayard, New Mexico, carry the Sherlock blanket roll equipment. They also wear 1890-pattern canvas infantry leggings, and carry M1873 Springfield rifles. The man second from left has knocked his 1889-pattern campaign hat into a non-regulation "Montana peak." (NARA)

The buffalo soldiers did not immediately receive these improved arms. According to Private William Branch, his company of the 25th Infantry was carrying unconverted Civil War surplus arms as late as 1874. Remembering the action at Anadarko, Indian Territory, in that year, he recalled: "We got de ole fashion muzzle loaders. You puts one ball in de muzzle and shove de powder down wid de ramrod."

Regarding accoutrements, both the cavalry and the infantry were issued with surplus Civil War equipment upon organization. For the cavalry, this probably consisted of waist belts of black harness leather, minus shoulder strap, with eagle buckle; Blakeslee cartridge boxes slung suspended from shoulder straps; and saber scabbards secured to the waist belt via a Stuart saber attachment. A black leather percussion pouch was possibly also attached to the waist belt for pistol ammunition. Canteens with gray wool covers were suspended from white cotton slings. Saddles were of the McClellan model of 1859.

The infantry probably wore black leather waist belts, fastened by a stamped brass "US" oval plate. Slung from this would have been the experimental M1866 cartridge box for either 19 or 20 rounds of .50cal ammunition. A M1855 bayonet and scabbard would also have been attached to the belt, plus a percussion pouch containing extra rounds.

By 1873, most of the original Civil War surplus accoutrements and saddles issued to the 9th and 10th Cavalry were wearing out. Indeed, Company A of the latter unit was using 30 condemned saddles. From 1873 through 1875, various companies of both black cavalry regiments, along with their fellow white units, received variations of an experimental M1872 brace accoutrement system, with orders to give it "a thorough trial." Similar to the brace system used by the British Army at that time, the basic pattern developed for US horse soldiers consisted of a black leather waist belt with shoulder braces, to which was attached the Dyer carbine pouch, pistol cartridge pouch, swivel pistol holster, and saber. The supporting braces held a carbine sling attachment at front and rear. The 24th and 25th Infantry were among the foot soldiers to receive infantry versions of this equipment during the same period, combining "the knapsack, haversack, canteen, cartridge-box, waist-belt, and the bayonet-scabbard" into one system. Neither system proved popular, although the belts continued to be worn without the braces.

Equally unpopular was the Palmer infantry brace system with McKeever cartridge boxes, designed by Lieutenant George Palmer, 16th Infantry. Issued for experimental purposes in 1874, these were found to be cumbersome in the field and were seldom used, becoming obsolete by 1878.

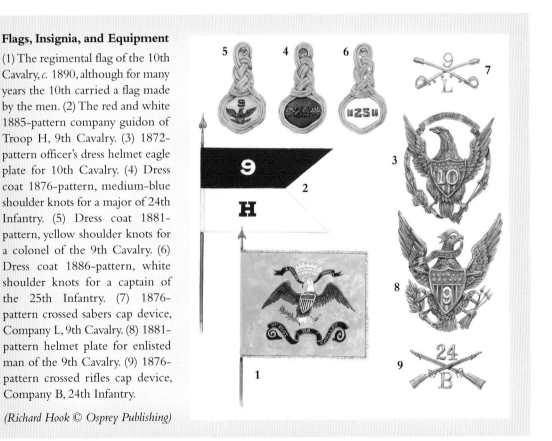

Flags, Insignia, and Equipment

(1) The regimental flag of the 10th Cavalry, c. 1890, although for many years the 10th carried a flag made by the men. (2) The red and white 1885-pattern company guidon of Troop H, 9th Cavalry. (3) 1872-pattern officer's dress helmet eagle plate for 10th Cavalry. (4) Dress coat 1876-pattern, medium-blue shoulder knots for a major of 24th Infantry. (5) Dress coat 1881-pattern, yellow shoulder knots for a colonel of the 9th Cavalry. (6) Dress coat 1886-pattern, white shoulder knots for a captain of the 25th Infantry. (7) 1876-pattern crossed sabers cap device, Company L, 9th Cavalry. (8) 1881-pattern helmet plate for enlisted man of the 9th Cavalry. (9) 1876-pattern crossed rifles cap device, Company B, 24th Infantry.

(Richard Hook © Osprey Publishing)

PART II

BUFFALO SOLDIERS 1892–1941

INTRODUCTION   92

FRONTIER DUTIES, 1892–98   93

CUBA, 1898   96

THE PHILIPPINES, 1899–1902   113

THE MEXICAN BORDER, 1914–17   121

WORLD WAR I, 1917–18   131

UNIFORMS & EQUIPMENT   145

THE INTER-WAR YEARS   152

OPPOSITE
Enlisted men of Company G, 25th Infantry, photographed at Fort Missoula, Montana, at some date before 1895 – note the chasseur-pattern 1889 forage cap. The man at left has a tan woven infantry cartridge belt, its 1887-pattern H-shaped "US" plate visible under his open jacket. (Elrod Collection, K. Ross Toole Archives, University of Montana – Missoula)

INTRODUCTION

On August 18, 1918, Sergeant William Butler, Company L, 369th Infantry, won the Distinguished Service Cross and the French Croix de Guerre for breaking up a German raiding party in US trenches near Maison-de-Champagne. (NARA)

The African American soldier played an important part in the operations of the US Army during the so-called "age of American Imperialism" from 1898 through 1916, and two years later went on to distinguish himself in the trenches of World War I.

In the Spanish–American War of 1898, black troops charged fearlessly up Kettle Hill alongside Teddy Roosevelt and his Rough Riders. As conflict with the Spanish developed into the Philippine Insurrection, black regulars and volunteers became embroiled in the long drawn-out struggle with the Filipino nationalist forces and the dreaded Moro warriors of the island of Mindanao. In Mexico during 1916, black cavalrymen and infantry went on campaign against Mexican revolutionaries under Pancho Villa, and the former conducted the last US cavalry charge in battle at Aguas Calientes in April of that year.

With the involvement of US troops in World War I in 1917, soldiers of the African American 92nd and 93rd Divisions saw combat in France; four regiments earned collective citations for the French Croix de Guerre for their outstanding bravery, while numerous individual soldiers won gallantry decorations, including the Distinguished Service Cross. By the war's end, a total of 5,000 black soldiers had been wounded and 750 killed in the bitter fighting of the summer and fall of 1918. Every foe that encountered him – whether Spanish, Filipino, Mexican, or German – learned to respect the bravery of the buffalo soldier.

FRONTIER DUTIES, 1892–98

For eight years following the end of the Indian Wars in 1891, the four regular regiments of buffalo soldiers continued to garrison various frontier posts and to police the tamed American West. The 9th Cavalry was headquartered at Fort Robinson, Nebraska, throughout this period. The 10th Cavalry was based at Fort Assinniboine, Montana, with troops also stationed at Fort Keogh. The 24th Infantry was in New Mexico with headquarters at Fort Bayard, but subsequently removed to Fort Douglas, Utah, in October 1896. The 25th Infantry operated out of Fort Missoula, Montana, and Fort Buford, North Dakota, plus several other stations.

During this period African American troops were often included among those used to bring under control the civil unrest caused by industrial strife. Early in 1892 a confrontation developed between the mine owners and labor unions in the Coeur d'Alene mining district of Idaho. Scenes of disorder and anarchy culminated on the Fourth of July with the American flag being riddled with bullets and spat and trampled upon by strikers; and by July 11 several mines had been blown up, with consequent loss of life. Federal aid was invoked, and Regular Army troops were quickly on their way to the area, including a provisional battalion from the 25th Infantry consisting of Companies F, G, and H, commanded by Captain W. T. Sanborn. Although strikers blew up the tracks of the Northern Pacific Railroad, the buffalo soldiers finally managed to reach the troubled area via the Coeur d'Alene City, Harrison & Union Pacific Railroad on July 14. Making camp at Wardner Junction, they were immediately assigned to guarding trains, scouting, furnishing escorts, and making arrests.

In April 1894, elements of the 25th Infantry and 10th Cavalry were among troops dispatched to intercept a train on the Montana & Pacific Railroad carrying members of "Coxey's Army," a group of unemployed workers led by Jacob Sechler Coxey, who were on their way to protest in Washington DC. The local press would subsequently comment on "the excellence of the negro as a soldier. During the entire period that the guard was on duty, no act of the troops was open to criticism, and there was not a single instance of an unjust exercise of authority." The *Army & Navy Journal* of August 25, 1894, stated that the railroad authorities were "naturally loud in their praise of the troops, and the majority of strikers admit that if the soldiers had to be called out there could have been none better than … the 25th Infantry." During July of that year, four companies of the 24th Infantry, plus two companies of the white 1st Cavalry, were assigned to guard mail trains on the Sante Fe Railroad.

In the summer of 1896 the entire 10th Cavalry was in the field rounding up Cree Indians under Little Bear, who had fled from their reservations in Canada and were committing minor depredations over the border in the United States. Large numbers of Cree were escorted back north and handed over to the Canadian authorities. One of the leaders of this assignment was Lieutenant John J. Pershing, commanding Troop D. Later known as "Black Jack," the future commander of the American Expeditionary Force (AEF) acquired that nickname for earlier service with the 10th Cavalry.

The detachment of the 25th Infantry, commanded by Lieutenant James A. Moss, that tested the use of the bicycle in rugged terrain in 1896. After the end of hostilities in Cuba in 1898 the 25th's 100-strong bicycle company was sent to perform riot duty in Havana. (K. Ross Toole Archives, University of Montana – Missoula)

In June 1897, the 10th Cavalry got a new commander when Colonel J. K. Mizner was promoted to brigadier-general, and Colonel Guy V. Henry took command. That same year, Troops A, E, and K were called out to the Tongue River Indian Agency to resolve a disturbance among the Cheyenne. Thanks to the diplomacy of the officers, and respect among the Indians for their old adversaries, the buffalo soldiers made four arrests and the outbreak died down. At the end of 1897, the Army consolidated the 10th Cavalry at Forts Assinniboine and Keogh, where they remained until the outbreak of the Spanish-American War.

BICYCLE TRIALS, 1896

It was the Italian Bersaglieri light infantry who first used the bicycle for military purposes in 1875; and in 1891 the "push bike" made its first martial appearance in America when the Connecticut Militia formed a Signal Corps bicycle unit. Four years later, General Nelson A. Miles – a member of the League of Military Wheelmen – promoted the use of the bicycle for reconnaissance purposes in the Regular Army. By November 1895, the US Signal Corps had adopted it as a means of distributing telegraph and telephone wires. In 1896 a detachment of the 25th Infantry, commanded by Lieutenant James A. Moss of Company F (and later CO of the 367th Infantry in World War I), was selected to conduct extensive trials of the bicycle in mountainous country.

During the following year, Moss led his 21 men on a 1,900-mile journey from Fort Missoula, Montana, to St Louis, Missouri. When a civilian asked one of the riders where they were going, the soldier replied: "The Lord only knows. We're following the lieutenant." Taking 41 days, the buffalo soldiers rode through heat, snow, and rain, and successfully proved the practicality of military cycling. Their mounts were 32lb Spaulding safety bicycles with Goodrich tires, Christy Anatomic saddles, tandem spokes, and reinforced forks. The men each carried a Krag-Jorgensen rifle weighing 10lb, a cartridge belt with 50 rounds, a canteen, blanket, and half-shelter tent, in addition to rations. After reaching St Louis on July 24, 1897, Lieutenant Moss informed the *Army & Navy Journal*:

> The trip has proved beyond peradventure my contention that the bicycle has a place in modern warfare. In every kind of weather, over all sorts of roads, we averaged 50 miles a day. At the end of the journey we are all in good physical condition. Seventeen tires and half a dozen frames is the sum of our damage. The practical result of the trip shows that an Army Bicycle Corps can travel twice as fast as cavalry or infantry under any conditions...

CUBA, 1898

The buffalo soldiers' first combat deployment since the end of the Indian Wars followed the outbreak of war between the United States and Spain following an accidental explosion that sank the USS *Maine* in Havana Harbor on February 15, 1898. Cuban guerrillas had been in rebellion against their Spanish overlords since 1895, and the American public had become increasingly alarmed by the inhumane methods used by the Spanish government in trying to quell this revolt. Convinced that his warship had been sabotaged, President William McKinley received permission from Congress on April 19 to use the US Army and Navy to force Spain to renounce its sovereignty over Cuba.

Commanded by Major-General William Shafter, the US force that prepared to invade Cuba consisted of V Corps, and included all four black regular regiments. The 9th and 10th Cavalry formed part of the Cavalry Division, under ex-Confederate cavalry leader Major-General Joseph Wheeler, US Volunteers (USV), while the 24th and 25th Infantry served in the 2nd Division. Twelve African American volunteer units also filled out the ranks of the US Army during the Spanish-American War. These included four of the ten "Immune Regiments," whose ranks were filled with those supposed to possess immunity from yellow fever, or likely to be exempt from "diseases incident to tropical climates" – a dangerous fiction.

The four regular regiments were ordered to mobilize during March–April 1898. The 9th and 10th Cavalry and 24th Infantry assembled at "Camp Thomas" in Chickamauga Park near Lytle, Georgia, while elements of the 25th Infantry proceeded to Key West, Florida. This was the first time in their history that the buffalo soldiers had been ordered to the southeastern United States, and the first time that the bulk of the American people even realized that their standing army included regiments composed wholly of black soldiers. On April 30 the *Army & Navy Journal* reported that the "Buffalo soldiers, colored, 25th Inf [were] the admiration of all the colored belles" in Chattanooga as they passed through on their way to Chickamauga Park.

Having served at remote frontier posts for many years, the African American soldiers, in their turn, were unused to seeing poverty-stricken blacks. Walking down Meeting Street, Chickamauga, Sergeant J. P. Smith, 10th Cavalry, spied a 12-year-old black boy dressed in rags, and insisted on taking him into a clothing store where he "bought him a complete outfit, hat, shoes and clothing, for the sum of $10, and made him put them on." However, the black soldiers were not so popular with the whites. Racial tension was nothing new for the Southeast, but the sudden arrival of self-confident black soldiers unaccustomed to suffering blatant discrimination created an explosive atmosphere. Soon after they reached that city, an editorial in the *Tampa Morning Tribune* seemed to promise trouble: "The colored infantrymen stationed in Tampa ... have made themselves very offensive to the people of the city... The men insist upon being treated as white men are treated."

The African American regiments were next moved to the staging area near Tampa, where a six weeks' wait in May–June seemed interminable. The 10th Cavalry, the last to arrive, was located at Lakeland about 22 miles east

Armed with M1896 Krag-Jörgensen rifles, the 24th Infantry train in full marching order prior to departure for Cuba in 1898. (Library of Congress, LC-USZ62-119314)

George W. Prioleau, Chaplain of the 9th Cavalry, wrote to *The Gazette* (Cleveland, Ohio) from Port Tampa, Florida, on May 13, 1898, describing the mixed reception the buffalo soldiers received as they transferred southeast in preparation for the invasion of Cuba:

Yesterday, May 12, the Ninth was ordered to be ready to embark at a moment's notice for Cuba... We are here waiting for the order to march. Possibly before you shall have been in receipt of this communication, the Ninth, with the Twenty-fourth and Twenty-fifth infantries and eight batteries of artillery will be in Cuba. These men are anxious to go. The country will then hear and know of the bravery of these sable sons of Ham.

The American Negro is always ready and willing to take up arms, to fight and to lay down his life in defense of his country's flag and honor. All the way from northwest Nebraska this regiment was greeted with cheers and hurrahs. At places where we stopped the people assembled by the thousands. While the Ninth Cavalry band would play some national air the people would raise their hats, men, women and children would wave their handkerchiefs, and the heavens would resound with their hearty cheers. The white hand shaking the black hand. The hearty "goodbyes," "God bless you," and other expressions aroused the patriotism of our boys... These demonstrations, so enthusiastically given, greeted us all the way until we reached Nashville. At this point we arrived about 12.30 a.m. There were about 6,000 colored people there to greet us (very few white people) but not a man was allowed by the railroad officials to approach the cars. From there until we reached Chattanooga there was not a cheer given us, the people living in gross ignorance, rags and dirt. Both white and colored seemed amazed; they looked at us in wonder... Had we been greeted like this all the way... there would have been many desertions before we reached this point.

– *The Gazette,* Cleveland, Ohio (May 13, 1898)

of Tampa, while the 9th encamped at Port Tampa. The 24th Infantry was situated on the "Heights" outside the city. On June 7 orders were finally received to embark for Cuba. The 24th Infantry sailed on the *City of Washington*, while the 25th boarded the *Concho* with the 4th US Infantry and 2nd Massachusetts Volunteers. Required to leave their horses behind for lack of shipping space, the cavalry regiments discovered that they would be expected to fight as infantry. The 9th Cavalry sailed on the *Miami*, while the 10th was transported on the *Leona*, with the exception of Troops C and F who sailed on the *Alamo*. The contingent from the 10th Cavalry consisted of the 1st Squadron commanded by Major S. T. Norvell, and composed of Troops A, B, E, and I; and the 2nd Squadron, under Major Theodore J. Wint, consisting of Troops C, D, F, and G. To their disappointment, most of the other personnel remained at Lakeland in charge of the horses and baggage.

The exception to the general dismounting of the troopers was a detachment of 50 men from Troops A, H, and M commanded by Lieutenant C. P. Johnson, which was assigned to perform a "special mission" in Cuba as mounted troops. Accompanied by the Cuban General Munez, 375 assorted Cubans, and a large quantity of arms and munitions for General Maximo Gomez, these buffalo soldiers sailed from Tampa aboard the *Florida*, under escort from the gunboat *Peoria*, on June 21.

Reproduced in *McClures Magazine* in September 1898, this gouache painting by William Glackens depicts the 25th and 12th Infantry taking the stone fort of El Viso, near El Caney, on July 1, 1898. The lone figure struggling up the hill in advance of the main body of troops may possibly be journalist James Creelman, who later falsely claimed that he – not the buffalo soldiers – had captured the Spanish flag. (Anne S. K. Brown Military Collection, Brown University Library)

LAS GUÁSIMAS

Finally sailing from Tampa on June 8, the flotilla of 32 ships carrying nearly 17,000 men of the main expedition made landfall at Siboney on the southeast tip of Cuba on June 22. As soon as they were disembarked, Shafter's brigades began pushing inland along the road from Siboney toward Santiago de Cuba. Overtaking Brigadier-General Henry W. Lawton's 2nd Infantry Division, advanced elements of the dismounted Cavalry Division under Major-General Wheeler fought the first engagement of the campaign on June 24 at Las Guásimas, a junction of two trails about 3 miles inland. Deployed in two columns, eight troops of the 1st US Volunteer Cavalry (the "Rough Riders"), commanded by Colonel Leonard Wood, with future president Lieutenant-Colonel Theodore Roosevelt as second in command, proceeded along an overgrown jungle trail to the left, while four troops each of the 1st and 10th Cavalry, led by General Wheeler, followed two separate routes on their right.

Without a trail to follow, and advancing "as blind men would through the dense underbrush," the buffalo soldiers took time to hack their way through

the jungle, and got into battle about 20 minutes after the first US troops engaged the enemy. With orders to fight a rearguard action, the Spanish opened fire with their Krupp mountain gun detachment and smokeless-cartridge Mauser rifles, and held back the American advance for about an hour. Fanning out, the US troopers groped their way forward and eventually flushed the Spaniards out of their positions; the 10th Cavalry, commanded by Lieutenant-Colonel T. A. Baldwin, suffered one man killed and eight wounded. In the heat of the moment the absent-minded ex-Confederate Joe Wheeler's reaction to the Spanish withdrawal was to jump up and shout, "Come on, boys, we got the damned Yankees on the run!" Nothing now lay between Shafter's beachhead and the outer defenses of Santiago de Cuba.

EL CANEY

The key to the capture of the city was the San Juan Heights, which were held by entrenched Spanish troops. On July 1 the attack on these positions was assigned to the 2nd Division, supported by the dismounted Cavalry Division. Meanwhile, as diversions, a brigade commanded by General H. Duffield, with Navy support, followed the railroad line down the coast from Siboney toward Santiago, while the 1st Infantry Division, including the 25th Infantry, marched north to capture an entrenched Spanish position at El Caney. Both of these detached forces were eventually to march back to the Heights in support of the main attack.

Commanded by General Joaquin Vara de Rey, the Spanish defenses at El Caney consisted of a stone fort, four wooden blockhouses, and a stone church that had been loop-holed and garrisoned; these works were interconnected by slit trenches and surrounded by barbed wire. The Spanish positions on San Juan Heights were similar, consisting of several blockhouses linked by trenches to those on neighboring Kettle Hill. According to General Shafter's plan, El Caney should have fallen within two hours, but 520 Spanish troops managed to hold back some 6,600 Americans for about eight hours.

According to Spanish lieutenant José Muller, the defenders "threw forth a hail of projectiles upon the enemy, while one company after another, without any protection, rushed with veritable fury upon the city." The 12th Infantry attacked the stone fort from the east, while the 25th, commanded by Lieutenant-Colonel Aaron S. Daggett, approached from the southeast. In the aftermath, both regiments claimed to have received the surrender of the Spanish strongpoint. According to a report by Lieutenant James A. Moss published in the *Army & Navy Journal*, Companies D, E, G, and H of the 25th Infantry advanced about 600 yards toward the fort "by a series of rushes over exposed ground, crawling up streams, working their way through 'Spanish dagger' [cactus], thick underbrush ... during which they were subjected to most galling front and flank fires from several different sources."

Reaching the crest of a small hill about 150 yards from the fort, these men delivered a general fusillade for about 15 minutes, before orders were given for only marksmen and sharpshooters to fire. "For ten minutes or more," continued Moss, "these men poured lead into every door, porthole and rifle pit in sight, the mortar, brick and earth fairly flying! The Spaniards were now panic stricken and demoralized, and with neither hats nor rifles were frantically running from the stone fort to the rifle pits, and from the rifle pits to the stone fort, while our men were shooting them down like sheep."

Men of the 9th Cavalry in quarantine at Camp Wikoff on Montauk Point, Long Island, after their return from the Cuban campaign. The trooper with the bandana standing second from right is Augustus Walley, one of four enlisted men in the regiment eventually to be awarded a retrospective Silver Star for bravery at San Juan Heights in July 1898. (USAMHI)

At this point the buffalo soldiers observed a white flag being waved from the fort, but continuing Spanish flanking fire from a nearby blockhouse made it impossible for them to advance any further to accept the surrender. Meanwhile, a company of the 12th Infantry rushed forward, poured into the fort through a large hole created by the US artillery, and received the white flag. At the same time, Privates T. C. Butler, Company H, and J. H. Jones, Company D, 25th Infantry, entered the fort and took possession of the Spanish flag. When he presented a piece of this flag to Lieutenant Vernon A. Caldwell, 25th Infantry, Butler informed that officer: "I went off ahead of the company, and when the artillery blew that hole in the wall I went in and got the flag, and along came a white man dressed something like an officer and made me give it to him, but I tore a corner off the flag anyway." This white man was probably James Creelman, war correspondent for the *New York Journal*, who claimed to have been "the first American inside the walls of the fort," and who was shot through the shoulder while "recovering the Spanish flag." The 25th Infantry sustained eight killed and 27 wounded at El Caney, and Private Conny Gray, Company D, earned the Certificate of Merit (CM) for "fearlessly exposing himself, under a heavy fire, applying a first-aid bandage and carrying his wounded captain a considerable distance to shelter, and then rejoining his company, participating in the action to its close."

SAN JUAN HEIGHTS

The main assault on San Juan Heights on July 1 was actually an attack on several different defended hilltops. General Sumner's dismounted Cavalry Division – composed of the 1st, 3rd, 6th, 9th, and 10th regular regiments, plus the 1st US Volunteer Cavalry (USVC) – went up that part of the range north of the sunken road, known as Little San Juan Hill or Kettle Hill. The 1st Brigade, 1st Division, under General Hawkins – the 6th and 16th Infantry – assaulted the main section of the Heights afterwards named "Blockhouse Hill." The 3rd Brigade, 1st Division, commanded by Colonel Wickoff (but led by Lieutenant-Colonel E. P. Ewers after Wickoff was killed) – the 9th, 13th, and 24th Infantry – attacked that part of the Heights south of the Santiago road. The 10th, 2nd, and 21st Infantry of Colonel Pearson's 2nd Brigade scaled San Juan Hill immediately to the south of Hawkins' brigade.

While waiting for orders to attack, the buffalo soldiers came under heavy fire when an observation balloon of the US Signal Corps was towed down the road and hovered above them. At this point the men were ordered to slip off their blanket rolls and haversacks, which were left under guard. The first line, consisting of four troops of the 9th Cavalry under Colonel John M.

Sergeant J. C. Pendergrass, Troop A, 10th Cavalry, describes the participation of his unit in the victory at San Juan Hill:

On the morning of the 27th our brigade proceeded with the regiment to Servilla, and late in the afternoon of the 30th to El Paso and took position in front of the defense covering the city of Santiago. At 4:30 a.m., July 1, batteries of artillery, American and Spanish, began firing, and we being the support to one battery were subjected to a galling fire until about 6:30, when the dismounted cavalry was ordered forward. By this time the heat from the sun was almost unbearable, and quite a number of men, both officers and enlisted, fell on the way from its effects, and all the while the Spanish were throwing volley after volley into us, and men of every rank fell at each volley. All this time we were unable to locate the enemy, being in a dense jungle of about two miles.

About 9:20 we got in about 1000 yards of them when our small arms fire began, while our advance was rapid and was too rapid for the Spanish force, who were buried in entrenchments up to their necks. After our fire got well under way, our shots were so effective that the enemy was unable to harm us to any great extent. When a Spanish soldier put up his head to fire, sometimes as many [as] six of our bullets would strike his head at once, and in the pit dead everyone fell. This action on our part wholly destroyed the discipline of the enemy so they would not show any part of their body, but would simply stick their rifles above their entrenchments and fire without aim; while our sight was true almost every time.

By about 11:00 o'clock the San Juan hills were ours and the city of Santiago, and the Spanish troops were annihilated, though the fire was incessant until 10:00 a.m. the 3rd.

— *Illinois Record*, Chicago (September 3, 1898)

Hamilton, took cover in the sunken road. When the Rough Riders caught up with them Lieutenant-Colonel Roosevelt, still mounted on his charger "Little Texas," informed a captain in command of the black troopers that they "would not take these hills by firing at them," and that the position must be rushed. The captain replied that he could not do so without orders and did not know the whereabouts of his commander. "Then I am the ranking officer here," Roosevelt replied, "and I give the order to charge!" When the regular still hesitated to follow orders from a volunteer officer, Roosevelt said, "Then let my men through, sir." With that, the Rough Riders began to pass through the regulars, many of whom jumped up and joined in the advance.

Entitled "Forgotten Heroes," this painting by Fletcher R. Ransom depicts Troop C, 9th Cavalry, commanded by Captain Taylor, leading the charge up Kettle Hill during the battle for Santiago de Cuba on July 1, 1898. It was published in *Harper's Weekly* on October 15 that year – coincidentally, the same issue carried illustrations of the battle of Omdurman on September 2, including the charge of the 21st Lancers in which Winston Churchill took part. (Ron Field Collection)

Corporal John R. Conn, who was farther along the line with Company H, 24th Infantry, recalled:

The orders from our colonel were: "Twenty fourth Infantry, move forward 150 yards and lie down." With a last look at our arms and ammunition – yes and a little prayer – we started, and such a volley as they sent into us! It was then that Sergeant [D. T.] Brown was shot almost at the river bank. We had to cut and destroy a barbed wire fence … someone sounded "Let us charge" on the bugle. When that pack of demons swept forward the Spaniards stood as long as mortals could stand, then quit their trenches and retired to the trenches around Santiago.

The cavalrymen had the shortest distance to cover once they had crossed the San Juan river and reached the foot of the Heights. As the black troopers waded the river, the 10th Cavalry's regimental sergeant-major, Edward L. Baker Jr, left the cover of the bank to save a wounded comrade from drowning, for which he was later awarded the Medal of Honor. The 9th and 10th Cavalry went up Kettle Hill with the Rough Riders to their right. Troops A, B, E, and I of the 10th, under Major Norvell, formed the first line, followed by Troops C, F, and G led by Major Wint. Having crossed the river farther down, Troop D of the 10th attached itself to Hawkins' infantry brigade and joined in the assault on "Blockhouse Hill." Corporals John Walker and Luchious Smith were at "the head and front of the assault," and both were later awarded the CM; this was subsequently replaced by the Distinguished Service Medal (DSM).

Elsewhere along the line, other elements of the cavalry also began to stumble up the steep 120ft hill. Irregularities in the 30-degree slopes partially masked the defenders' view; grabbing tufts of grass, the US troopers scrambled upwards, with men of different units becoming intermingled. According to the *Army & Navy Journal*, several musicians of the 6th and 10th Cavalry lifted their bugles as they climbed and "blew the 'Star Spangled Banner' into the Spanish lines."

Major Wint and Adjutant First Lieutenant Malvern Hill Barnum, 10th Cavalry, were both wounded, and Lieutenant W. E. Smith of Troop G was killed. Lieutenant Frank R. McCoy, Troop A, was severely wounded at the height of the action, and was commended for gallantry; Lieutenant Richard L. Livermore of the same troop was commended for bravery for capturing the blockhouse where he was wounded. Three Spanish bullets struck Captain John Bigelow Jr, commanding Troop D, when he was only 75 yards from the blockhouse. Lieutenants H. O. Willard, Troop B, and H. C. Whitehead, Troop F, were also wounded. Corporal John E. Lewis of the 10th's Troop H recalled that "About every troop … lost its officers … and non-commissioned officers took their places and led the troops on to a victory."

In the first line of that regiment, Farrier Sherman Harris, Troop I, kept in advance and picked out the best cover for the men in his immediate rear.

Entitled "Packing up in a Hurry," this engraving depicts the 25th Infantry preparing for departure from Cuba during August 1898. (Anne S. K. Brown Military Collection, Brown University Library)

Sergeant Thomas Griffith, Troop C, cut the barbed wire so the buffalo soldiers and Rough Riders could scramble through. Wagoner John Boland and Private Elise Jones also showed extreme courage during the advance. When Lieutenant T. A. Roberts, commanding Troop G in the second line, fell wounded, Trumpeter James H. Cooper and Private William J. Davis assisted him back to a dressing station under heavy Spanish fire.

Nearby, as he advanced with his men of the 3rd Cavalry, Color Sergeant J. E. Andrews took a bullet in the stomach. Calling in vain for a lieutenant to take the colors, he stumbled back down the hill, still clutching the flag. Following behind with Troop G, 10th Cavalry, Color Sergeant George Berry snatched it up and carried both regiments' colors to the top of the ridge. When questioned by *Harper's Weekly* in November 1898, Berry replied: "Where did my courage come from? It came from our 'war chief,' Captain [Charles G.] Ayres [Troop E]. When I saw him leading his men, waving his hat in the air, shouting out like a trumpet to the soldiers to follow, I took the two sets of colors and ran, calling as I ran: 'Dress on the colors, boys! Dress on the colors!'"

Meanwhile, on the main Heights men of the 24th Infantry under Captain Arthur C. Ducat and Lieutenant Henry G. Lyon scrambled toward a blockhouse defended by 35 Spaniards, but both officers and a number of men fell wounded before they reached the crest. Unable to break through the heavy wooden doors and planked-up windows, 19 men climbed on to the red tile roof to drop through a hole left by a shell. Four were killed at once; the remaining 15 captured the building after a few minutes of hand-to-hand fighting.

The 9th Cavalry had reached the crest of Kettle Hill, led by Captain Eugene D. Dimmick; now the troopers struggled over a wire fence and began to advance across the valley toward the second Spanish line. The Spaniards retreated long before the cavalrymen reached their trenches, and by 1.50pm the Americans had secured the entire length of the San Juan Heights. However, the Spanish artillery continued to shell them. Assigned with a detail of two men to temporary duty with the Gatling gun detachment under Lieutenant John H. Parker, 13th Infantry, Sergeant John Graham of the 9th's Troop E showed great courage toward the end of the day while saving that officer's life. In his recommendation for the Medal of Honor, Lieutenant Parker stated that Graham:

> ... rendered particularly valuable service in keeping the ammunition supply up at this time, and at one time, when a shell was about to explode in the battery, endeavored to shield his commanding officer, myself, with his own body. His services at this time, in keeping the ammunition going, were

particularly dangerous as it had to be carried some distance exposed to the view and fire of the enemy, but he so well performed this work that the Gatlings were enabled to drive the enemy's gunners away from their guns by directing a steady and continuous fire upon their pieces.

After the battle, First Sergeant Adam Houston, 10th Cavalry, recalled:

We had been on the hill about three hours and my gun was almost red hot. I had fired about 175 rounds of ammunition, and being very thirsty, I gladly accepted the [water] detail, as the hill was ours then and we had been shooting at nothing for about an hour. What a sight was presented as I re-crossed the

Kettle Hill, July 1898

The 10th Cavalry was one of three African American regiments that took part in the attack on San Juan Heights and Kettle Hill on July 1, 1898. During this action Color Sergeant J. E. Andrews of the white 3rd Cavalry took a bullet in the belly. He stumbled back down the hill, still clutching the national flag, until it was taken from him by Sergeant George Berry of Troop G, 10th Cavalry, who bore the regimental color. Berry then carried the colors of both the 3rd and the 10th up the slope. During the Cuban campaign the black troopers wore the dark-blue pullover flannel shirt with falling collar, three small front buttons, and two patch pockets fastened by single small buttons. Dark sky-blue trousers were supported by suspenders, worn with 1890-pattern drab canvas leggings. Headgear was the 1889-pattern drab campaign hat, minus insignia – these were not authorized until

July 25, 1898. Troopers were armed with M1896 Krag-Jörgensen carbines, and carried their ammunition in blue woven web 100-round Mills cartridge belts with brass wire C-clip fastening.

(Richard Hook © Osprey Publishing)

flat in front of San Juan. The dead and wounded soldiers! It was indescribable. One would have to see it to know what it was like, and having once seen it, I truly hope I may never see it again.

CASUALTIES AND RECOGNITION

In fact, 26 buffalo soldiers lay dead on the field, among several times that many wounded. The 24th Infantry suffered some of the heaviest casualties in the infantry assault on the main ridge, having two officers – including the CO, Lieutenant-Colonel E. H. Liscum – and 11 men killed, and six officers and 71 men wounded. Colonel Hamilton was shot dead leading the 9th Cavalry up Kettle Hill; seven enlisted men were also killed, and Lieutenant-Colonel Henry Carroll was wounded. Of 450 men of the 10th Cavalry, seven were killed, 72 were wounded, and four were listed as missing.

Shamefully, most of the battlefield accounts published in the weeks after the action ignored the deeds of the black troops in Cuba, and generally cast them in a supporting role. However, a report in the *Army & Navy Journal* dated September 2, 1898, indicates that the 1st USVC had found themselves in need of support after being pinned down by heavy fire: "The Rough Riders were in a bad position on San Juan Hill at one time, and it is generally admitted they could not have held their position but for the splendid charge of the Ninth Cavalry to their support. After the worst of the fighting was over a Rough Rider, finding himself near one of the colored troopers, walked up and grasped his hand, saying 'We've got you fellows to thank for getting us out of a bad hole.'" Frank Knox, another member of the 1st USVC, added, "I never saw braver men anywhere."

Sergeant Graham of the 9th Cavalry's Troop E received his CM for saving the life of Lieutenant Parker, and the CM was awarded to 29 other buffalo soldiers for the various actions in Cuba – one-seventh of the total awarded for the war. The CM was awarded to nine men of the 24th Infantry, plus one man in the 25th at El Caney. Seven CMs went to men of the 9th Cavalry and 12 to the 10th; two of these recipients were subsequently selected for commissions in the black regiments of US Volunteer Infantry (USVI) organized for later service in Cuba – First Sergeant Peter McCown of the 10th Cavalry became a second lieutenant in the 7th USVI, and Sergeant Elisha Jackson of the 9th, a second lieutenant in the 10th USVI. McCown would also serve later as a first lieutenant in the 48th USVI, a black regiment raised for service in the Philippines.

After World War I, the War Department began a systematic review of official reports and records of military service, and eight other black soldiers were retrospectively awarded the newly instituted Silver Star medal – third only to the Medal of Honor and Distinguished Service Cross (DSC) – for bravery during the Spanish–American War. These were Presly Holliday, Isaac Bailey, John Buck, and Augustus Walley, 10th Cavalry; and George Driscoll, Robert L. Duvall, Elbert Wolley, and Richard Curtis, 24th Infantry.

RESCUE AT TAYABACOA

While most black regulars were fighting on foot at El Caney and Santiago de Cuba, we must recall that Lieutenant Carter P. Johnson's 50-strong mounted detachment from Troops A, H, and M, 10th Cavalry, had been detailed to perform a "special mission" – the delivery of much-needed supplies to the Cuban rebels. Accompanying General Munez and his 375 soldiers, 65 mules and packs, rations, clothing, and ammunition, they sailed on the steamship *Florida*, accompanied by the steamship *Fanita* and escorted by the gunboat *Peoria*, on June 21. Arriving off the south coast of Cuba eight days later, they attempted a landing at the San Juan river, but found this impossible due to a long coral reef. Sailing down the coast toward Tunas, a landing party consisting of 28 Americans and several Cubans rowed ashore at Tayabacoa to reconnoiter the enemy fortifications. They hid their boats in the heavy jungle and began creeping inland, but they stumbled into view of a Spanish blockhouse, and came under heavy fire. As they fell back toward the shore several Americans fell wounded, and five or six Cubans were killed. When they reached the water they found their boats destroyed by enemy artillery, and were overrun by the Spanish.

Aboard the *Florida*, a detachment of Cubans was hastily organized to go ashore and rescue the captured soldiers. Four separate attempts were met with heavy fire, and the Cubans were forced to return to the ships. As darkness fell, Lieutenant George Ahearn, 25th Infantry, who had accompanied the expedition, agreed to lead one more rescue attempt. Going below, he asked for volunteers to make a fifth effort under cover of darkness; without hesitation, Privates George Wanton, Fitz Lee, Dennis Bell, and William H. Thompkins stepped forward. The five men rowed ashore, and as they secured their boat the Spaniards opened a heavy but blind fire. Ignoring the Mauser rounds cracking over their heads, the five volunteers slowly worked their way through the thick undergrowth. Eventually the Spanish ceased fire, and in the eerie silence Private Thompkins heard a quiet plea for help; following the sound, he found the missing men locked in a stockade.

As he smashed the gate, the Spanish opened fire once more. Two of the buffalo soldiers provided covering fire while the rescued prisoners were helped to the boat; all 16 surviving members of the advance party were recovered, and although the enemy continued firing, by 3.00am Lieutenant

Ahearn's volunteers and the rescued shore party were safely aboard the *Florida*. Lieutenant Johnson refused Private Wanton's offer to return to retrieve the bodies of their dead comrades.

Their problems were not over, however, for while attempting to get closer to the shoreline during the prolonged rescue mission, the *Florida* had run aground. For 24 hours she was at the mercy of Spanish batteries, since the gunboat *Peoria* was too small to haul the larger transport off despite efforts to lighten her. However, at about noon the next day the larger gunboat *Helena* (Commander W. T. Swinburne) unexpectedly hove into view, shelled the blockhouse, and successfully refloated the *Florida*. At Lieutenant Johnson's request, the commanders of the *Peoria* and *Helena* continued to lay down a

Undress & Campaign Dress, 1896–1902

(1) Private, Company G, 24th Infantry, *c.* 1899. He wears field service uniform, which includes an 1898-pattern khaki field dress blouse with "light sky-blue" facings on standing collar and shoulder straps. He is armed with an M1898 Krag-Jörgensen rifle with M1896 bayonet attached. (2) Corporal, Company B, 9th Cavalry, *c.* 1900. The mounted NCO wears field service uniform consisting of an 1899-pattern khaki coat with falling collar, regulation yellow shoulder straps, and five brass "eagle" buttons. His ammunition is carried in a drab-colored 1896-pattern Mills cavalry cartridge belt with C-clip fastener, supporting a holstered Colt M1892 .38cal Army revolver. (3) Private, Company G, 10th Cavalry, *c.*1896. The general issue field service uniform includes an 1883-pattern sack coat with five-button front and straight cuff seams, and an 1895-pattern undress cap with crossed saber branch insignia. He is cleaning his 1885-pattern McClellan saddle.

(Richard Hook © Osprey Publishing)

concentrated fire on the Spanish positions while the *Florida* and *Fanita* quietly steamed 40 miles down the coast to Palo Alto, where they successfully landed their men, horses, and supplies. The buffalo soldiers joined forces with General Gomez and fought the remainder of the campaign under his command, finally rejoining their regiment at Montauk in September 1898. For their conspicuous gallantry during the rescue at Tayabacoa, all four black troopers received the Medal of Honor on June 23, 1899.

COMPANY L IN PUERTO RICO

With the Spanish capitulation in Cuba on July 16, US forces turned their attention to Puerto Rico, the one remaining Spanish possession in the Caribbean. In charge of the operation was General Nelson Miles, commanding I Army Corps. American forces landed on July 25 and, in a 19-day campaign with very few US casualties, subjugated the Spanish garrison under Captain-General Manuel Macas y Casado. A unit of the landing force was the 6th Massachusetts Volunteer Infantry, commanded by Colonel Charles F. Woodward – in whose ranks were the only African American Volunteers to see combat during the war. Raised in Boston, Massachusetts, and mobilized under the first call for volunteers on April 23, 1898, Company L of the 6th Massachusetts was commanded by black officers Captain William J. Williams, First Lieutenant William H. Jackson, and Second Lieutenant George W. Braxton. It was also the only black unit in an otherwise white regiment. According to *Leslie's Illustrated Newspaper* of June 23, 1898, Company L was the best behaved and most thoroughly equipped company to be sent from Massachusetts; the piece concluded: "Every one of these colored troops is a marksman."

Part of the Provisional Division under Brigadier-General Guy V. Henry (the former regimental commander of the 10th Cavalry), the 6th Massachusetts landed at Guánica on the south coast of Puerto Rico on July 25. Although they faced only slight opposition, General Henry took nothing for granted, and ordered Brigadier-General Henry Garretson to assemble seven companies (A, C, E, G, K, L, and M) of the 6th Massachusetts, plus one company of the 6th Illinois, for a move on the railroad terminus at Yauco, 5 miles north of Guánica. Its capture would help secure the port of Ponce – a deeper harbor than Guánica – for three more invasion flotillas that were expected to arrive soon.

Approaching Yauco, Garretson ordered the Illinois company to occupy part of the Seboruco Hills on his right, overlooking a nearby hacienda thought to be occupied by Spanish troops. The Illinois men dug in and sent scouts toward the hacienda, and shortly afterwards Companies L and M of the

6th Massachusetts arrived as reinforcements. Meanwhile, some Spanish infantry dug in on another nearby hilltop detected the movement and opened fire at about 2.00am on July 26. Garretson immediately committed the remaining five Massachusetts companies to an attack; they swept the Spanish before them, suffering four wounded, including Corporal W. S. Carpenter and Private B. Bostic of Company L.

About a week later General Miles held an investigation into the conduct of the 6th Massachusetts during the first two days of the campaign – lack of discipline on a hard march from Guánica to Ponce had been reported to General Garretson (who was prejudiced against black troops, despite the reported high standards of Company L). Miles requested the resignation of Colonel Woodward and replaced him with Colonel Frank Rice, a regular officer.

RETURN TO THE UNITED STATES

During the remaining operations in Cuba the 24th Infantry remained on San Juan Heights until July 10, when it was moved half a mile, though still in an important position on the exposed left flank. Yellow fever soon broke out in the camps and, in line with the stereotypical view that blacks were physically better able to deal with tropical conditions, this regiment was ordered to the yellow fever camp at Siboney to serve as nurses and hospital orderlies. A report in the *Army & Navy Journal* of February 4, 1899, eventually commended the 24th Infantry for this service, stating that "its fearless attendance of the sick elicited the highest praises, and undoubtedly contributed materially to the excellent results of the medical service." A later reference to this service in the same journal stated that the "colored soldiers died daily at this post of duty." Sailing from Cuba on August 27, 1898, the 24th Infantry had been "reduced by bullets and yellow fever to fewer than 400 men," and received "an ovation on the wharf prior to its departure."

On their return to the United States, the buffalo soldiers joined their white comrades at Montauk Point on Long Island, New York, where they spent six weeks in quarantine to prevent the spread of diseases picked up in Cuba, such as malaria, typhoid, dysentery, and, in some cases, yellow fever. By the end of September, the 9th Cavalry had taken up station at Fort Grant, Arizona. After a short spell at Huntsville, Alabama, the 10th Cavalry was back in Texas by January 29, 1899, although they returned to Cuba for a further tour of duty in 1900. The 24th Infantry arrived back at Fort Douglas, Utah, on October 1, 1898. On their return from Cuba the 25th Infantry established their new headquarters at Fort Logan, Colorado, while other companies of the regiment were stationed in Arizona and New Mexico.

THE PHILIPPINES, 1899–1902

Following the Treaty of Paris of December 10, 1898, which ended the Spanish-American War and ceded Guam, the Philippine Islands, and Puerto Rico to the United States, hostilities broke out between American forces and Filipino insurgents under Emilio Aguinaldo on February 4, 1899. A Filipino force of about 20,000 attacked Manila, and the US garrison of about 11,000 fought fiercely to prevent being pushed into the sea. After much hard

Another dockside, another war: the 25th Infantry leave San Francisco for the Philippines on the transport *Pennsylvania* on July 31, 1899. (*Buffalo Soldier Regiment*)

fighting the Americans were able to throw the insurgents back, and General Arthur MacArthur (father of Douglas) followed up with a counterattack that ended in the occupation of Caloocan, north of Manila. The campaign then ground to a halt due to insufficient US troop strength – Army regulations required that volunteers, who made up 75 percent of the available force, be sent home because the war with Spain was over. Hence, Major-General Ewell S. Otis (nicknamed "Colonel Blimp"), commander of US forces in the Philippines, was compelled to stay on the defensive until the arrival of reinforcements.

On patrol duty 300 miles from Manila, Corporal Arthur E. Peterson, 48th USVI, reveals in the following letter much about the nature of the war being waged in the Philippines during 1900:

My company is stationed at this place some three hundred odd miles from Manila; in fact the whole regiment is somewhere in the vicinity. We are right in the heart of the mountains, and we have to patrol all over them every day, day after day, climbing mountains. Now, mountain climbing is not what it's cracked up to be, even under favorable conditions, but when it comes to climbing out here, when someone is shooting at you from behind a tree, or a stone, it is a mess. And, of course, the sun is boiling hot and to make things worse I am on guard every other night; that is I only get about three nights' sleep a week. And even those three cannot be termed sleep, because someone will fire a shot during the night and then there will be no more sleep for me that night. But even so we manage to get along all right and keep good health. My health is excellent but we have a few sick men in the company. They are suffering from dysentery. That is the disease that does more toward killing men than the enemies' bullets do and I am taking care not to get it. I am very particular about what I eat and drink and that is the main thing…

When we were coming up here marching in the hot sun, each man carrying seventy-five pounds of baggage, not counting gun and ammunition, there were two companies of us, about two hundred men. On the second day we struck a pretty hot pace and went thirteen miles without a rest or halt. The men just fell out like bees, and when we did stop, I believe there were 48 or 50 men left standing, and they are men too; if they were not, they never would have been in the army. When you see, 150 big, strapping young fellows fall out like that you can imagine how it was. I did not fall out. In fact, I did not feel very much fatigued. I could have gone further."

– *The Colored Citizen*, Topeka, Kansas (November 9, 1900)

Meanwhile, Congress authorized the organization of 25 new regiments of two-year volunteer infantry, the last two of which were the black 48th and 49th USVI, authorized via the Act of March 2, 1899. The black regulars also saw service in the Philippines: toward the end of June 1899 elements of the 24th and 25th Infantry were en route for Manila. Major J. M. Thompson and four companies of the 24th sailed from San Francisco aboard the *Zealandia* on June 22, 1899, arriving on July 24; two companies of the 25th sailed from the same port aboard the *Valencia* six days later, and further companies from both regiments followed shortly thereafter.

CAMPAIGNING IN LUZON

Within three days of arrival in the Philippines, the black regular infantry were in the Manila defenses, and helping to man 4 miles of trenches running from Caloocan to Block House No.5 on the Caloocan–La Loma line. After the rainy season passed, both units took part in MacArthur's offensive against the insurgent strongholds in Pampanga and Tarlac provinces of central Luzon. Marching toward the volcanic Mt Arayat, and reaching the town of Arayat on October 6, the 24th Infantry met the enemy and had a "hard fight." During this action First Sergeant Jacob W. Stevens and Sergeant Tennie Cranshaw, Company K, both earned the CM for commanding their men with "coolness and good judgment" during an insurgent attack near Santa Ana.

On October 9, the day that the 25th Infantry was ordered to march from the Caloocan–La Loma line for Bamban north of Mt Arayat, the insurgents made a demonstration against positions still held by that regiment. Private C. W. Cordin, Company B, recalled:

> As I was on outpost at the time, about a half mile from the company, doing picket duty ... we noticed a file of queer looking people coming out of the bamboo woods, and as about 200 Chinese coolies had been carrying bamboo

These NCOs of the 25th Infantry were photographed at Bamban, Luzon, in 1899. Sergeant William Chambers, Company M (left), and Commissary Sergeant D. P. Green (right), in drab campaign hats, dark-blue shirts, and khaki trousers and leggings, stand either side of Sergeant-Major A. A. Morrow, who wears a khaki blouse with what appear to be brown canvas fatigue trousers. (*Buffalo Soldier Regiment*) from these woods to our lines, to build our supply road, we did not pay much attention to them as they were dressed just as the Chinese coolies are. All at once they threw out their skirmish line. As the body of men did this another body to their left marched out of the woods as skirmishers, and before we could send word to the company, the insurgents opened the battle, and it seemed as if every bullet came towards us two lonely men. In a moment's notice we were down in our trenches that are near our picket tent. We must work, and this is where our target practice came into good play. We worked like demons … for about an hour we kept them from advancing. At the end of that time Company B came out to our outpost on the left, volley firing. This made the Filipinos sick and they soon scampered to the woods. We lost ten men killed and one wounded.

While stationed at Bamban and Mabalacat, the 25th Infantry received intelligence from Filipino deserters that O'Donnell, about 6 miles northwest of Bamban, was filled with insurgent soldiers and weapons. Guided by one of the deserters, about 400 picked men from Companies B, E, and K under Captain Harry A. Leonhauser set out for that place on the night of November 18, taking a roundabout route through the foothills for the sake of surprise. At about 4.00am the next morning, they encountered a palm-leaf shack and spied men moving inside. A detail of Company K under Lieutenant Bates silently surrounded the outpost and demanded its surrender, which was

A group photograph of Troop F, 10th Cavalry, commanded by Captain P. E. Trippe, taken possibly at Calbayog in Samar during their first tour of duty in the Philippines. The group shows a mixture of old issue 1898-pattern and 1902-pattern service uniforms – typical of the supply system of the day – with 1902-pattern hats. One of the officers wears the blue 1895-pattern cap and undress coat. (USAMHI – B. O. Davis Collection)

accepted. As the occupants passed rifles and ammunition out of the window, the barking of the village dogs gave the alarm, and the black troops rushed on to complete their mission.

In the *Denver Times* later that month, an officer who took part stated that:

> There was an immediate move toward the town, and a few scattered shots were fired as our troops entered. We were in the town now and the colored soldiers showed a grim and great earnestness in their work of gathering in prisoners, rifles and bolos (long-bladed knives). Strong black arms caught fleeing insurgents upon the streets and hauled them from under beds and beneath houses. Native women screamed in alarm and on their knees offered money and food to the American troops.

At 6.00am the command regrouped, bringing in as prisoners the entire Filipino garrison consisting of seven officers and 200 men. They used bull carts from the village to carry away about 225 rifles and nearly 10,000 rounds of ammunition.

While posted in northern Luzon the black regulars spent much of their time on long scouting expeditions and patrols. On December 7, 1899, Corporal John H. Johnson, Company F, 24th Infantry, and Privates Earnest Stokes, Lig J. Clark, Benjamin H. Goode, and Amos Stuckey of Company H earned the CM for "most distinguished gallantry in action" during a scout near Naguilian on the west coast of the island.

On January 5, 1900, Companies B, K, and M, 25th Infantry, again under the command of Captain Leonhauser, left their camp at Magalang and attacked the insurgent stronghold of General Aquino at Camansi near Mt Arayat. According to the report on this operation, "The troops scaled heights of great difficulty, and crawled through dense undergrowth. Lieutenant William T. Schenck, 25th Infantry, particularly distinguished himself in leading the advance, as did also Lieutenant A. C. Martin, and the enemy was driven off with what was believed to be considerable loss." Sergeant James R. Lightfoot, Company K, received the CM for "distinguished gallantry displayed in the advance upon a concealed enemy" during this action. The insurgent barracks were destroyed with large quantities of stores; American losses amounted to only one man killed – Corporal M. Washington of Company B.

According to Lieutenant Schenck, the insurgents "evidently had all they wanted of the 'soldados negros'. After we had gotten the wounded dressed we started back and I covered the retreat with the scouts." The battle report concluded: "Five American prisoners fell into our hands [i.e. were rescued], but not until they had been shot and so brutally boloed that but two recovered."

On January 6–7, 1900, a force of about 1,000 insurgents attacked the village of Iba on the west coast, which was occupied by Company F, 25th Infantry, commanded by Captain Joseph P. O'Neil. The buffalo soldiers held their ground in three "defensible buildings" including a church. At the signal of a lighted candle in the church window, O'Neil ordered his men to sally forth and form up with "bayonets charged." According to the report of Colonel Burt, the officer "ordered the trumpeter to sound the 'Charge' and his men raised a yell and with Captain O'Neil at the head they went at the enemy and cleaned them out in a handsome manner."

Scouting in the Philippines, 1899

This scene depicts the advance guard of a scouting expedition across the Zambales Mountains of western Luzon, conducted by Companies F, H, I, and M, 25th Infantry under Captain Joseph P. O'Neil; supplies were carried by local porters. In typical field service dress of the period, some men have non-regulation flannel scarves tucked into the collars of their 1883-pattern dark-blue pullover flannel shirts. They all wear the 1889-pattern drab campaign hat and khaki trousers. Two men wear the 8th Army Corps insignia on the front of their hats, while the foreground man carries a toothbrush in one of the ventilation slits he has cut in his. Some men unofficially punched their hats into the "Montana peak" shape. The sergeant is distinguished by narrow off-white chevrons pinned to his upper shirtsleeves, as authorized on July 25, 1898/ September 14, 1899. They are all armed with M1898 Krag rifles with M1896 bayonets. Their ammunition is carried in Mills cartridge belts, and the rest of their equipment consists of 1885-pattern drab canvas haversacks, tin canteens in drab duck covers, and, slung on their backs, 1878-pattern blanket bags of drab canvas, to which are attached 1874–1901 pattern quart-sized tin mugs.

(Richard Hook © Osprey Publishing)

On July 4, 1900, a 40-strong scouting party of the 24th Infantry encountered a large group of insurgents near Manacling. According to the *Army & Navy Journal*:

> The rebels had the little body of colored troops "horse-shoed," but they fought their way out with little loss to their party and much damage to the insurgents. The American colored men fought like demons and soon had their antagonists on a sprint in all directions. The insurgents left 16 killed and 30 wounded on the field. Lieutenant Mitchell was seriously wounded, and one enlisted man was killed and two wounded. Lieutenant Mitchell and the men were highly praised for their tact and bravery.

On August 11, 1900, elements of the 24th Infantry captured 165 insurgents, led by Roberto Grassa, who probably belonged to the band that had attacked them the previous month.

Meanwhile, by March 1900 the black 49th USVI, commanded by Colonel William H. Back, saw action at the northern end of Luzon. Four companies of that regiment left Manila on the transport *Aztec* and landed at St Vincent, from whence they marched overland to Aparri, where they established their regimental headquarters and were soon joined by four more companies. On March 20, a patrol of 30 black volunteers from this regiment encountered a band of insurgents and killed two, capturing arms and ammunition. During another patrol, Lieutenant Gilmer of the 49th began to suspect that the Filipino guide who claimed to know the location of a band of "insurrectos" was leading them into an ambush. Halting his men in a bamboo thicket, he ordered the guide to exchange clothing with one of the buffalo soldiers, and gave him a rifle and ammunition belt. The party proceeded and came to a river, which the guide insisted had to be crossed in order to attack the insurgents. As the guide was forced out into the water at gunpoint, shots rang out from the opposite bank and the insurgents revealed their position. The black volunteers then flanked the enemy, and after "a hot fight, won the day, capturing rifles and ammunition."

LATER SERVICE

Between October 1900 and June 1901, about 1,000 further clashes occurred between US forces and Filipino insurgents, but after the capture of Emilio Aguinaldo in March 1901 these encounters decreased. However, US forces remained in occupation of the Philippines, and elements of all four black regular regiments completed further service there between 1901 and 1918. Eight troops of the 9th Cavalry were in the Philippines by September 1900, and Sergeant Richard Miller, Company F, was subsequently awarded the CM for "distinguished conduct" when attacked by "several bolomen" near Tagbac on December 17 of that year. A squadron of the 10th Cavalry served in Samar and Panay from May 1901 until June 1902, and the entire regiment returned in 1907 to undertake a two-year tour of duty. The 9th was back in the islands in 1902, taking part in expeditions against the Moros, a fierce Mohammedan people of Mindanao and the Sulu Archipelago, who had never been completely subjugated by the Spanish. The 24th Infantry returned to the Philippines in 1906; on July 24 of that year Sergeant John W. Ash and Corporal Preston Askew, Company E, earned the CM for "conspicuous gallantry in action" near Tabon-Tabon in the jungles of Samar, against Pulajanes – followers of Papa Faustino, who claimed to possess messianic powers. The 25th Infantry began their second tour in the Philippines on September 13, 1906, and served against hostile Moros on Mindanao until 1909. A further six buffalo soldiers were awarded CMs for life-saving actions in non-combat situations in the Philippines between 1899 and 1914.

THE MEXICAN BORDER, 1914–17

Following the Mexican Revolution of 1910, in 1911 fighting erupted between the "constitutionalist" army of Venustiano Carranza and the rebel forces of Francisco "Pancho" Villa. By late 1915, Villa hoped for American support to obtain the presidency of Mexico, but instead the US government recognized the Carranza regime. An irate Villa swore vengeance, and began attacking Americans in hopes of provoking President Woodrow Wilson's intervention in Mexico. Villa believed that this would discredit the Carranza government with the people of Mexico, and reaffirm his own popularity.

The 10th Cavalry sailed from the Philippines to the United States on May 14, 1909, and arrived in New York harbor on July 25. On July 27 it moved to Fort Ethan Allen, Vermont, where it remained (apart from a spell at the Cavalry Camp of Instruction at Winchester, Virginia) until December 8, 1913, when it was ordered back to Fort Huachuca near Tombstone, Arizona. Arriving at its old garrison, the regiment promptly found itself back on duty on the Mexican border which, according to regimental historian Major E. L. N. Glass, was in "a more than usual turmoil."

NACO, 1914

Both the 9th and 10th Cavalry were ordered to protect American lives and property when fighting occurred between the rival Mexican armies outside Naco, a small town that straddled the border between the United States and Mexico, during October 1914. Colonel William C. Brown, leading four troops of the 10th, arrived on the scene during the night of October 7. He was joined by six troops and the machine-gun platoon from the 9th Cavalry, under Colonel John Francis Guilfoyle, who took overall command. Brown deployed west of that part of Naco which lay on the American side of the border, while Guilfoyle occupied the eastern sector. By December 1914, this force had been increased to seven troops from each regiment, plus a machine-gun company, for a total of 1,050 men.

During this highly confusing campaign it was difficult for the US soldiers to distinguish between the entrenched pro-Villa rebels (who included Yaqui Indians) under General Maytorena, and the Mexican federal forces commanded by General Benjamin Hill. However, they maintained a neutral stance while observing the fighting from their own trenches and rifle pits, with "machine guns all set in action." To make matters worse, American civilians crowded into Naco to watch the fighting. According to Major Glass, the African American troopers had "great difficulty … in holding back the crowds of visitors from Bisbee and Douglas who flocked to see the 'battles', in automobiles, wagons and [on] horseback."

The fighting at Naco continued until January 1915, with Mexican bullets ripping through the frame buildings and military tents in and around town on a regular basis. Seven members of the 10th Cavalry were wounded by stray bullets during the performance of this duty, while the 9th sustained one dead and two wounded. Indeed, as the officers of the 10th enjoyed their Thanksgiving meal in a tent about 800 yards from the US Army trenches, their menu contained the caution "Guests will please be careful in dodging stray bullets not to upset the soup." On April 7, 1915, the buffalo soldiers were commended for their "splendid conduct and efficient service" at Naco by Secretary of War Lindley M. Garrison.

The regiments remained on border patrol duty during the remainder of 1915, and continued to encounter hostility from Mexican troops and guerrillas. At Lochiel, Arizona, on August 22, a detachment of government

A detachment of the 10th Cavalry search for Pancho Villa during the Punitive Expedition of 1916. The mount second from left can be seen to wear the first-pattern M1904 McClellan saddles used during this campaign. (Fort Huachuca Museum)

African Americans persisted in their willingness to serve their country, despite being vulnerable to racism and facing a lack of equal opportunity to progress through the ranks. One of the finest black soldiers of his time, Medal of Honor winner J. William McBryar, volunteered first for duty on the Mexican border in 1914 and then again in 1916, as tension mounted between the United States and Germany:

Bee, McNeil Island, Wash.

June 10, 1914

The Adjutant General, U.S.A.
      War Department
      Washington, D.C.

Sir:

I take pleasure in offering my services to the U.S. Government if needed in connection with our present entanglement with the Mexican Republic.

I first enlisted in the regular Army in Jan'y 1887, and was assigned to the Tenth U.S. Cavalry, Troop K.

Was appointed a Lieutenant for the 25th U.S. Infantry, to the 8th and the 49th U.S. Vol. Infantries during the Spanish American War and the Philippine Rebellion and served in each regiment until mustered and served fifteen years altogether in the regular and volunteer forces of the United States,

Very respectfully,

      Wm McBryar.

– NARA

soldiers crossed the border and attempted to rustle cattle, but was thwarted by patrols of Troop K, 10th Cavalry. On November 3–4, four troops of the 10th, under Colonel Brown, protected the citizens of Douglas, Arizona, during fighting between the rival factions at Agua Prieta, Mexico. On November 21 two enlisted men of Troop F, at an observation post near Monument 117, exchanged fire with Mexicans, and Private Willie Norman was wounded. The next day five armed Mexicans rode into a camp at the Santa Cruz river and fired on another detachment of Troop F, who replied with revolver fire. On November 25, Mexican troops crossed the border again and attacked an outpost manned by members of the same troop near

Major Charles Young as commander of 2nd Squadron, 10th Cavalry, during the Punitive Expedition. In June 1917, Young was promoted colonel, but was then retired – allegedly on medical grounds, which he promptly proved false by riding on horseback from his Ohio home to Washington DC. The racial prejudice of the day would not tolerate a black general in France – the command for which Young was obviously qualified. Cynically restored to active duty in November 1918, he died in Liberia in 1922. (NARA)

Mascarena's Ranch. On the same day, elements of this troop occupied the western outskirts of the border town of Nogales, Arizona, which was under attack from both Mexican factions.

PUNITIVE EXPEDITION, 1916

On March 9, 1916, the confrontation reached a new level when Mexican guerrillas led by Pancho Villa raided Columbus, New Mexico; 19 Americans were killed, including seven troopers of the 13th Cavalry. The following day the Southern Department commander, Major-General Frederick Funston, ordered the 10th Cavalry veteran Brigadier-General John J. Pershing, commander of the 8th Cavalry Brigade, to apprehend the perpetrators and bring back "Villa, dead or alive." For his mission into Chihuahua – which at first had the grudging acquiescence of the ineffective Mexican government – Pershing organized a provisional division designated as the Punitive Expedition, US Army. Designed to pursue bandits in hostile and barren northern Mexico while protecting its lines of communication with infantry, this division differed considerably from the organizations outlined in the Field Service Regulations. It consisted of two provisional cavalry brigades, each made up of two cavalry regiments and a field artillery battery, and one infantry brigade of two regiments. Also included were two engineer companies, plus medical, signal, transport, and air units as divisional troops.

Aguas Calientes

The 2nd Cavalry Brigade, under Colonel George A. Dodd and consisting of the 7th and 10th Cavalry and Battery B, 6th Field Artillery, rendezvoused at Culberson's Ranch, New Mexico, on March 16, 1916. There they were joined by the Machine Gun Troop of the 10th Cavalry, commanded by Captain Albert E. Phillips. Meanwhile, the 24th Infantry, about 1,800 strong, left Columbus on March 28 for service in Mexico guarding the steadily lengthening lines of communication of the mounted troops.

The Machine Gun Troop, 10th Cavalry, provided valuable covering fire for the charge at Aguas Calientes on April 1. The pack saddle invented by their CO, Captain Albert E. Phillips, can be seen on the mule at left center. (Fort Huachuca Museum)

Although cut off from the main column by a heavy snow storm on April 1, the advance guard of Dodd's column surprised a 150-strong party of Villistas by riding 55 miles in 17 hours to attack their encampment at Aguas Calientes, near Parral, about 300 miles inside Mexico. Under cover of the overhead fire of the machine guns, Troops F and H of the 2nd Squadron, under Major Charles Young, charged an adobe hut held by the guerrillas. As they increased their speed to a gallop, withholding their fire, the buffalo soldiers began to yell – and the Mexicans ran off into the brush. Three Villistas were killed, and 40 of their horses were captured; the black troopers sustained no casualties, but several of their mounts were killed. During the next few days the 10th Cavalry followed the trail, but the Villistas broke up into smaller groups when they left the mountains, and disappeared once again.

Santa Cruz de Villegas

By April 1916 the Carranza regime was growing hostile to the American military presence, and Mexican government troops began to attack Pershing's units. On April 12, Major Young's squadron of the 10th rode to the aid of two troops of the 13th Cavalry and one company of the 6th Infantry, under Major Frank Tompkins, which had come under fire from government troops and an angry mob at Parral, the home town of Pancho Villa. Tompkins' command was forced to retire about 8 miles toward Santa Cruz de Villegas, where he made a stand. According to the report of Colonel Brown: "The village of Santa Cruz was entered quietly and prepared for defense. The roofs of the buildings were manned by riflemen and the enemy kept at 1,200 yards range. At 7.55[pm] I arrived with Major Young's Squadron, and the Machine Gun Troop, Tenth Cavalry, and assumed command. The enemy was still on the hill to the south when we arrived, as was shown by the sounding of their bugles after ours had been sounded."

A member of the relief column, Captain George B. Rodney, Troop G, 10th Cavalry, recalled that the:

> ... sound of our hoof beats brought Tompkins to the gates and he gave us a warm welcome. He had been wounded in the arm and he had injured a leg by falling over some hasty entrenchments that he had been supervising, and he was glad to see us. As we splashed through the ford he shouted to us. I can hear his words yet. Major Charles Young, one of the six Negro officers of the army and our Squadron Commander, was riding by me at the head of the advance guard when Tompkins sighted him and called out, "By God! They were glad to see the Tenth Cavalry at Santiago in '98, but I'm a damn sight gladder to see you now. I could kiss every one of you!"

Forty Mexican troops, plus one civilian, were killed in this action, while the Americans sustained two killed and six wounded, plus one man missing.

Carrizal

Towards the end of May 1916, about 10,000 Mexican government troops were massing south and west of Juarez in order to "replace" Pershing's force, who had outstayed their welcome in Mexico. The Carranza government announced that no opposition would be made to US forces retiring north toward the border, but that any troops venturing to move in any other direction would be opposed. By that time the 10th Cavalry was encamped at Colonia Dublan, where they would be based for the remainder of their time in Mexico. On June 11, trouble boiled over between the buffalo soldiers and a large group of Carranza soldiers

The mule-mounted "pack platoon" stand in the background while a section of the Machine Gun Troop, 10th Cavalry, operate their M1909 Benet-Mercié machine rifle. This French design, rechambered for the US .30-06 cartridge, featured a feed mechanism that avoided the Maxim patent on flexible webbing belts by using long metal stripper clips like the Hotchkiss machine guns; the strips were prone to jamming if not properly handled. (NARA)

who objected to a black trooper talking to a Mexican girl. Although greatly outnumbered and surrounded, the Americans fought their way out, killing three of the Mexicans but losing 13 of their own men taken prisoner.

Five days later an expedition was sent eastward to check on Mexican troops concentrating around Villa Ahumada. Captain Charles T. Boyd, in command of Troop C, with Henry R. Adair as lieutenant, was ordered to reconnoiter the vicinity of the Santa Domingo Ranch but to avoid contact with Mexican forces. Similar orders were issued to Captain Lewis S. Morey, commanding Troop K. The two columns converged on the evening of June 20 at a ranch at Ojo Santo Domingo, about 60 miles east of Colonia Dublan, where they gathered intelligence on Mexican dispositions from the American ranch foreman. However, Captain Boyd felt that his orders required him to take a look for himself, so the two troops rode out at dawn on the 21st for Villa Ahumada via Carrizal. (It has been claimed that in ordering this mission General Pershing actually sought to provoke the Carranza regime into providing the US with a *casus belli*.)

Carrizal, June 1916

During the Punitive Expedition into Mexico, Troops C & K, 10th Cavalry, were defeated by superior numbers of Carranza regime troops at Carrizal on June 21, 1916. The troopers wore 1911-pattern olive-drab wool pullover shirts, drab campaign hats with "Montana" peak and yellow worsted cords, olive-drab breeches, and 1910-pattern drab canvas or leather leggings. They were armed with M1903 .30–06 rifles, and M1911 Colt .45cal semi-automatic pistols carried in 1912-pattern swivel holsters, with leg straps, suspended from drab 1910-pattern mounted cartridge belts.

(Richard Hook © Osprey Publishing)

Arriving outside the town of Carrizal at 6.30am, Boyd discovered a government force awaiting his arrival drawn up for battle, consisting of three squadrons of the Mexican 2nd Cavalry Regiment, estimated at "several hundred." They were deployed behind a row of cottonwoods, along a stream bed, and in the town, which was fronted by a barbed wire fence. Between the Americans and the Mexican defenses was a water-filled ditch.

The Mexican commander and his staff rode out and parleyed with Boyd, informing him that their orders were to prevent the Americans from advancing any further to the east. Boyd replied that his orders required him to pass through the town. The Mexican commander invited him into Carrizal for a conference but, fearing a trap, he declined. Both officers returned to their units; the American captain informed his troopers that his orders were to travel east to Villa Ahumada, 8 miles beyond the town, and added, "I am going through ... and [intend to] take all you men with me." At this, some of the buffalo soldiers cheered, and struck up "spirited songs" to show the Mexicans they meant business. Boyd gave orders for the advance; Troop C was formed on the left in line of skirmishers, with one platoon of Troop K to their right, and another on the extreme right, echeloned a little to the rear.

Corporal H. C. Houston, Troop K, recalled:

> We were within 500 yards of the enemy, then we dismounted and our horses moved to the rear and we moved forward, the Mexican cavalry started riding around both flanks and when we were about 200 yards from the enemy, we received a heavy volume of fire from rifle and machine guns and we knew that the ball was opened then. We then received the order to lie down and commence firing, using the battle sight (which is the way we aim our rifles when we are fighting at close range). All of our men were taking careful aim, and Mexicans and horses were falling in all directions but the Mexican forces were too strong for us as they had between 400 and 500 and we only had 50 men on the firing line, so even though we were inflicting terrible execution, they outnumbered us too greatly [for us] to stop their advance around our right flank.

After about an hour of firing, Troop C was ordered to advance toward the irrigation ditch beyond which a Mexican machine-gun section had been posted, while Troop K closed in from the right, where they were busy holding off the flank attack. Captain Boyd was wounded in the hand and the shoulder as he ran toward the ditch, and received a fatal wound in the head as he climbed up the opposite bank. Meanwhile, a squad of Mexican troops left the town and, going round to the rear of the buffalo soldiers, captured their horses.

In a situation that was rapidly becoming desperate, Lieutenant "Hank" Adair continued to lead Troop C toward the houses of the town. Finding that his men were running short of ammunition, Adair went back to get the belts from the wounded, but during his return he was struck by a bullet just above the heart. Seeing his officer fall, Sergeant Peter Bigstaff, a veteran of the Cuba campaign, went to his aid. According to a graphic account by newspaper columnist John Temple Graves, Bigstaff:

> ... fought in deadly shamble side by side with the white man, following always, fighting always as his Lieut. fought. And finally when Adair, literally shot to pieces, fell in his tracks, his last command to his black trooper was to leave him and save his own life. Even then the heroic Negro paused in the midst of that hell of courage for a final service to his officer. Bearing a charmed life he had fought his way out. He saw that Adair had fallen with his head in the water and with superb loyalty the black trooper turned and went back to the hailstorm of death; lifted the head of his superior officer out of the water, leaned his head against a tree, and left him there dead with dignity when it was impossible to serve him any more.

At about 9.00am, Troop K on the right was forced to fall back about 1,000 yards, with Captain Morey wounded in the shoulder. Joined by stragglers from Troop C, these men then scattered and escaped to safety as best they could. Morey and five troopers made their way to San Luis ranch, where they found a squadron of the 11th Cavalry. From there the wounded officer was driven in a motor truck to Pershing's headquarters. American losses amounted to 14 men killed, including two officers, and 23 taken prisoner, including

Men of the 10th Cavalry captured at Carrizal on June 21, 1916, photographed in captivity; some have been stripped of their shirts, leggings and shoes. They were released on June 29, and even their horses and equipment were returned the next day – the Caranza regime was clearly anxious not to escalate the situation. (Fort Huachuca Museum)

their Mormon scout and interpreter Lemuel H. Spillsbury. The Mexicans sustained 30 killed, including General Felix Gomez plus ten other officers, and 43 wounded. The Mexican government troops took their American prisoners to Chihuahua town, where they were imprisoned briefly before being turned over to the American authorities eight days later.

Pershing had his *casus belli*; but although a desire for revenge for the losses at Carrizal was widespread throughout the country, and particularly among African Americans, the US government was preoccupied with America's impending entry into World War I. Hence the 10th Cavalry spent the remainder of 1916 at Colonia Dublan, training and perfecting its equipment. The Punitive Expedition had succeeded in dispersing the Villistas and protecting US border settlements from Mexican raids, though not in actually coming to grips with Pancho Villa (who would eventually be assassinated in an ambush outside Parral on July 23, 1923). With the onset of winter in 1916, the men of the 10th were set to work building more comfortable quarters. On January 30, 1917, the regiment joined the main column in the final withdrawal from Mexico, and arrived back at Fort Huachuca on February 14, 1917.

FIFTIETH ANNIVERSARY

While encamped at Dublan, the 10th Cavalry celebrated its 50th birthday with a pageant organized by Lieutenant-Colonel Charles Young. According to the *Army & Navy Journal* of August 12, 1916:

… a non-commissioned officer, clad in heraldic trappings, recited stanzas of blank verse composed by Colonel Young, which gave a synopsis of the scenes presented. The first two episodes of the pageant contrasted the men as they appeared and drilled fifty years ago and as they appear today. The third, in which fifty troopers apparelled as Indians appeared, illustrated a brilliant feat by an officer of the 10th, Lieut. Powhatan Clark, who returned under fire during a fight with Indians to rescue a wounded trooper [in 1886]. Private [George] Wanton, of the Machine Gun Troop, one of the four Medal of Honor men of the regimental rolls [see above, "Tayabacoa"], was the central figure in the fourth episode. He was escorted across the field of honor by a guard bearing wreaths on their saber points. The fifth illustrated the part the 10th took in the battle of Santiago, Cuba. The sixth was presented by a troop, which carried banners bearing the names of the battles in which the regiment has fought and those of its commanders who became generals. At the close of the celebration the call to colors was sounded and regimental spirit reached a climax in a great burst of cheering, ending with singing of "Glory, Hallelujah."

WORLD WAR I, 1917–18

African Americans were called to the colors once again when the United States declared war on Germany on April 6, 1917. Of approximately 400,000 African American soldiers who served in the US Army in the Great War, about 200,000 were sent to Europe, of whom 42,000 saw combat. The remainder performed valuable service as labor and stevedore battalions within the Services of Supply (SOS). Around 367,700 of the total came into the service through the operation of the Selective Service Act of May 18, 1917 – i.e. they were draftees.

Besides these, about 5,400 were already in the Regular Army, while another 2,500 served in the National Guard of several states. However, reflecting the attitudes of that time, the War Department announced that it would not assign any of the four all-black regular regiments to combat roles overseas because they feared that the presence of these units might cause trouble in France (the 24th Infantry had recently been involved in race riots at Houston, Texas). Consequently, the Army dispersed these regiments throughout the US or American-held territory. The 9th Cavalry was assigned to Stotsenberg Camp in Luzon, Philippines, for the duration of the war. The 10th Cavalry spent the war years patrolling the Mexican border around Fort Huachuca, Arizona. In the summer of 1917, the 24th Infantry received orders to relocate to several camps in Texas and New Mexico. The 25th Infantry, stationed at Schofield Barracks in Hawaii, hoped for service in France until early summer of 1918, when they received orders to transfer to Camp Little at Nogales, Arizona, for the remainder of the war.

The National Guard units drafted for the war included the 15th New York, 8th Illinois, 1st Separate Battalion of the District of Columbia, 1st Separate Company of Maryland, 9th Battalion of Ohio, 1st Separate Company of Connecticut, Company L of the Massachusetts National Guard,

Garrison Life, 1902–14

(1) Sergeant, Company G, 24th Infantry, c.1904. The 1902-pattern full dress consists of a 1902-pattern single-breasted, six-button, dark-blue dress coat, with three small gilt "eagle" buttons on each cuff. The collar insignia are the unpopular US coat of arms and "crossed rifles." The 1902-pattern full dress dark-blue cap has a slightly belled crown, and a detachable blue woolen band trimmed with two 1in bands of sky blue. A breast cord of light blue mohair is attached to his coat. Trousers are dark sky-blue kersey with 1in-wide white seam stripes. He holds an M1898 Krag rifle with leather sling, and his equipment consists of a dark russet 1904-pattern waist belt with squared bronze box buckle, supporting a fourth pattern McKeever cartridge box at the back. (2) Private, Troop D, 10th Cavalry, c. 1906. Service dress now features the 1902-pattern five-button olive-drab cotton coat (exact shades varied considerably).

Its falling collar displays dull-finish bronze "U.S." and crossed sabers insignia. The four front "choked-bellows" pockets are expandable by means of a concealed pleat around the pocket's edge, the pocket having the appearance of a widened horseshoe shape. His 1902-pattern olive-drab service cap bears "10" over crossed sabers over "D" in dull-finish bronze metal. He is armed with a .38cal M1903 Colt Army double-action revolver with cord attachment, and the M1860 light cavalry saber with 1885-pattern black leather knot, in a "browned" scabbard. His russet enlisted man's saber belt with bronzed brass roller buckle supports the revolver cartridge box and 1892-pattern holster. Footwear consists of 1904-pattern russet calfskin Blucher-style garrison shoes, worn with canvas leggings. (3) Private, Troop L, 9th Cavalry, c. 1913. Uniformed for dismounted service, he wears a 1912-pattern five-button olive-drab garrison coat with four conventional patch pockets, and olive-drab cotton breeches. His 1907-pattern button-type collar insignia have "U.S." on the left and "9" over crossed sabers over "L" on the right. The 1911-pattern campaign hat with "Montana" peak has a yellow branch-of-service cord and acorns. Pattern 1910 russet leather strap leggings are worn above his garrison shoes. He is armed with an M1903 .30-06 Springfield rifle with brown leather sling, and a .38cal revolver in an 1912-pattern swivel holster with leg strap. His belt is the Mills 1903 pattern, with 1907-pattern suspenders.

(Richard Hook © Osprey Publishing)

and Company G of the Tennessee National Guard. When the United States became a belligerent on April 6, 1917, several of these units had only recently seen service on the Mexican border in support of the regulars.

AFRICAN AMERICAN OFFICERS & FORMATIONS

As the United States mobilized for war, the federal authorities showed little interest in commissioning any more African American officers in addition to the tiny handful then serving. However, due to the campaigning of leaders such as Dr Joel E. Springarn, Chairman of the Executive Committee of the National Association for the Advancement of Colored People, Dr W. E. B. DuBois, editor of black newspaper *The Crisis*, and Colonel Charles Young, 10th Cavalry, a separate reserve camp was established for the training of black officers at Fort Des Moines, Iowa, on June 15, 1917. From the ranks of the four regular regiments, 250 NCOs were shortlisted for training at this facility, and a further 1,000 recruits were selected from the various states and the District of Columbia on a pro rata basis. Most of the latter came from institutions such as Howard University and the Tuskegee Normal and Industrial Institute. These student officers were put through four months of intensive training under Colonel Charles C. Ballou and his staff, plus a group of black NCOs from the regular regiments.

Finally, on October 14, 1917, Colonel W. T. Johnson of the Adjutant-General's Office arrived at Fort Des Moines with commissions for 639 officers – 106 captains, 329 first lieutenants, and 204 second lieutenants. These officers subsequently reported for duty at training camps in Iowa, Kansas, Illinois, Ohio, Maryland, New Jersey, and New York, and became part of the all-black 92nd Division, commanded by Major-General Ballou, which was organized on November 29, 1917. This formation eventually consisted of the 365th through 368th Infantry, supported by machine-gun, artillery, and mortar battalions, plus engineer and field signal troops. While the company-grade officers and entire enlisted personnel of this division were black, the staff and field officers, and the officers of the artillery, quartermaster, engineer, and supply units were, with few exceptions, white.

The all-black 93rd Division (Provisional), commanded by General Roy Hoffman, was organized at Camp Stuart, Newport News, Virginia, in December 1917. This formation lacked a full complement of combat units and support elements, and never attained full divisional strength. Three of its infantry regiments were composed of National Guard. The 15th New York was subsequently designated the 369th Infantry, and the 8th Illinois (also known as "Chicago's Old 8th") became the 370th Infantry. Separate

The color guard of the 15th NY National Guard – soon to be designated 369th Infantry – parade in New York City in 1917. They wear "Montana peak" campaign hats, British-style olive-drab overcoats, and 1910-pattern canvas leggings. They are equipped with 1903-pattern infantry cartridge belts, and armed with M1903 Springfield rifles. (NARA)

battalions and companies of guardsmen from DC, Connecticut, Maryland, Massachusetts, Ohio, and Tennessee made up the 372nd Infantry; and the fourth regiment, which became the 371st Infantry, was composed of draftees from North and South Carolina. During December 1917 these four regiments were assigned to the 185th and 186th Infantry Brigades, and a small divisional headquarters was established, although the latter was disbanded in May 1918.

OVER THERE, 1918

The first American combat troops, black or white, to arrive in France belonged to the 15th New York of the 93rd Division. The division sailed from Hoboken, New Jersey, on December 12, 1917, aboard the USS *Pocahontas*, arriving at the port of Brest in northwestern France 15 days later (despite experiencing engine trouble, an onboard fire, and a collision with a British oil tanker). Additional units of the division arrived in various stages during March and April 1918.

When the 93rd arrived in France the situation was desperate for the Allies, after nearly four years of trench warfare and casualties numbered in the high hundreds of thousands. French Army morale had almost collapsed in 1917, throwing an even heavier burden on the British Expeditionary Force (BEF) in the northern half of the 400-mile Western Front; the British had held up, but were badly weakened by their losses in the Third Battle of Ypres that autumn. With the entrance of the US into the war, the Allies breathed a collective sigh of relief and welcomed the "doughboys" of the American Expeditionary Force (AEF) into the fray; however, there was an inevitable conflict at command level. The Allied generals wanted American formations placed at their disposal as quickly as possible, while AEF commander General Pershing was determined that US troops would only enter battle as an integrated and separate American army when they were fully equipped and trained. This process would take many months to complete.

Integration into the French Army

General Pershing did agree to help fill the depleted French ranks to a limited extent, and the troops he loaned included the four regiments comprising the 93rd Division — the French had a well-established tradition of successfully integrating units from their colonies in Algeria, Morocco, and Senegal into their field armies. More importantly for Pershing, this arrangement would partially avoid the difficulty of integrating black and white American troops in the frontline trenches.

The 93rd Division joined the French Fourth Army approximately two months after its arrival in France, and served in this command until the close of hostilities. The French military trained, armed, equipped, and organized the dispersed units as French soldiers. Under the French plan, a regiment consisted of three battalions, and each battalion had three rifle companies and one machine-gun companies (under the US plan there was only one machine-gun company per regiment). For reasons of logistical commonality, the US equipment carried by the black soldiers was mostly replaced with French helmets, rifles, pistols, machine guns, personal accoutrements, and gasmasks; the French also provided draft horses and wagons.

The buffalo soldiers adjusted quickly to their new assignment, but not without some difficulties. There were problems over communication (except for those who hailed from the Cajun areas of Louisiana), monetary exchange, and provisions. Used to three substantial meals a day, usually consisting of meat stew and cornbread, the black soldiers took some time to become accustomed to the French Army ration of soup and bread served only twice daily.

African American "Doughboys" at rifle practice behind the lines in France in 1918. (Courtesy Anne Clarkson)

Private Henry Johnson, Company C, 369th Infantry, was one of the first two American soldiers to receive the French Croix de Guerre for bravery during World War I. On May 14, 1918, Johnson and Private Needham Roberts were on sentry duty when they fought off a party of about 12 Germans using a rifle, grenades, and a bolo knife. Both men were wounded, and both received the Croix de Guerre; Johnson was also promoted to sergeant. (NARA)

369TH INFANTRY: "HARLEM HELL FIGHTERS"

The war service of the 15th New York, which was redesignated the 369th Infantry after transfer to the French Army, began disappointingly. Instead of a posting to the frontline, they were assigned to the French 16th Division and sent to St Nazaire on the western coast of France, where they joined black labor battalions of the SOS. For nearly two months the regiment unloaded ships, guarded German prisoners, laid railroad track, and constructed roads, storehouses, docks, hospitals, and dams. The 369th felt insulted by this "pick and shovel" placement, and morale suffered.

However, on March 10, 1918, the 369th were finally ordered to the war zone, and after only three weeks of instruction in the use of French arms at Givry-en-Argonne, the black soldiers moved up to the frontlines in a region just west of the Argonne Forest near the Aisne river. For nearly a month they defended a 3-mile sector against several German assaults. Although the 369th comprised less than 1 percent of US troops in France, it held 20 percent of the front held by American troops at that time.

After a brief respite in the reserve lines, the 369th was next placed in the path of one of the German spring offensives, at Minacourt. In desperate fighting the Allies finally halted the German onslaughts, and on July 18, 1918, they were ready to launch their massive counterattacks. Thus began the Aisne–Marne offensive, which lasted until August 6. The 369th Infantry helped drive the Germans from their entrenchments at Butte-de-Mesnil, and repulsed a subsequent counterattack. By August 3 the Allies had eliminated the Marne salient and had forced the Germans to retreat behind the Vesle and Aisne rivers.

While leading his platoon in an assault near Sechault on September 29–30, First Lieutenant George S. Robb was severely wounded by machine-gun fire, but rather than go to the rear for treatment he remained with his platoon until ordered to the dressing station by his commanding officer. Returning within 45 minutes, Robb remained on duty throughout the entire night, inspecting his lines and setting up outposts. He was wounded again early the next morning, but once more remained in command of his platoon. Later the same day a bursting shell added two more

France, 1917–18

(1) Private first class, Company C, 367th Infantry, *c.* December 1918. Out of the line following the Armistice, he wears service dress of the 1912-pattern olive-drab wool service coat with five-button front and standing collar with disc-type insignia: "U.S." on the right, and crossed rifles on the left with "367" above and "C" below. The "Buffalo" patch of the 92nd Division is sewn on his left shoulder. A brass National Guard "expert rifleman" badge is pinned on his left breast. His olive-drab 1918-pattern overseas cap has a blackened bronze branch-of-service disc at left front. He is armed with the M1903 .30-06 rifle, and has a 1910-pattern dismounted "rifle belt." This held 100 rounds: two 5-round stripper clips in each of ten pockets. His trousers are 1912-pattern olive-drab wool, his footwear 1917-pattern russet-brown "Pershing" trench boots. (2) Corporal, Company B, 369th Infantry, 1918. For combat service in the trenches, he wears a 1917-pattern khaki coat fastened with five subdued "national seal" or "eagle" buttons; the bronze collar discs are blackened. His helmet is the M1915 French "Adrian," painted horizon-blue but lacking any frontal crest. He is armed with the 8mm Berthier M1907/15 rifle, and he has been issued 1914-pattern French brown leather equipment, a 4-pint canteen with horizon-blue cover, the M1917 ARS gas respirator, and a cotton musette bag. (3) Captain, 370th Infantry, 1918. His officer's service dress consists of the 1912-pattern winter cap; 1911-pattern five-button olive-drab service coat with paler cuff braid, and four patch pockets; olive-drab breeches, russet leather leggings with adjustable top strap, and russet campaign shoes. He has service chevrons on his left forearm, and wears the pattern-1906 russet leather officer's belt and shoulder strap.

(Richard Hook © Osprey Publishing)

wounds, the same shell killing his company commander and other officers. He then assumed command of the company until relieved shortly thereafter. Lieutenant Robb was subsequently awarded the Medal of Honor.

From September 26 to October 5, the 369th – now transferred to the French 161st Division – participated in the Meuse–Argonne offensive. Prompted by the successful reduction of the Marne salient, the Allies next hoped to sever the main German line of supply to the Western Front, destroying vital railroads and junctions, particularly at Aulnoye and Mezieres. After suffering more than six hours of shelling with heavy artillery and poison gas on September 26, the 369th went over the top "shouting like maniacs and pouring over the embankments through the few remaining strands of barbed wire." Flanked by native French on the right and Moroccans on the left, the 369th was met by heavy machine-gun fire and grenades. The African American troops suffered horribly, but the survivors continued to push the Germans back 4 miles, until they evacuated the town of Ripont. Finally, the 369th Infantry was the first Allied unit to set foot on German soil after the Armistice, reaching Blodelsheim on the Rhine on November 18. Their tenacity and fearlessness in battle on September 26 earned this regiment the nickname "Harlem Hell Fighters." France awarded the entire unit a collective Croix de Guerre with silver star. Additionally, 171 members received individual awards for exceptional gallantry in action.

370TH INFANTRY: "BLACK DEVILS"

Distinguished for being the only combat regiment to have all-black officers, the 370th Infantry, originally commanded by Colonel Franklin A. Denison and nicknamed by the French the "Diables Noirs," did not see action until July 1918, as part of the French 36th Division on the Meuse–Argonne front, where they manned the St Mihiel sector. On July 16, Lieutenant Harvey Taylor received six wounds during a raid, earning the Croix de Guerre. During September four detached companies of the 370th served with the French 232nd and 325th Infantry of the 59th Division, taking part in the capture of the Mont des Singes or "Monkey Mountain." During these operations a platoon of Company F, 370th, led by Sergeant Matthew Jenkins, especially distinguished itself by resisting enemy attacks for 36 hours while blocked in a fortified tunnel. As a result, Sergeant Jenkins received both the DSC and the Croix de Guerre.

By October the 370th was involved in the main attack on the Hindenburg Line. On October 4 a reconnaissance was ordered to locate enemy machine-gun nests in the Bois de Mortier. Captain Chester Sanders and 20 volunteers

Under the heading, "Colonel Hayward Praises Negro Troops," this report was published in a Baltimore newspaper in December 1918:

Writing to the governor of New York Col. [William] Hayward commends the bravery of the Fifteenth New York Infantry [369th Infantry] in the fierce fighting which marked the opening of the great offensive in the Argonne–Verdun Sector in the closing days of last September.

Every fiendish device known to the Germans were used against the Negro troops. Gass [sic], shrapnel, high explosives, machine guns and aerial minnies [mortar bombs] were hurled at the Americans. For twelve days and twelve nights the regiment was under constant fire often on scant rations or none, but in the face of it all they pushed ahead nine or ten miles.

We finally on the fourth day gained the height overlooking the marvellous plain and valley and I saw what I am sure has never been given to man to see before. I saw four divisions of our troops attack abreast (twelve regiments). The two artillery forces, ours and Boche, firing from behind, laid down terrible barrages on each other's infantry. It was like a double belt of flame, smoke, tossed up earth, men and debris for four kilmeters [sic] that I could see.

Suffice it to say we got cited, the regiment will receive the Croix de Guerre for its colors and each officer mentioned personally."

– *The Afro-American*, Baltimore, Maryland (December 6, 1918)

crossed the Oise–Aisne Canal and penetrated into the woods about 30 yards east of the Vauxaillon–Bois de Mortier road. Drawing attention from several enemy machine-gun posts, the patrol retired to the French lines under heavy fire and shelling without the loss of a man.

The regiment then took part in the crossing of the Oise–Aisne Canal and River Ailette and the capture of the town of Bois de Mortier. The 370th suffered its greatest loss that month while stationed at Chantrud Farm, near Chambry, when a German shell landed among a large group gathered around a field kitchen, killing 34 and wounding 52 men. The 370th had the honor of fighting in the last battle of the war, capturing a German wagon train half an hour after the Armistice went into effect on November 11.

During their combat service the "Black Devils" suffered 20 percent casualties but lost only one man taken prisoner. Although the 370th was not awarded a collective Croix de Guerre, 71 individuals received the medal and another 21 the DSC.

371ST & 372ND INFANTRY: WITH THE "RED HAND" DIVISION

After brief retraining, both the 371st and 372nd Infantries were assigned to the Verdun sector in early June 1918, to reinforce the much depleted French 157th Division, which used the "blood red hand" on its flags and insignia. The first combat assignment of the 371st was to fill a gap between the French 161st and 2nd Moroccan Divisions. In heavy fighting, often hand-to-hand, it captured 60 prisoners, three field guns, two anti-tank rifles and large quantities of ammunition. Subsequently the regiment forced the Germans from Bussy Farm and assisted in the capture of Ardeuil and Montfauxelle.

On September 28 the 371st Infantry attacked Hill 188 in the Champagne–Marne sector. As Company C led the way across no-man's-land some Germans stopped firing and climbed out of their trenches, holding up their arms as if surrendering; but as the African American troops moved toward them the Germans jumped back under cover and sprayed the advancing black soldiers with machine-gun fire, shooting down well over 50 percent of the company. Corporal Freddie Stowers rallied the survivors and, though mortally wounded, led them on to knock out the machine-gun nest and capture a second trench line, causing heavy enemy casualties. His commanding officer recommended him for a posthumous Medal of Honor, but the nomination was "misplaced." Finally, after two congressmen resurrected the case in 1988, President George Bush awarded the medal posthumously, and it was presented to Corporal Stowers' two surviving sisters in 1991, a full 73 years after his heroic death.

A lieutenant and men of the 369th in a practice trench north of Ste Menehould on May 4, 1918. They wear French helmets and are armed with French weapons. The sergeant (foreground) has a Lebel M1886/93 rifle fitted with the 50mm Vivien-Bessière grenade launcher; he has retained his US pistol belt and clip pouch, and therefore presumably his Colt .45cal semi-automatic pistol on the right hip. The other soldiers are armed with Berthier M1907/15 rifles (the butt of which was too flimsy to take the shock of the VB launcher), and French brown leather equipment. At left background, one soldier mans an M1915 CSRG ("Chauchat") automatic rifle. (NARA)

During the same action, Private Burton Holmes showed extreme bravery for which he was posthumously awarded a DSC. Wounded and with his automatic rifle seized up, he acquired a replacement weapon from company HQ and returned to the firing line, where he engaged the enemy until he was killed. The next day, at Ardeuil, Privates Charlie Butler, Willie Boston, Bruce Stoney, and Tillman Webster crawled 200 yards out into no-man's-land under heavy machine-gun fire to rescue an officer lying seriously wounded in a shell hole; Butler and Boston received the DSC and Croix de Guerre with bronze star, and Stoney and Webster were awarded the DSC.

Of the fighting in the Champagne–Marne sector during the same period, Private Frank Washington, Company B, 371st, recalled:

I went over the top in the fighting on September 29 and 30. We advanced after the usual barrage had been laid down for us. We went up to the Germans,

Maison-en-Champagne, September 1918

The 369th Infantry advance toward Maison-en-Champagne on September 26, 1918, an action that brought many of the 171 individual awards of the Legion of Honor and Croix de Guerre earned by the unit. The infantry squads making a rush toward a German machine-gun position wear French helmets, 1917-pattern khaki coats with blackened bronze collar discs, and matching trousers with drab canvas leggings; the sergeant (center) has acquired a British sleeveless brown leather jerkin for additional warmth. He is armed with an M1903 .30-06 rifle, and has US web equipment; the other men carry Berthier M1907/15 rifles, plus French brown leather equipment and 4-pint canteens. They all carry British "small box" respirators in canvas bags.

(Richard Hook © Osprey Publishing)

and my platoon found itself under the fire of three machine guns. One of these guns was in front and running like a millrace. The other two kept a-piling into us from the flanks, and the losses were mounting. We got the front one. Its crew surrendered and we stopped. The other guns kept right on going, but we got them, too.

Ravaged by a 45 percent casualty rate, the 371st Infantry were much relieved when their combat tour ended and they were sent to a reserve area in the Vosges. One soldier described the regiment's march from the frontlines: "A dirty, tired, haggard, nerve-shattered bunch of men we were, but as we moved to the rear and the din of battle grew fainter we breathed easier and knew that for the time being at least, we were safe from the death that had stared us in the face for days. It was a quiet and somber column of men that pulled out of that sector." The 371st remained in the relative quiet of the Vosges until the Armistice. During its participation in the Champagne offensive this regiment captured three German officers, 90 men, and large amounts of weaponry including eight trench mortars, 37 x 77mm guns, 47 machine guns, a munitions depot, and several railroad cars. All this came at a heavy price; the regiment lost four officers and 122 men dead, and another 41 officers and 873 men wounded. For its extraordinary bravery the regiment was awarded the Croix de Guerre with palm (the latter distinction marking a citation in Army orders, as opposed to corps, divisional, or unit orders). Additionally, three officers won the French Légion d'Honneur, 123 men earned individual Croix de Guerre, and 26 won the DSC.

The 372nd Infantry also fought bravely during the American assault in Champagne. Reaching the frontlines on September 28, the regiment helped drive the Germans from Bussy Farm and joined the 369th in their attack at Sechault, where enemy resistance was heaviest. As a result, the 1st and 3rd Battalions incurred such heavy losses that they had to be combined into a single unit. The 372nd next relieved the 371st at Trieres Farm on October 1, and assisted in the capture of Monthois, an important railway center and supply base. Here the regiment again met strong resistance and was often forced to repel the enemy in hand-to-hand fighting. The 372nd was finally relieved by the French on October 7; in less than two weeks' frontline service the unit had suffered nearly 600 casualties, many of whom were shell-shocked rather than physically wounded.

Colonel Quillet of the French 157th Division remarked of the 372nd that the regiment possessed the "finest qualities of bravery and daring which are the virtues of assaulting troops." In General Order No. 234 of October 8, divisional commander General Goybet informed the regiment: "In these nine hard days of battle you have pushed ahead for 8 kilometers, through powerful enemy organizations, captured close to 600 enemy prisoners, taken 15 guns, light and heavy, 20 infantry mortars, close to 150 machine guns and a very important supply of engineer and artillery ammunition, and brought down by rifle fire three aeroplanes." The 372nd Infantry was awarded a unit Croix de Guerre with palm; in addition, 43 officers, 14 NCOs and 116 privates received either the Croix de Guerre or the DSC.

92ND DIVISION: "THE BUFFALOES"

On August 12, after completing brief training, the 92nd Division, aka the "Buffalo Division," moved to the St Die sector near the Rhine, southeast of Metz, where they joined the French 37th Division. Two weeks later the 92nd Division engaged the enemy for the first time when it assaulted and captured German positions. On August 30 the Germans counterattacked near the town of Frapelle, and elements of "The Buffaloes" beat them back. The following day the division repeated their success at Ormont, despite being bombarded with more than 12,000 shells in a two-hour period.

On September 20, the division was ordered to the Argonne Forest, northwest of Clermont, where they took part in the Meuse–Argonne offensive. Due to lack of sufficient training and equipment, and unfamiliarity with the terrain, elements of the 368th Infantry failed to maintain contact with the US 77th Division on their flank, and the attack stalled. During an assault on Binarsville the next day these same troops failed to press forward and withdrew in confusion. The poor performance of the 368th in September 1918 led to an unfair and completely unjustified campaign to

A soldier of the 3rd Battalion, 366th Infantry, nicknamed "Big Nims," holds a British 1916-pattern "small box respirator" during a gas alert exercise at Ainvelle in the Vosges region. The British gasmask was more practical for African Americans than some earlier French types which required wearing nose clips. (NARA)

Aboard the transport
Stockholm on their return
to the United States in
January 1919, each of
these soldiers
of the 369th wears the
overseas cap, has a
Croix de Guerre pinned
to his chest, and sports
two overseas service
chevrons on his left
forearm. (NARA)

discredit and dishonor the contribution that all African American soldiers made to victory in World War I. Thirty black officers were relieved from duty and five were court-martialed; of the latter, four received death sentences, while a fifth was given a life sentence. All five were eventually freed.

Meanwhile, the soldiers of the Buffalo Division continued to prove themselves in battle during the closing days of the war. For example, during the Allied attack on Pagny, a stronghold of the German line opposite Metz, on November 10, two battalions of the white 56th Infantry became hopelessly entangled in the enemy's barbed wire and were being slaughtered by German machine guns. Advancing on their right, the 1st Battalion, 367th Infantry, under Colonel James A. Moss (the bicycle enthusiast of the old 25th Infantry) was ordered to give covering fire while the remains of the 56th Infantry withdrew. In true "buffalo soldier" tradition, two black machine-gun companies quickly laid down a covering fire that silenced the German batteries, and the 56th retired leaving a third of their men dead or wounded. The 367th held the position until relieved by reinforcements, following which they continued their advance toward Pagny. The whole white battalion would have been destroyed but for the timely intervention of the black machine-gunners; for this action the 1st Battalion, 367th Infantry, was awarded a collective Croix de Guerre.

UNIFORMS & EQUIPMENT

By the early 1890s, the US Army was still wearing the 1882-pattern uniform with various modifications. For campaign purposes, this consisted of the dark-blue, five-button blouse or "sack coat," dark-blue 1883-pattern wool flannel overshirt, sky-blue kersey trousers prescribed in 1884, and chasseur-pattern 1889 forage cap. In 1895, headgear was replaced by a distinctive round-topped forage cap with sloping visor. Also worn was the 1899-pattern drab or black service (campaign) hat, and the lace-up brown canvas leggings introduced in 1890. The 1880-pattern cork "Summer Helmet" covered with white wool cloth was issued in hot weather. The buffalo soldiers involved in the Spanish-American War in 1898 wore combinations of this clothing. Indeed, a correspondent of the *Army & Navy Journal* visiting an encampment at Lakeland, Florida, during June 1898 reported that "The troops are still sweltering in their heavy blue cloth uniforms, but it is allowable to leave off the blouse."

Canvas fatigue clothing was made available on a large scale at the beginning of the 1898 conflict, and supplemented the blue woolen clothing until khaki cotton drill could be supplied in sufficient quality and quantity. Originally adopted in 1884, the fatigues consisted of a five-button "sack coat" and trousers of 6oz cotton duck dyed brown. A British correspondent of the *Hong Kong Telegraph*, reporting from the Philippines in August of that year, described this uniform as "a coarse brown canvas, beside which our Indian campaigning dress khaki is as silk beside floor matting. The color is darker than khaki, and I think better for invisibility; but the material is altogether too much like coal sacks."

Although the khaki drill service uniform adopted by the US Army in 1898 was originally intended for officers only, it was quickly issued to enlisted men as well. Made of a lightweight yellow-brown cotton drill, the five-button blouse had flapped breast and hip pockets, and pointed cuffs. Waist belts made of the same fabric, secured by buttons at the front and supported by loops at the back, were also a distinctive feature on many of these garments. General Order No.51 of May 23, 1898, stipulated that the collar and shoulder strap of the blouse for both officers and men were to be faced with the branch of service color. Hence, uniforms issued to the two black cavalry regiments were faced yellow, while those worn by the infantry were faced light blue. A photograph of a black trooper wearing a khaki cotton drill uniform indicates that the buffalo soldiers also had unofficial facing color on pocket flaps. This uniform, later minus facing color except for shoulder straps, and combined with the dark-blue overshirt, was worn throughout the Spanish–American War and the Philippines Insurrection.

An olive-drab service uniform was introduced to the US Army via General Order No.130 of December 30, 1902, but issue of some old uniform items continued until at least 1904, via General Order No.122 dated July 13 of that year. Worn by the black units serving on Samar and Mindanao islands

Flags, Insignia, and Equipment

(1) Blue silk regimental flag of the 369th Infantry

(2) Field flag of the French 157th Division, with small silk US national flag attached

(3) Blackened bronze collar disc insignia, 1907-pattern, for Company H, 370th Infantry

Late 1918 & 1919 shoulder patches:

(4) 370th Infantry, "Black Devils"

(5) French 157th Division, as worn by 371st & 372nd Infantry

(6) AEF 92nd Division

(7) AEF 93rd Division

(8) 1902-pattern full dress cap, Troop F, 10th Cavalry

(9) 1905-pattern band musician cap insignia, 9th Cavalry

(10) 1915 Croix de Guerre, with silver star for citation in divisional orders

(11a & b) 1896-pattern blue woven Mills cartridge belt worn at San Juan Heights, 1898, by trooper 62 of Troop D, 9th Cavalry

(Richard Hook © Osprey Publishing)

in the Philippines from about 1904, the new uniform consisted of a blouse with falling collar and four "choked-bellows" pockets, and breeches that fitted closely below the knee and were fastened with tapes or laces. Headgear consisted of the 1902-pattern service (campaign) hat, with cord in branch of service color – yellow for cavalry and white for infantry.

In line with US Army regulations, black enlisted men began wearing bronze collar disc insignia in 1907 to replace the crossed rifles and sabers insignia they had worn on the collar since 1901. The 1907 pattern called for the letters "U.S." on the right collar disc and branch insignia on the left, with the regimental number above and the company letter below. This style would last until 1917, when the regimental number was taken off the left disc and placed below the "U.S." on the right disc.

Items of a new service uniform, consisting of olive-drab breeches, overshirt, and service coat with four patch pockets and stand-up collar, were issued to the black regiments serving both in the Philippines and on the Mexican Border from about 1912 onwards. Made at first of blanket wool, the 1912-pattern uniforms were worn without the coat in the summer months, until a uniform of cotton material was prescribed. Headgear began to change to the 1911-pattern campaign hat with "Montana" peak.

Due to difficulty in supplying troops operating deep in Mexican territory during the Punitive Expedition, much of the clothing worn by the 10th Cavalry was in tatters by April 1916. Regimental veterinarian Dr Charles D.

Two of these black lieutenants aboard the transport *Ulna* wear a version of the British-style olive-drab overcoat approved for US officers in June 1907. (Center) Lieutenant H. A. Rogers has had his coat altered to fasten on the left; he wears a 1912-pattern pistol belt, with 1910-pattern first aid packet pouch. Both he and Lieutenant William Andrews (left) display overseas service chevrons stitched over the "chicken guts" on their left forearms; Lieutenant Andrews also has a wound chevron on his right sleeve. (Right) Medical Officer Lieutenant J. N. Rucker wears, over his 1904-pattern russet leather waist belt, a 1917-pattern MO's web belt with one large and one small pocket on each side. The large pocket contained a pad of diagnosis forms and a small field surgery kit, the smaller a syringe plus six ampules of morphine. (NARA)

Published in *Harper's Weekly* in August 1898, this photo shows men of either the 9th or 10th Cavalry as they looked during the Spanish-American War. (Right) The dark-blue five-button blouse, sky-blue kersey trousers, and drab campaign hat. (Left) The khaki drill service uniform with yellow facing color, including – unofficially – on the pocket flaps. (Center) A waterproof coat of the type issued to enlisted men. (Anne S. K. Brown Military Collection, Brown University Library)

Captain O. C. Troxel describes the clothing worn by the Second Squadron and Machine Gun Troop, 10th Cavalry, during the Punitive Expedition in Mexico during 1916:

As to clothing: Each man started with the authorized allowance in his pack. Unfortunately the men had gotten so used to going out for border duty and wearing their oldest clothes that many did the same thing this time. This made conditions worse than they should have been. Hoods of stirrups were used to tack on as half soles of shoes, when tacks were available. Breeches were patched so long as patches would hold together, the men gambling to see whose shelter half [tent] was to be cut up for the purpose. Occasionally the quartermaster bought and issued civilian clothing of all descriptions, and for hats the men took the lining of the saddle bags, in the cases where hats were lost or completely torn up. I got my patches from the lining of my overcoat.

– "The Tenth Cavalry in Mexico," *US Cavalry Journal* (October 1917)

McMurdo graphically described the situation in a wire sent to Fort Huachuca: "Send me a pair of trousers. Am getting sunburned." As a result of the shortage, the regiment purchased civilian trousers from local merchants in Parral.

Goggles were worn by many American troops during the Punitive Expedition to protect against sand storms and glare in the Chihuahua desert.

The woolen version of the 1912-pattern uniform was worn by the African Americans in the AEF in France during World War I. This was supplemented by the 1916-pattern shirt, 1917-pattern wool breeches, and 1918-pattern service shoes. The African American enlisted infantry replaced their canvas gaiters with olive-drab wool puttees, while the many new black officers wore leather leggings. Headgear consisted of the 1911-pattern "Montana" peak campaign hat. An olive-drab wool "overseas" cap began to replace this in France in 1917, and was mainly worn in the rear areas; a branch-of-service collar disc was worn on the left side. Two slightly different styles of this cap were in use. The British version was folded in the center and issued unstitched, but the wearer could have the two ridges sewn together to produce a neater appearance. Another version with taller peaks at front and back was based on the French *bonnet de police* fatigue cap. African American troops in France were also sometimes issued either the British Mk I or US M1917A1 steel helmet painted a drab color. These were later embellished with painted versions of divisional patches. Most African American units assigned to French Army formations were issued the French M1915 "Casque Adrian" helmet painted horizon-blue.

ARMS

By the outbreak of the Spanish-American War, the single-shot, black powder, breech-loading .45cal Springfield carbine and rifle carried by the black regulars during the Indian Wars had been replaced with .30cal Krag-Jörgensen carbines and rifles using smokeless powder. This weapon was also issued to the volunteer regiments in the Philippines by 1901. The bolt-action .30–03 1903 Springfield rifle, with five-round charger and rod bayonet, began to replace the Krag in 1904; a barrel length of 24in permitted this rifle to be standard issue to both cavalry and infantry. However, its issue was suspended due to dissatisfaction with its sliding rod bayonet. After further trials, a knife bayonet replaced this, and a new sharp-pointed "spitzer" bullet, with superior ballistic performance, replaced the round-nose .03–03 cartridge. By the end of 1906 both the 24th and 25th Infantry had received this improved M1906 .30–06 with knife bayonet. The 10th Cavalry received their Springfields in March 1907 before leaving for duty in the Philippines. The African American combat troops attached to the French Army in 1918 were armed primarily with the 8mm M1907/15 Berthier rifle.

As to hand guns, the M1911 Colt .45cal semi-automatic pistol supplanted the .38in revolver after the latter showed itself incapable of stopping a charging Moro warrior in the Philippines. As a stop-gap, .45cal single-action Colts of Indian Wars vintage were taken out of storage and shipped across the Pacific.

Cavalry trooper wearing the full dress introduced in 1902. His six-button coat is piped yellow on collar, shoulder straps and cuffs. His "bell-crown" cap has a detachable band trimmed with two stripes of yellow facing material, while yellow worsted cords and tassels adorn his chest. His sword belt, fastened by an 1872-pattern plate, supports the M1872 Light Cavalry saber. (Herb Peck Jr Collection)

First Lieutenant Benjamin O. Davis Sr, Troop F, 10th Cavalry, wearing the 1912-pattern full dress uniform; note the crossed sabers with regimental number on his forearm below the rank knot. This officer became the first African American general in the US Regular Army when he was promoted brigadier-general (temporary) on October 25, 1940. (USAMHI)

The 9th and 10th Cavalry were still armed with the US M1872 Light Cavalry saber in 1892, and mainly carried this weapon until it was replaced by the 1906 pattern. The 9th were issued some of the short-lived 1905 experimental sabers for trial in 1906/7. The further development of the latter weapon led to the introduction of the M1913 cavalry trooper's sword, also known as the "Patton" sword after its designer George S. Patton (who saw active service as an aide to Brigadier-General Pershing in Mexico). The "Patton" sword was intended to be used as a thrusting weapon rather than a slashing saber; carried in a webbed khaki scabbard, it was attached to the cavalryman's saddle rather than his belt.

As they were required to serve dismounted due to the lack of space for horses in the transports, the enlisted men of the 9th and 10th Cavalry did not take their sabers to Cuba in 1898. Still officially required to take their swords into the field in 1916, the black cavalry, like their white comrades, found them to be useless encumbrances in the type of warfare waged against Pancho Villa during the Punitive Expedition, and sent their weapons back to base. The *Army & Navy Journal* reported that a truck train arrived at Columbus, New Mexico, on April 11 carrying "a load of sabers."

The machine gun was incorporated into the US Army in 1906, a platoon-size unit being organized in various cavalry and infantry regiments. Established at Fort Robinson, Nebraska, in July 1906, the MG Platoon of the 10th Cavalry, commanded by First Lieutenant A. E. Phillips, developed the technique of direct overhead and indirect machine-gun fire used extensively during World War I. During the Punitive Expedition, the 10th Cavalry's MG Troop was armed with the over-complicated gas-operated M1909 Benet-Mercié machine rifle, chambered for the .30–06 cartridge. During World War I, black machine-gun units used a variety of weapons, including the French Hotchkiss M1914 and the US M1915 version of the British Vickers. Light machine guns (automatic rifles) were the French M1915 CSRG ("Chauchat"), and to a lesser extent the M1917 Lewis.

ACCOUTREMENTS

During the 1890s, the buffalo soldiers wore woven looped cartridge belts of Mills manufacture, secured by H-shaped "US" plates; these were gradually replaced with those introduced *c.*1894 with a wire C-fastener. During the first decade of the 20th century, the looped belts began to be replaced with the web infantry and cavalry versions of the 1903-pattern cartridge belt, featuring pockets to accommodate the five-round clips required for the M1903–06 rifles. This was later supplemented and replaced by the 1910-pattern dismounted woven cartridge or "rifle" belt. Black troops assigned to the French Army were issued 1914-pattern French brown leather equipment.

Two unidentified African American soldiers of the AEF. The infantryman at right has either a British Mk I or a US M1917A1 helmet. The man at left, possibly of the 371st Infantry, wears a French "Adrian" helmet; his respirator is the French M1917 ARS. (Larry Strayer Collection)

THE INTER-WAR YEARS

With the exception of the four black Regular Army units, all African American troops were deactivated or returned to their National Guard status with little or no American recognition for their efforts upon return from Europe at the end of the Great War in 1918. Retained in the United States throughout the world conflict, the 24th Infantry became involved in what was to be the last Mexican border skirmish of any consequence, when it rushed to El Paso and briefly crossed into Mexico for 24 hours to disperse bandits in June 1919. Stationed at Camp Furlong, near Columbus, New Mexico, this regiment was drastically reorganized in 1921–22, as a result of the Army Reorganization Act of 1920. In 1921 its 3rd Battalion, which had been relegated to duty at various isolated posts in the aftermath of the Houston race riot of 1917, was disbanded as the result of general Army budget cuts. In 1922, all but its Headquarters Company, Service Company, and Company D were transferred to the 25th Infantry, the Provisional Battalion of which was also based at Camp Furlong. What remained of the 24th was moved to the Infantry School at Fort Benning, Georgia, to serve as School Troops. Segregated from the rest of the post, they were classified as riflemen and machine gunners, but mainly performed duties involving manual labor. In 1927, the 1st and 2nd Battalions, 24th Infantry, were brought up to strength less their machine-gun companies. From October 1, 1933 to October 16, 1939, the regiment was assigned to the 7th Infantry Brigade, 4th Division, while remaining at Fort Benning. In March 1940, it was returned to full strength with the reactivation of the 3rd Battalion. After the United States declared war on Japan and Germany on December 8 and 11, 1941, the 24th began intensive training in preparation for overseas deployment.

Based at Camp Stephen D. Little near Nogales, Arizona, from 1918 through 1923, the 25th Infantry also underwent various reorganizations, and was transferred to Fort Huachuca, already garrisoned by the 10th Cavalry, in September of the latter year. The entire 25th Infantry formed the regular "cadre" of the reactivated all-black 93rd Infantry Division at Fort Huachuca in 1942 for service in World War II.

The 9th Cavalry finally returned from the Philippines in 1922 and was stationed at Fort Riley, Kansas. On March 1, 1933, this regiment was assigned to the 3rd Cavalry Division, and helped police and patrol the Mexican border until October 1940, when it was assigned to the 4th Brigade, 2nd Cavalry Division, commanded by Brigadier-General Benjamin O. Davis Sr. Based in Camp Funston at Fort Riley, Kansas, this unit also included the 3rd Cavalry Brigade, composed of the all-white 2nd and 14th Cavalry regiments, and as such was the first integrated division in the US Army. In February 1941, the 4th Cavalry Brigade was training for possible deployment to Europe.

From 1918 through 1931, the 10th Cavalry served along the Arizona–Mexico border, being assigned to the newly activated 1st Cavalry Division in 1921, and transferred to the 2nd Cavalry Division two years later. In 1931, the

Back in New York City in 1919, the 369th Infantry parade, "present arms" and sing the National Anthem as they return their colors to the Union League Club. (NARA)

regiment was broken up. The Machine Gun Troop was sent to Washington DC to perform escort duty. The 1st Squadron was assigned to the United States Military Academy at West Point, New York, to replace the detachment of the 9th Cavalry that had been there since 1907 teaching the cadets horse riding skills and mounted drill instruction on Cavalry Plain, now known as Buffalo Soldier Field. The 2nd Squadron went to Fort Leavenworth to tend the horses for the equitation class at the Commanding General Staff School and the third squadron was ordered to Fort Riley to perform the same duty at the Cavalry School.

With the activation of US forces during 1941, the 9th and 10th Cavalry were regrouped as the 4th Cavalry Brigade, 2nd Division, and took part in manoeuvres in Arkansas during August of that year. However, with the Japanese attack on Pearl Harbor on December 7, 1941, and the entrance of the United States into World War II, neither regiment was assigned abroad; both were sent southwest to patrol the Texas-Mexico border as part of the Southern Land Frontier Sector, and remained as such until this command was deactivated in 1943.

After the number of African American soldiers had dropped to less than 4,000 by 1939, and in response to growing black demands for a greater representation in the military, the US Army began accepting black volunteers in proportion to their demographic presence, which was 10.6 percent of the

Three men of Troop C, 10th Cavalry, set up a light machine gun for action during Second Army maneuvers in Arkansas during August 1941. (NARA)

On army maneuvers in Louisiana on September 12, 1941, Private Chester Burnett, Troop G, 9th Cavalry, from Aberdine, Mississippi, cleans the hoof of his horse, while Staff Sergeant Columbus Rudisal, of Goffney, South Carolina, looks on. (NARA)

US population. To absorb the larger numbers of African Americans being admitted, the Army formed several new all-black units, primarily in the service and technical forces. Organized in 1939, the 47th and 48th Quartermaster Regiments were followed in 1940 by the 1st Chemical Decontamination Company and the 41st General Service Engineer Regiment, as well as a number of artillery, coastal artillery, and transportation units. The first black armor unit was established as the 78th Tank Battalion at Fort Knox, Tennessee, on January 13, 1941, but was redesignated as the 758th Tank Battalion on May 8 of that year, and not activated until June 1, 1941, "with negro enlisted personnel." On February 10, 1941, the 366th Infantry Regiment was reactivated at Fort Devens, Massachusetts, and became the first all-black Regular Army unit officered by African Americans only.

PART III

AFRICAN AMERICAN TROOPS IN WORLD WAR II

INTRODUCTION	158
US ARMY	160
US NAVY	195
US MARINE CORPS	206
OTHER MARITIME SERVICES	213

OPPOSITE
Private Lloyd A. Taylor, an Army Air Corps dispatcher at Mitchel Field, New York City, posed with a Chinese-language primer. The caption states that this former medical student at Temple University studied languages as a hobby, and had already mastered Latin, Greek, Spanish, French, German, and Japanese. Although an extreme case, Taylor's current employment is a stark reminder of the potential wasted by the Army's racial prejudices in the 1940s. (NARA)

INTRODUCTION

During World War II, hundreds of thousands of African Americans served in segregated units in the US military. The racial policies of the armed forces in the 1940s relegated most of them to tasks that were often both more physically demanding and more demeaning than those assigned to European Americans. Although each branch of the military had different policies regarding the admittance and employment of African Americans, the end of World War II found black Americans serving in every branch and in every theater of the war.

While the majority of the approximately half-million African Americans who served overseas during World War II were draftees, overall they demonstrated the same enthusiasm (or lack thereof) for military service as their white counterparts. For many African Americans their service in World War II was filled with irony: they were being asked to fight fascism and racism abroad, while they themselves endured racism at home. While the purpose of the two ugly signs was very different, it remains true that the world's justified outrage at the painting of the word *Jude* on German Jewish storefronts in the 1930s did not carry over to the use of the word "Colored" on public amenities in the American South.

As we have seen, the Selective Service Act of 1940 allowed for the induction of a number of African Americans equal to their percentage of the national population, which translated into 10.6 percent. However, since the majority of African Americans were generally ranked in the lowest two intelligence classes, the military resisted inducting that predetermined percentage. The Army argued that if 10.6 percent of all draftees were African American, it would have to organize ten of its combat divisions completely with African Americans. The question of what to do with "excess" African Americans was a perpetual problem for the US military during the war.

While President Franklin D. Roosevelt favored desegregation of the military, he was prevented from acting upon his wish because the Democratic Party, his political power base, was considered a Southern party. If all of the Southern legislators withdrew their support from President Roosevelt he would find it impossible to pass any legislation. Instead, on June 25, 1941, Roosevelt signed Executive Order 8802, which prevented discrimination on the basis of race, creed, color, or national origin by any corporation possessing a defense contract with the US government. Despite protests from business owners and labor unions, too much money was at stake for them to risk the government's wrath by non-compliance; for their part, the Southern legislators were generally unaffected by Executive Order 8802, because so little industry was located in their region.

Members of a ground crew of the 332nd Fighter Group in Italy fit a drop tank to the wing of a P-51D Mustang. Left to right: Tech Sergeant Charles K. Haynes, Staff Sergeant James A. Sheppard, and Master Sergeant Frank Bradley. The fighter group used auxiliary fuel tanks for long-distance flights while escorting bombers over German territory. (NARA)

US ARMY

The majority of the US military's segregated units were found in the US Army, and African Americans were represented in every one of the Army's combat, support, and service arms, including the Army Air Corps (later, Air Force). Despite their unequal treatment, it was in the Army that black Americans found opportunities for leadership unparalleled in the rest of American society at that time. Many African Americans reached senior leadership positions, and one officer reached the rank of brigadier-general. This achievement was all the more striking in that the pre-war US Army had fewer than 5,000 African Americans in just four regiments (24th and 25th Infantry and 9th and 10th Cavalry).

The most senior African American in the US Army at the outbreak of World War II was Benjamin O. Davis Sr. Born in 1880, Davis began his military career as a second lieutenant in the Separate Battalion (Colored), District of Columbia National Guard, in April 1898. Only two months later, he was offered the position of first lieutenant in the 8th USVI. After serving with the 8th Volunteers until March 1899, Davis enlisted in the ranks of the 9th Cavalry Regiment, and was promoted to corporal while serving as a clerk. He then passed a competitive examination for a Regular Army commission, and was sworn in as a second lieutenant in May 1901.

Over the next 40 years, Davis rose to the rank of colonel, and rotated between duties as the Professor of Military Science and Tactics at Wilberforce University in Ohio and the Tuskegee Institute in Alabama; tours as the US military attaché in Monrovia, Liberia; and relatively brief periods of command with the 369th Infantry Regiment, New York National Guard, and the 372nd Infantry Regiment, Ohio National Guard. Since the Army was determined to prevent Benjamin Davis from commanding white officers, his skills were underutilized, and he seldom served in positions that befitted his rank and

September 1941: African American Army Air Corps cadets report in to Captain Benjamin O. Davis Jr, the commandant of cadets at Tuskegee Field, Alabama. Davis was only the fourth African American to graduate from the US Military Academy at West Point, New York, and was the first black American to be rated as a pilot in the Air Corps. (NARA)

experience. During World War I, for instance, he was sent to the Philippines, where he served as the black 9th Cavalry Regiment's supply officer. On this blighted career path, Davis was following in the weary footsteps – from West Point, via the 9th Cavalry to Wilberforce, the Philippines, and Liberia – of Colonel Charles D. Young (1865–1922), the third black American to graduate from West Point, with the class of 1889.

Finally, in January 1941, Davis became the first African American general officer in American history, when he was promoted to brigadier-general and ordered to Fort Riley, Kansas, to take command of the 4th Cavalry Brigade in the 2nd Cavalry Division. After serving for a total of 42 years and reaching mandatory retirement age, Davis was surprised to be called back to active duty, to serve as an advisor on "negro problems" in the US Army's Office of the Inspector General. He retired on July 14, 1948, after 50 years of active duty. Despite his achievements, Davis's career clearly demonstrated many of the worst consequences of racial prejudice in the US Army. African Americans were welcome – provided that they remembered their pre-ordained place in the power structure. The spectacle of an African American in officer's uniform violated all of the preconceived notions of those days regarding intelligence and leadership abilities, qualities of which white Americans were raised to believe they had a monopoly.

US ARMY AIR CORPS/FORCE

The African Americans who served in the Army Air Force have probably received more attention than any other black American servicemen in World War II. The "Tuskegee Airmen" were seen as the most important "experiment" involving African Americans during the war, because these pilots were commissioned officers. While the Army had much experience with black enlisted men, there were very few African American officers (only five achieved officer rank in the Regular Army between 1865 and 1939), and many senior Army officers did not believe that African Americans had the necessary intellectual and leadership capabilities to serve in commissioned rank. The success of the "Tuskegee Airmen" was a major blow to these racist assumptions.

The first African American officer to be accepted for pilot training was Benjamin O. Davis Jr. The future general's son was also the first African American admitted to the US Military Academy at West Point during the 20th century. Entering West Point in 1932, Davis endured four years of "silencing," during which no other cadet spoke to him unless required to do so in the classroom or on duty (an ordeal which Charles Young had also suffered half a century before). In 1936, Davis graduated near the top of a class that included the future general officers William P. Yarborough, Creighton W. Abrams Jr, and William C. Westmoreland.

Davis had requested duty with the Air Corps, but he was informed that, since there were no "colored" units in that Corps, and the Army did not anticipate creating any, there was no need for a "colored" pilot. Instead, Davis was commissioned in the infantry and assigned to the 24th Infantry Regiment at Fort Benning, Georgia. After a year with the 24th Infantry and another year as a student at the Infantry School, he became the Professor of Military Science and Tactics at the Tuskegee Institute. Reflecting on his father's army career, Davis accepted this assignment with a sense of doom,

After long missions over enemy territory fighters often returned to base with only a few minutes' worth of gas left in their tanks; the officers' club of the 332nd Fighter Group was named "The Three Minute Egg Club" in honor of those pilots who got back just in time. Shown here are (left to right): First Lieutenants Clarence A. Dart and Wilson D. Eagelson, and Second Lieutenant William N. Olsbrook. Dart's service cap is a fine example of the "50-mission crush" beloved of AAF pilots. (NARA)

believing that he could also look forward only to years rotating between Wilberforce University and Tuskegee. Thankfully, after being promoted to general rank, Benjamin O. Davis Sr requested his son be assigned as an aide, and the younger officer moved to Fort Riley, Kansas.

After only a few months at Fort Riley, Davis found out that the Army was reversing its policy on African Americans in the Air Corps. Davis was among the first class of 13 black aviation cadets at the Tuskegee Army Air Field. After completing flight training, he was quickly promoted to lieutenant-colonel and made the commander of the newly formed 99th Pursuit Squadron – the first African American unit in the Air Corps.

All members of the black Air Corps units organized during World War II had to overcome racial prejudice on several levels. Initially, there were no African American instructors available for flight or other training, and white instructors generally tended to demand higher standards of black students

US Army Air Force

(1) Lieutenant-Colonel Benjamin O. Davis Jr, 99th Fighter Squadron; Sicily, August 1943. He wears the AN-H-15 summer flying helmet with goggles and oxygen mask/radio microphone, and the A4 summer flight suit under his leather A2 jacket and B3 lifejacket. (2) Captain, 477th Bombardment Group (Medium); United States, 1944. The heavier flight uniform worn for longer bomber missions in a roomier cockpit consists of the sheepskin B3 jacket and A3 trousers, and A6A boots. (3) Technical sergeant. This ground crew NCO wears the ubiquitous one-piece herringbone twill (HBT) fatigue coverall, worn throughout the Army for dirty jobs around mechanical equipment, with his rank insignia inked on the sleeve; his headgear is the baseball-style B1 summer mechanic's cap.

(Raffaele Ruggeri © Osprey Publishing)

October 1944: Lieutenant Andrew D. Marshall, a Mustang pilot in the 332nd Fighter Group with the Fifteenth Air Force, was shot down by flak during a strafing mission over Greece. Greek partisans hid him from the Germans until the British III Corps invaded Greece a few days later. (NARA)

than they did from other Americans. An example of this attitude is the fact that only five of the first 13 African American aviation cadets completed the program, which was a significantly higher failure rate than encountered among white cadets. Even after an African American training cadre had been established, black aviation cadets had to endure segregated facilities that were certainly "separate" but far from "equal." The officers' club at the Tuskegee Army Air Field refused to admit African Americans, but there was no corresponding African American officers' club. Following the creation of the Army Air Forces (AAF) in July 1941, all Army aviation-related issues came under the direction of General Henry H. "Hap" Arnold. Like the rest of the AAF, Arnold considered African American pilots to be an "experiment," and felt no need to deviate from established US Army rules regarding their segregation and treatment.

Even before the 99th Pursuit Squadron (later renamed the 99th Fighter Squadron) completed its training and left for combat duty in the Mediterranean, the 332nd Fighter Group – which ultimately included the 99th, 100th, 301st, and 302nd Fighter Squadrons – was organized to accommodate the further training of African American aviation cadets. Unfortunately, the influx of officers, cadets, and enlisted men caused Tuskegee Field to become hopelessly overcrowded, a situation that was only slightly eased by the departure overseas of the 99th. The attitude of the surrounding white community did nothing to help the situation at the airfield. The "Jim Crow" system that reigned throughout the South in those days was very much alive in Tuskegee; this caused great resentment among the African American officers, many of whom were from the North and had never before experienced such overt racism.

Another problem that contributed to the cramped facilities at Tuskegee was an excess of non-flying personnel. Early in 1942, since the nation was now at war, the Air Corps stopped discharging individuals who had flunked out of flying school; instead, these men were retained at Tuskegee, despite having no suitable employment. Unlike failed white officer candidates, who were reassigned to other aviation programs, there was no other place for African Americans. By September 1943, the majority of the 286 failed officer candidates were still at Tuskegee, and suffering from very low morale. By the end of that October, Tuskegee reported an excess of 90 officers, most of whom were second lieutenants. By then, an average of seven African American officer candidate school graduates were arriving each month for non-flying assignments at Tuskegee.

Into combat

Though the 99th Fighter Squadron entered combat in the Mediterranean theater in June 1943 as part of the 33rd Fighter Group, its missions tended to center on strafing and dive-bombing, since there were still serious doubts within the AAF hierarchy about the abilities of its pilots. Despite being assigned these support missions rather than those that entailed a high risk of aerial combat, the 99th still had to put up with criticism for a lack of aggressiveness, insufficient air discipline, and not operating as a team. In September 1943, Lieutenant-Colonel Davis was recalled from Sicily to assume command of the 332nd Fighter Group. At the same time he had to defend the 99th against the allegations that had been lodged by its superiors in the 33rd Fighter Group, who recommended that the squadron be relegated exclusively to coastal patrol duties.

This recommendation went up the chain of command and was endorsed by Lieutenant-General Carl Spaatz, the commander of Allied Air Forces under General Dwight D. Eisenhower, and by General Arnold, the commander of the US Army Air Forces. However, before General George C. Marshall, Chief-of-Staff of the US Army, made a decision regarding the future of the 99th Fighter Squadron, he ordered the Army's G-3 (Operations) to carry out a study of the squadron's performance. Lieutenant-Colonel Davis defended his unit by pointing out that, because of segregation, the African Americans could not profit from the experience of white pilots. The men of the 99th were well trained and qualified, and could have become members of any squadron and functioned well in combat; however, segregation meant

Commanding the 332nd Fighter Group, Colonel Benjamin O. Davis [Jr] explains to a reporter how his black pilots enjoyed fighting the Luftwaffe:

The willingness of his fliers to mix with the enemy was revealed here last week… Col. Davis told how his pilots shot down nine enemy planes, destroyed eighteen on the ground and strafed oil barges, trains and destroyed or damaged a fleet of trucks during a single five-hour mission to Budapest last October. He stated that the four squadrons of his unit were on a mission strafing river [and] rail traffic along the Danube when west of the city a pilot spotted a plane and went down to investigate… The colonel, who formerly commanded the 999th Fighter Group [correction: 99th Fighter Squadron], said the pilot shot down the lone plane and called for the rest of his squadron when he saw an airfield below where fliers were practicing landings and take-offs. Before the dog fight was over, it was related, four ME-109s and four Heinkel 11s had been blasted from the air… The colonel said that in less than a year the 332nd has flown more than 100 missions and firmly established itself as a hard-flying, straight-shooting unit.

– *The Afro-American*, Baltimore, Maryland (January 6, 1945)

that they all started at the same level of inexperience. The final report of the G–3 found no qualitative difference between the 99th and white fighter squadrons assigned to the same theater and missions, and this effectively silenced the squadron's critics.

In January 1944, the 332nd Fighter Group as a whole deployed to Italy under the command of the newly promoted Colonel Benjamin O. Davis Jr. In July the 99th Fighter Squadron joined the 332nd, and the group ultimately participated in combat over Italy, Romania, the Balkans, France, and Germany. It compiled an impressive combat record – flying more than 15,000 sorties, destroying more than 400 enemy aircraft, and never losing a bomber to enemy aircraft in more than 200 escort missions. Through their actions in combat these African American pilots earned the respect and acceptance of their white AAF counterparts.

The 477th Bombardment Group (Medium) was the only other African American combat unit in the AAF. Unfortunately, its officers and men never had the chance to prove themselves in combat, due to almost constant racial animosity. The 477th – comprising the 616th through 619th Bombardment Squadrons – began its training at Selfridge Field, Michigan, but racial problems were created by the base commander, who prohibited African

American officers from using the officers' club. The unit was then moved twice, first to Godman Field, Kentucky, and then to Freeman Field, Indiana, in an attempt to isolate them rather than to solve the racial problems. As a result of the AAF's policy of segregation, the 477th was plagued with both manpower surpluses and shortages. Three months after the group's original (and missed) deployment date, the 477th was short 26 pilots, 43 co-pilots, two bombardier-navigators, and no fewer than 288 gunners. As a result, training took 15 months – five times the normal time – and the group was still not prepared for combat.

The racial climate in the group became increasingly volatile as whites tried to enforce segregation, and the result was a series of incidents at the Freeman Field officers' club. A total of 101 African American officers were arrested for attempting to enter the club against the orders of the base commander. The Army Chief of Staff, General Marshall, had to intervene personally, and ordered the release of the African American officers, who received only an administrative reprimand.

After the end of the war in Europe, Colonel Benjamin O. Davis Jr and his African American officers replaced the entire white command structure of the 477th and of Godman Field, where the group had been transferred after the officers' club incident. Some African American officers argued that the segregationists had ultimately won, because the AAF had thus created an all-black base. Nevertheless, African Americans did gain the opportunity to advance in rank and had command opportunities never before envisioned.

On April 25, 1945, the same day that the US First Army met up with the Soviet Red Army at Torgau on the River Elbe, M5A1 Stuart tanks of the 761st Tank Battalion park in the town square of Coburg, Germany; each tank battalion's Company D usually had these light tanks. The statue is of Prince Albert of Saxe-Coburg-Gotha, the consort of Queen Victoria. (NARA)

The 477th Bombardment Group was preparing for combat in the Pacific when the war ended.

ARMORED FORCE & TANK DESTROYERS

While only a few African American tank units were organized, and though the tank destroyers were a short-lived branch of the Army, these units included African American officers, and proved that they could master complex machinery as easily as white Americans. Several tank destroyer units were manned exclusively by African Americans, from the commander down to the lowest private. The success of these units helped to prove that African American officers had leadership potential equal to that of whites.

The 761st Tank Battalion was the first African American armored unit in combat. The battalion landed over Omaha Beach, Normandy, on October 10, 1944; it had six white and 30 African American officers, and 676 black enlisted men. From November 7, when it was committed to combat, the battalion spent 183 days in action; during this time the members of the 761st won 11 Silver Stars and 69 Bronze Stars.

On its first day in combat the lead tank of Company B was set on fire, the tank commander killed and another crewman severely wounded. A corporal from the crew manned a machine gun in the disabled tank, silencing several enemy machine-gun positions and a German antitank team. The tank was hit twice more, but the crew remained with it. By the end of only their second day in combat, the 761st had certainly earned the right to their motto "Come Out Fighting."

During November the 761st Tank Battalion suffered 24 killed in action, 81 wounded in action, 44 non-battle casualties, and 14 tanks lost. Tanks could be recovered and repaired, or replaced, but men were not so easy to come by. During

March 28, 1945: correspondent Ted Stanford of the *Pittsburgh Courier* interviews First Sergeant Morris O. Harris, a tanker of the 784th Tank Battalion. Here Harris is leaning on an M3 halftrack; each tank company had one halftrack in its maintenance section, and others were on the table of equipment of headquarters, recon and mortar platoons. (NARA)

November no replacements arrived, and the battalion ended the month with a shortage of 113 men. On December 4 the first replacements arrived, but these were not trained tankers and had to receive on-the-job training. Though African American soldiers anxious to see combat requested transfers to the 761st, the battalion remained perpetually short of trained personnel. During the Battle of the Bulge, the battalion aided in the breakthrough to the surrounded 101st Airborne Division. By the end of the war in Europe the 761st was in Austria, where it met up with Soviet troops. The battalion remained in Germany until it was inactivated on June 1, 1946.

Not every tank and tank destroyer unit had the same leadership and motivation as the 761st Tank Battalion; one of the worst examples of failure in these respects was the 827th Tank Destroyer Battalion. The 827th arrived in the European theater in November 1944 following a canceled deployment to the Pacific in spring 1944 – canceled because the battalion was deemed insufficiently trained. Just before the 827th departed for Europe the commanding and executive officers were replaced, in the belief that new leadership might improve the unit. All of the senior officers in the battalion shared the opinion that the unit would never perform adequately in combat and should be converted to a non-combat role or inactivated. By the time it was shipped to Europe, the 827th had been on active duty for two years, during which time it had had eight different commanders, had been organized under four different tables of organization and equipment, and had been re-equipped with main weapons four times. This degree of turmoil would have been difficult for any unit, but it was worse for the 827th for other reasons.

June 28, 1944: men of the 333rd Field Artillery Battalion dig in one of their 155mm M1 howitzers soon after arriving in Normandy; each such battalion had three batteries each with four howitzers. This unit was one of ten non-divisional African American field artillery battalions to see combat as corps or army assets. The 155mm howitzer could send a 95lb shell out to a maximum range of 9 miles. (NARA)

Approximately 80 percent of the battalion's enlisted personnel ranked in the two lowest classes of the US Army's standardized intelligence tests. As a result, the battalion had never been able to form a strong cadre of noncoms, and the officers did not fare much better. African American junior officers were expected to motivate their men beyond any reasonable standard; when they "failed," they were removed and replaced with white officers, most of whom were either Southerners or had previously served with African American tank destroyer units that had been inactivated – and who therefore already had a negative attitude toward the future of the unit. Not surprisingly, these new white officers were no more successful in leading and motivating the 827th than their black predecessors. The commander then determined that the enlisted men, rather than the officers, were to blame for the unit's problems. In September 1944, as the unit prepared to move to Europe, preparations were disrupted by two courts-martial, one involving an ax murder. Both cases indeed demonstrated the degree of indiscipline within the unit; neither officers nor NCOs were able to control their men.

After arriving in France, the battalion performed a five-day march in December 1944 over icy roads to join the Seventh Army. So many accidents, breakdowns, cases of speeding and column-breaking, slow starts, and late arrivals occurred that when the battalion arrived many of its vehicles immediately went in for significant repairs. It was an inauspicious beginning, and things would only get worse.

On December 20, the 827th was attached to the 12th Armored Division. The battalion was placed in reserve for three days, during which it saw no action, but experienced problems with discipline among its crews, many of whom left their vehicles unguarded to gather firewood and build fires against the bitter cold. On January 6, 1945, the battalion was ordered to assist the 79th Infantry Division; but before the 827th could move out, an officer and an enlisted man shot each other when the officer attempted to break up a fight among the soldiers, and a disgruntled soldier attacked the first sergeant of another company. The sergeant, while shooting at his attacker, accidentally hit another

March 21, 1944, Italy: Private Jonathan Hoag of the 92nd Division is decorated with the Croix de Guerre by General Alphonse Juin, commanding general of the French Expeditionary Corps, for courage while treating wounded even though he himself was wounded. Hoag wears the Fifth Army shoulder patch on his early pattern field jacket. (NARA)

innocent enlisted man. In yet another company, the company commander reported that approximately 75 percent of his men were missing.

Between January 8 and 20, the companies of the 827th performed at varying levels – some better than could possibly be expected, and others very

Armor & Artillery Units; Northwest Europe, Winter 1944–45

(1) Staff sergeant, Field Artillery. The M1 steel helmet was worn at most times and places where there was any danger of enemy artillery attack. The high-neck olive-drab wool sweater has a low standing collar and five-button front; it is worn with standard issue wool pants in light shade olive-drab, canvas leggings, and leather-soled russet field shoes. The only unusual feature is the rank insignia sewn to the sweater sleeves, typical of the latitude allowed by units in the frontlines. (2) Corporal, Tank Destroyer Force. His field jacket in light olive-drab poplin is the "Parsons" type (often but erroneously called the M1941 – it had no such official designation); despite the introduction of the longer, greener-colored M1943 field jacket by late 1944, the original model was widely used until the end of the war. On the left sleeve he displays the shoulder sleeve insignia of the whole TD

Force above his rank chevrons. His dark shade olive-drab wool pants are tucked into "buckle boots" – the M1943 combat service boot, not yet widely available in the European Theater of Operations (ETO) and the object of much trading and larceny. (3) Major, 761st Tank Battalion. The steel shell of a large-size M1 helmet is worn here – against sniper's bullets and shell fragments – over the top of the hard leather M1942 armored forces helmet, with its integral radio earphones; in this case the major's rank insignia is soldered to the helmet front. The so-called tanker's jacket – actually the "winter field jacket" – bears the universal Armored Force shoulder insignia with the addition of the battalion number in black. The jacket is worn here over the winter combat trousers; windproof, water-repellent, and fully lined with blanket material, these had high bib tops at front and rear. The shoulder holster rig for the M1911A1 .45cal semi-automatic pistol was more convenient in the tight confines of a tank turret than a conventional waist-belt holster.

(Raffaele Ruggeri © Osprey Publishing)

poorly. In one incident, on January 14, a tank destroyer that was parked in a barn where antitank mines were stored caught fire. When ordered to drive the burning vehicle out before the mines exploded, the crew refused. Instead, white infantrymen ran into the barn and carried the mines out before the whole structure caught fire.

The 827th's problems resulted in an investigation by the Inspector General's office, and this disclosed some instructive facts. Some companies of the 827th had acquitted themselves well, despite their own officers' low expectations; this was especially creditable when seen against the background – they were strafed by German aircraft, and fighting in support of white American infantrymen who were themselves disorganized and confused. Nevertheless, every white officer of the 827th expressed doubts about his men's abilities and courage. The Inspector General made three primary recommendations. These were: first, that the 827th be withdrawn from the line, given additional training, and then be returned to combat; second, that the men refusing to engage the enemy be tried by court-martial; and third, that the commanding officer be replaced. The commanding general of VI Corps, to which the battalion was attached, recommended instead that the unit be disbanded, and his superior, the commanding general of Seventh Army, agreed. The Sixth Army Group did not concur. It seems that the investigating officer had questioned only the officers, and not the enlisted men of the 827th. A new investigating officer interviewed enlisted members of the battalion, and found that most of them were competent in their tasks, but that the overwhelming majority did not

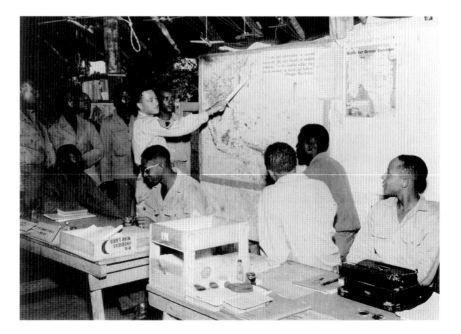

November 1944: Members of the S-3 (Operations) section of the 477th Antiaircraft Artillery Battalion (Air Warning) study maps at Oro Bay, New Guinea. (NARA)

want to go back into combat. After the German surrender in May 1945, the issue of the 827th was finally settled when the battalion was named as a surplus unit so that it could be returned to the United States.

It is important to be clear about the reasons for the problems within the 827th. These were mostly the result of poor training, poor discipline, and poor leadership, exacerbated by frequent changes in organization, equipment, and officers. Nevertheless, parts of the battalion performed well enough that fair-minded officers concluded that more skillful leadership at crucial points in the battalion's life would have resulted in a far more effective unit.

CAVALRY

More than 10,000 African American cavalrymen served during World War II. After the Army decided to dismount the horse cavalry, however, they were uncertain what to do with these troopers. On February 25, 1943, the 2nd Cavalry Division was reactivated with African American enlisted personnel. Despite being trained as a combat division, and despite the need for more combat troops in Italy, after the 2nd Cavalry Division began arriving in Oran, Algeria, on March 9, 1944, it was inactivated and its personnel used to create support and service units. A small number of black cavalrymen traded their horses for armored cars and saw combat in Italy and the Pacific, as the division reconnaissance troops of the 92nd and 93rd Infantry Divisions.

FIELD, COAST, & ANTIAIRCRAFT ARTILLERY

During World War II, African American soldiers were found in all three artillery branches in the US Army. The Army had distinguished between field and coast artillery since 1901. The differences between the two were self-evident: field artillery was mobile and employed on the battlefield, while coast artillery was generally immobile and designed to protect the American coast from invasion. Before World War II, a new type of unit was created from within the coast artillery: Antiaircraft Artillery (AA), whose importance was dramatically emphasized by events in Europe in 1939–40 and in the Pacific theater in 1941–42.

During World War II, the Army organized 27 African American field artillery battalions. While 11 of these battalions were assigned to the African American 2nd Cavalry, 92nd and 93rd Infantry Divisions, and nine (including the three assigned to the 2nd Cavalry) were later reorganized as engineer battalions, the remaining ten were organized as separate battalions generally coming under corps commands. These units were equipped with either 105mm or 155mm howitzers, and were attached at random to divisions in need of non-division artillery support assets.

Cavalry, 1943–44

(1) First sergeant, 2nd Cavalry Division. This senior NCO wears the early-war service uniform of the remaining horsed cavalry units: the M1939 olive-drab wool service coat, wool elastique breeches, olive-drab wool shirt with khaki tie, and olive-drab garrison cap with the yellow arm-of-service piping of the cavalry. His chevrons and rockers of rank are worn on both sleeves, the divisional insignia on the left shoulder, and a slanting service stripe on the left forearm, marking a completed three-year enlistment. His russet riding boots are of non-regulation pattern. (2) Brigadier-General Benjamin O. Davis Sr, 2nd Cavalry Division. The commanding general of the 4th Cavalry Brigade also wears service uniform, but with the M1911 service hat, its black-and-gold cords and "acorns" indicating general officer's rank. His winter service coat in "chocolate" (OD shade No.51) wool elastique has the half-inch ring of contrasting

olive-drab shade No.53 mohair braid around the cuffs which was displayed by all officer ranks. The star of his individual rank, and the officers' cut-out "U.S." cyphers, are pinned to the epaulettes and both upper lapels respectively; he wears the 2nd Cavalry Division shoulder sleeve insignia, but not the cavalry-branch sabers on his lower lapels. His riding breeches, in a contrasting light shade of drab, are worn with regulation elkhide legging-topped laced riding boots and spurs. (3) Second Lieutenant Jack Roosevelt Robinson. In 1947, "Jackie" Robinson would become famous as the first African American to play major league baseball, with the Los Angeles Dodgers. In World War II he served originally as an enlisted man in the 761st Tank Battalion, but then attended Officer Candidate School and was commissioned second lieutenant. However, Robinson did not ship out to Europe with his battalion – because he was court-martialed for refusing to sit at the back of a public bus in the area traditionally reserved for "coloreds." After being acquitted, he accepted an honorable discharge, and began playing professional baseball with the Kansas City Monarchs in the Negro League. Lieutenant Robinson is depicted wearing the M1943 field jacket in olive-drab shade No.7, over a khaki shirt and light shade olive-drab tie. When the service coat was not worn – as here – a single officers' cutout national cypher and arm-of-service insignia were to be pinned to the right and left shirt collar respectively.

(Raffaele Ruggeri © Osprey Publishing)

At the outbreak of the war, the Army had more "traditional" than AA coast artillery units. By the end of the war, however, coast artillery functions had largely vanished as the reality of modern airpower became apparent. (The coast artillery also included additional searchlight and barrage balloon battalions, the latter to defend American troops and installations on the ground by preventing enemy low-altitude strafing runs.) As the war progressed, coast and AA artillery units within the United States increasingly became "caretakers" for stateside installations. Just as the war demonstrated that tanks were better than tank destroyers at killing other tanks, so it also proved that aircraft were better than artillery at destroying other aircraft. This downgrading of their role led to a large number of coastal and AA units being manned by African American

A reporter for *The Afro-American* of Baltimore, Ollie Stewart accompanied Allied troops as they liberated Paris during August 1944:

We were about three miles from the German lines. Heavy gunfire was continuous and German ack-ack was spattering mushroom bursts of flak as our planes dived over their lines and our observation grasshopper planes sailed placidly along, spotting the Germans guns and radioing back their positions.

When a white colonel saw colored troops in the midst of all this, he said: "This is the first time that I have ever seen quartermasters up so close to the front line."

Sgt Eugene W. Jones, of 1611 W. Butler Street, Philadelphia, replied: "Sir, we are not quartermasters, we are field artillery and we have just been given a firing mission. Want to watch us lay one on the target?"

That was my introduction to the first colored 155-mm. howitzer outfit in France, one of the best groups of artillerymen in the army, white or colored. Two battalions have been in action for weeks and had a big part in the taking of La Saye du Puits. Another unit operating 155-mm. Long Toms has just arrived.

These hard-working gunners will tell you frankly that they know they are good. Their officers told me that they are good. White infantrymen who won't budge unless these guys are laying down a barrage say that they are good, and German prisoners ask to see our automated artillery that comes so fast and so accurate."

– Black History Museum website:
http://www.blackhistorymuseum.org/: "This is our war" – excerpts from Ollie Stewart

September 1943: the headquarters staff of the 92nd Infantry Division established in an ancient Greek temple of Neptune in Italy. Sitting at the improvised desks are (front to back): Sergeants James Shellman, Gilbert A. Terry, John W. Phoenix, Curtis A. Richardson and Leslie B. Wood. In front of the desks are (front to back): Tech Sergeant Gordon A. Scott, Master Sergeant Walter C. Jackson, Sergeant David D. Jones, and Warrant Officer Carlyle M. Tucker. (NARA)

soldiers, who were generally not trusted by the Army hierarchy to perform more critical tasks. In turn, as manpower shortages became more apparent, African American coast and AA artillery units were often reorganized as engineer and quartermaster elements, in order to maintain the flow of supplies to combat units (see below, Support and Service Troops).

INFANTRY

The largest percentage of African American combat soldiers was found in the infantry, and more than 20,000 black infantrymen fought in Europe and the Pacific. Not only did many African Americans serve in segregated infantry units, but some were part of an experiment that involved the creation of the first racially integrated units in American military history. This experiment was so successful that it helped to justify President Harry S. Truman's decision to integrate the US military in 1948.

92nd Infantry Division

On October 15, 1942, the 92nd Infantry Division was reactivated at Fort McClellan, Alabama, with the 365th, 370th, and 371st Infantry Regiments, the 597th through 600th Field Artillery Battalions, and Engineer and Medical Battalions both numbered 317th. The 370th Infantry was the first unit of the division to arrive in Italy, and went into combat on the Arno river front north of Rome on August 24, alongside the 1st Armored Division; the other division units went into action on October 6.

During the northern Italian campaign, the 92nd "Buffalo" Division saw significant action, and suffered 2,997 battle casualties including 548 killed and 206 missing; only 56 men were listed as prisoners. It was reorganized in March/April 1945, when the 365th Infantry became a replacement training unit and the 371st was assigned rear security duties; for the last few weeks of the war it had one black regiment (370th), one white (473rd), and one "Nisei" Japanese-American regiment (442nd Regimental Combat Team).

Though the 92nd Division represented less than 2 percent of African American troops in the Army, it received disproportionate media attention. This was not always from positive motives; the division's combat performance was mixed, and there were always those who were eager to slander African American GIs generally by seizing on particular incidents. As with so many other black units, the core of the problems suffered by those of the 92nd Division was poor leadership (starting with the division commander, Major-General Edward M. Almond), and inadequate training. The white officers assigned to the formation were unhappy to be there; significant numbers of them were – deliberately – selected from among Southerners, many of whom proved unable to see beyond their ancestral prejudices.

93rd Infantry Division

The regiments of this formation had seen more combat in World War I than any other American units. Reactivated on May 15, 1942, at Fort Huachuca, Arizona, the 93rd Division included the 25th, 368th, and 369th Infantry Regiments, with the 593rd through 596th Field Artillery Battalions and the 318th Engineer and Medical battalions. The division was deployed to the Pacific, arriving on Guadalcanal progressively between January and March 1944. It served in New Guinea, the northern Solomons and the Bismarck Archipelago; however, owing to Army prejudice against African American units, much of the division would spend the war performing labor and security duties. The 25th Infantry did see combat when it was attached to the "Americal" Division in March–April 1944 on Bougainville island. The 93rd

September 7, 1944: a combat patrol from the 92nd Infantry Division advance, some 3 miles north of Lucca, Italy. The bazooka team have just fired an AT rocket; the M9A1 model bazooka had a maximum range of 300 yards. By this date each rifle company had five bazookas, and they were also issued on a generous scale to other battalion and regimental sub-units for antitank defense. (NARA)

Cavalry Reconnaissance Troop was also attached to XIV Corps to raid, patrol, and maintain perimeter positions. In April 1945, the 93rd Division occupied Morotai, Dutch New Guinea, and recorded scattered skirmishes along the northwestern coast of the island, where the division continued its labor and security missions. Since the Army prevented the 93rd as a whole from seeing any significant combat, the division's wartime battle casualties amounted to only 138 men killed and wounded.

24th Infantry Regiment

Operating as a separate regiment, the 24th Infantry was destined to serve in the Pacific Theater, to which it was deployed from San Francisco in April 1942. Its first destination was the New Hebrides Islands, but from there it headed out to the Solomons and Guadalcanal. The Solomons duties were tough – the 24th had to secure US basing areas and airfields against the constant depredations of the Japanese, and fighting was intense. They were also responsible for protecting additional landings of men and supplies to the Solomons beachheads.

In 1944, the 1st Battalion of the 24th Infantry was attached to the 37th Infantry Division, and later the Americal Division, its destinations including Bougainville. At the end of the year, the battalion joined its parent regiment once more for the occupation of Saipan and Tinian. This posting involved direct combat duties, principally in mopping-up operations. The regiment's final World War II posting was to Kerama Island Group off Okinawa in July 1945, where it took the first formal surrender of a Japanese military garrison, on Aka Shima. With the end of the war, the 24th took up occupation duties on Okinawa itself, and also on mainland Japan.

November 1944: soldiers of an 81mm mortar platoon from the 92nd Infantry Division in action against targets near Massa in northern Italy. The weapons company of each of the three battalions of each infantry regiment had six of these mortars. (NARA)

555th Parachute Infantry Battalion

This unit was born as a test company, activated at Fort Benning, Georgia, on December 30, 1943, as the 555th Parachute Infantry Company. The Army authorized the formation of a company with African American officers and enlisted men; all members of the company were to be volunteers, with an enlisted cadre selected from the 92nd Infantry Division. On November 25, 1944, after months of training, the company moved to Camp Mackall, North Carolina, where it was reorganized and redesignated as Company A of the 555th Parachute Infantry Battalion.

In May 1945, the 555th was sent to the West Coast of the United States to fight forest fires. Stationed at Pendleton Field, Oregon, the battalion's paratroopers participated in dangerous missions throughout the Pacific Northwest during the summer and fall of 1945. Nicknamed the "Triple Nickles" or the "Smoke Jumpers," the battalion returned to Camp Mackall in October 1945. The 555th then transferred to Fort Bragg, North Carolina, where it remained for the next two years and was attached to the 82nd Airborne Division. On December 15, 1947, the battalion was inactivated and most of its personnel were reassigned to the 3rd Battalion, 505th Airborne Infantry Regiment.

Volunteer infantry replacements

By December 1944, the US Army was experiencing severe shortages of infantry replacements in Europe. The shortfalls of riflemen began in July 1944, soon after the invasion of France. The problem was so severe that the Army began retraining enlisted men from other specialties to serve as infantrymen. The German Ardennes offensive of mid December further exacerbated the situation. The only readily available and relatively untapped

May 1944: African
American soldiers of the
25th Infantry Regiment,
93rd Division, advance
cautiously through thick
bamboo jungle off the
Numa-Numa Trail on
Bougainville, Solomon
Islands. (NARA)

source of manpower was the African American service and support units
already serving in the European theater.

The suggestion of drawing upon these units for volunteer infantry
replacements was welcomed by the Supreme Allied Commander, General
Dwight D. Eisenhower; however, since integration was still unacceptable to
many senior officers and politicians, he had to find a way to hide his real
intention. Therefore, a request was put out for volunteers from all service and
support units, regardless of race; publicly, it was stated that if there were more
black volunteers than were needed for existing African American combat
units, those men would be used in other organizations.

The call for volunteers was issued on December 26, and since white units
had already been combed out for infantry replacements, the overwhelming
majority of the volunteers came from among those for whom the appeal was
originally intended – African Americans. Within two months almost 5,000 of
them signed up, but since the Army could not afford to strip too many service
and support units, the number accepted was initially limited to 2,500. As part
of the arrangement the volunteers had to give up any rank they possessed in
their previous units; thus, a first sergeant in a quartermaster unit would have
to be willing to become a private in order to serve as an infantryman.

In January 1945, the first volunteers gathered for six weeks of infantry
conversion training. After training, the African American infantrymen were
organized into 53 platoons, each with a white platoon leader and platoon
sergeant. The platoons were divided between two armored divisions (the 12th
and 14th) and eight infantry divisions (the 1st, 2nd, 8th, 9th, 69th, 78th, 99th,
and 104th). Each platoon included about 60 men – almost 50 percent more

than the normal strength, in order to provide replacements for battle casualties. Three volunteer platoons were assigned to each division, one for each of its infantry regiments.

At the end of the war it was made clear to the African American volunteers that the experiment had ended, and the majority of them were reassigned to African American units. The experiment was carefully scrutinized by Eisenhower's head-quarters. In July 1945, after the cessation of the war in Europe, a survey was undertaken among the white officers and platoon sergeants who had had contact with the African American platoons. In addition, an anonymous question-naire was submitted to more than 1,000 white enlisted men to determine their attitudes toward the black riflemen. (Interestingly, no African Americans were interviewed.)

March 1944: a stick of 16 African American soldiers ride a C-47 transport on the way to one of their required five qualifying jumps before being awarded their "wings" at Fort Benning, Georgia. All ranks of the entire 555th Parachute Infantry Battalion would be African Americans; they would make dangerous jumps, but against forest fires in the Pacific Northwest rather than any human enemy. (NARA)

More than 80 percent of the white officers and NCOs interviewed believed that African American soldiers had performed "very well" in combat, and an almost equal number believed that African Americans could perform as well as white infantrymen if they had the same training and experience. Nearly all the white soldiers were surprised that, despite initial apprehension, the white and black infantrymen worked well together. The majority of the officers thought that the experiment should be continued and expanded, rather than retaining the segregated African American units.

Recommendations based on these findings were opposed by many senior Army officers, including the Army Chief of Staff General George C. Marshall and General Omar N. Bradley, the senior American field commander in Europe. Bradley argued that most of the African American platoons had participated in only minor combat operations; that they were made up of African Americans of "above average" intelligence; and that racial tension had arisen when the "integrated" companies were in rest and recreational areas.

Marshall agreed with Bradley regarding the unusual quality of the volunteers and the uniqueness of the emergency that had prompted their employment. (It should be noted that both Marshall and Bradley, while professional Army officers of the highest caliber, haled from Southern states – Virginia and Missouri, respectively.)

Nevertheless, the volunteer platoons exploded many racial myths – and first, that of African American cowardice. If that were true, then why were thousands of black soldiers willing to trade the safety of duties in the rear – and many of them, their NCO pay and status – for combat in the snowy forests of the Bulge? Second, the myth that close contact between the races would result in conflict; in fact, there were very few racial incidents in the "integrated" companies. The last myth to be exposed was the belief that Southern officers were better suited to lead African American units, because of their experience of contact in civilian life. Since the placement of the volunteer platoons was not dependent on preconceived segregationist notions, platoon leaders and company commanders had been chosen fairly randomly, and included many Northern officers. The success of the volunteer platoons could therefore have little to do with the regional background of the officers.

In the end, the most long-term effect of the lessons of the volunteer platoons in the Battle of the Bulge would not be felt until July 26, 1948, when President Harry S. Truman signed Executive Order 9981, which provided equal treatment and opportunity for all members of the US military regardless of race.

April 1944, beside the East–West Trail, Bougainville: Sergeant John C. Clark and Staff Sergeant Ford M. Shaw, from Company E, 25th Infantry, clean their Garand rifles. The constant damp and filth of the jungle, and the M1's relatively complex semi-automatic action, made this a frequent and very necessary precaution. (NARA)

Infantry, 1944–45

(1) Private first class, 555th Parachute Infantry Battalion; Camp Mackall, NC, spring 1945. A paratrooper of the only African American airborne unit, posing proudly in dress uniform after earning his "silver wings" – displayed on his left chest. He wears the garrison cap with light blue infantry piping, and on the left front the combined parachute-glider patch introduced in 1943. (This position could also be used to display enameled regimental badges, but they were seldom seen.) As prized as paratrooper insignia, was the authorization to wear the pants bloused into highly polished "Corcoran" jump boots. (2) First Lieutenant Vernon J. Baker, 370th Infantry Regiment, 92nd Infantry Division; Viareggio, Italy, April 1945. Lieutenant Baker is depicted in field uniform of M1 helmet with camouflage net, shirt with rank and infantry insignia, M1943 field jacket with 92nd Division "Buffalo" insignia, and M1943 trousers. He carries the .30cal M1 carbine with two-

magazine butt pouch, and the M1936 pistol belt supports a .45cal pistol in its russet leather M1916 holster, a two-magazine pistol ammo pouch and first aid pouch. Vernon Baker was a platoon leader in the 370th Infantry; on April 5 and 6, 1945, in mountainous terrain near Viareggio, he crawled forward and destroyed three German machine-gun nests and an observation post, killing or wounding a dozen of the enemy. He then covered the evacuation of his company's casualties by occupying an exposed position and drawing the enemy's fire. Initially Baker was awarded the Distinguished Service Cross, the Army's second highest award for valor, but in 1997 his and similar decorations to six other African American soldiers were retrospectively upgraded to the Medal of Honor. Vernon Baker was the only one of the seven soldiers still alive to receive his award. (3) Private, 370th Infantry Regiment, 92nd Infantry Division; Naples, Italy, August 1944. A soldier of the first combat unit of the division to disembark in Italy, wearing summer field uniform of helmet, light olive-drab wool shirt with divisional sleeve insignia, olive-drab wool pants, canvas leggings and field shoes (note that privates did not receive rank insignia until 1968). He is armed with the Garand M1 .30cal rifle, and wears full web gear: M1923 rifle belt, canteen in M1917 cover, and M1928 haversack with integral suspenders, meatcan pouch and M1910 T-handle "intrenching tool."

(Raffaele Ruggeri © Osprey Publishing)

SUPPORT & SERVICE TROOPS

By far the largest number of African Americans in the US Army served in support and service units. Every one of the Army's support and service arms contained African American soldiers, who were frequently called upon to perform hazardous and crucially important duties with little or no recognition for their efforts. The majority of these duties were physically demanding, and some were considered beneath the dignity of white soldiers.

On February 13, 1944, members of Company A, 66th Medical Training Battalion, wrote to Truman K. Gibson, civilian aide to Secretary of War Henry L. Stimson, describing the treatment of black troops at a training camp in Texas:

Camp Barkeley is one of the largest army camps in Texas and the only MedicalReplacement Training Center in the south … approximately two hundred of us, were the first Colored to be stationed here, now however, there are roughly over five hundred of us… None of our commissioned officers are Colored despite the fact that located here are Officer Candidate and Medical Administration schools… Up until a few weeks ago, we … could only attend [an open air theatre] when the weather was favorable. By protest, we acquired the right to attend any theater of our choice but are forced to contend with being segregated … on the local buses we are compelled to sit in the back, threatened by the drivers if we refuse. Despite the fact that buses run all day back and forth to camp at regular one half hour intervals, we have only three which we may ride. Our buses are crowded to the extent that it is practically impossible to close the doors and yet extra buses has been refused us… Our living quarters are terrible being formerly C.[ivilian] C.[onservation] C.[orps] barracks, located just in from of the camp cess pool. When I first arrived, our sector actually looked like a garbage dump in comparison with the rest of the camp. We spent three weeks cleaning the place before we could begin training…

It was to my amazement, a short time ago, when I had the opportunity of visiting the German concentration camp here at Barkeley to observe a sign in the latrine, actually segregating a section of the latrine for Negro soldiers, the other being used by the German prisoners and the white soldiers. Seeing this was honestly disheartening. It made me feel, here, the tyrant is actually placed over the liberator.

– Lowry G. Wright et al., "Letters from African American Soldiers during World War II"

Crewed by African
American GIs, US Army
2½-ton trucks and a
Dodge weapons-carrier
wind precariously along
a mountainside on the
Ledo Road, the only land
supply route between
Allied rear bases in India
and troops in northern
Burma and China.
(NARA)

Many African American units were converted to new designations or specializations when they arrived overseas. In most cases they performed tasks for which they had never been specifically trained. The African American units in greatest demand and most consistently employed were those of the engineer and quartermaster branches of the service. While it might be imagined that such troops would require a fair amount of specialized training, they generally needed nothing more than physical strength and the ability to operate a motor vehicle. Although the first units shipped were generally less well trained than those that followed, the sense of urgency early in America's participation in the war put a higher value on simply filling immediate needs.

These units, who received little attention or fame, were in fact often among the first to arrive in combat zones. For instance, black engineers arrived before other American ground units at Port Moresby, New Guinea, the most vital single bastion of resistance to the Japanese operations there. Right across the immense expanses of the Pacific, they arrived just behind initial landing forces in order to construct airfields, and the roads and anchorages necessary to keep a steady stream of supplies moving forward to the troops on the frontlines.

Equipped with bulldozers, trucks, or simply on foot, they moved across the icy wilderness of Alaska, the jungles and hills of the China–Burma–India theater and the coral reefs of the Pacific, building the infrastructure necessary for the military transportation without which combat operations were simply impossible.

Drivers from the 666th Quartermaster Truck Company, who chalked up 20,000 miles each without an accident after arriving in the ETO. Soldiers like these were instrumental in successfully supplying the US Army via the Red Ball Express. Left to right: Tech 5 Sherman Hughes, Tech 5 Hudson Murphy, and Private First Class Zacariah Gibbs. Note that all have acquired the M1944 "Ike" jacket. (NARA)

African American Port and Amphibious Truck companies found themselves attached to Army and Marine units for the invasions of Pacific islands such as Saipan, Tinian, Iwo Jima, and Okinawa. During the battle of Iwo Jima, beginning on February 19, 1945, two US Army Port companies and three Amphibious Truck companies (equipped with DUKWs) were attached to V Amphibious Corps (Marine). Port companies manned harbors throughout the world, even in places where no port had ever before existed. In Normandy on June 6, 1944, the African American 320th AA Balloon Battalion set up barrage balloons to protect the invasion fleet and the troops on the beaches from low-flying German aircraft. At the same time, amphibious truck, quartermaster, and ammunition companies began unloading and transporting the supplies without which the beachhead could not have been established and defended.

African American transportation companies were attached to infantry and armored divisions as they fought their way eastwards across Europe. Many of these companies became semi-permanent elements of these divisions, even serving as temporary infantrymen when circumstances required. For instance, during the drive across France, the 57th Ordnance Ammunition Company was engaged by 65 Germans at the French town of Peronne, with no other

American units in support. The soldiers of the company killed 50 and captured the remaining 15 Germans; four men were cited for bravery during this encounter, and were awarded two French Croix de Guerre, one Silver Star, and one Bronze Star.

The logistic lifeline of the advancing armies was, notoriously, stretched out perilously long and thin during the many months that the original Normandy beachhead remained the only available disembarkation point. This lifeline depended upon the quartermaster truckers, who sped supplies forward along the roads of Northwest Europe by the priority traffic system christened the "Red Ball Express." In the end, the sheer quantity of work performed by African American units was more than planners had ever envisioned before the war. Many of these small units changed their designations and functions as needed; some of them – such as the dump truck companies – were always in demand. In total, more than 4,000 small African American service and support units were organized during World War II.

In March 1944, before the invasion of France, the majority of the nearly 700,000 African American soldiers were still in the United States, but by December 1944 more than two-thirds of them were overseas. The trend continued, and by April 1945 the figure had risen above 70 percent. Of the approximately 470,000 black soldiers serving overseas in December 1944, around 170,000 were quartermaster troops, 110,000 were engineers, and 65,000 were transportation troops.

Private William A. Reynolds displays a machine-gun bullet that lodged above the windshield of his ambulance when he was strafed by a German plane near the front in France. He wore the spent bullet on his dog-tag chain for good luck. (NARA)

India, July 1943: African Americans off duty in crisp khakis, enjoying a rickshaw ride. For all the demeaning treatment they often endured, the war did bring nearly half a million black Americans an opportunity to see far countries and other cultures – some of which gave them food for thought. (NARA)

For the most part the quartermaster, truck, and service companies, the laundry and dump truck companies, and the engineer and port units spent their overseas service in harbors, base camps, and depots; they performed routine duties, with few if any opportunities for heroism. Though their service was in the main rather unexciting, they were no more or less efficient than similar units of any race. Interactions between African American and white soldiers, and between black American troops and foreign civilians, were generally more often positive than negative. The efficiency of most African American units was never as high as it could have been if the training and leadership they were given had truly been equal to that of white units; but likewise, their efficiency was generally never as poor as white segregationists continually claimed.

ARMY UNIFORMS

The uniforms worn by African Americans during World War II did not differ from those worn by their white counterparts. The "dress blues" uniform was not a required purchase item for Reserve, National Guard, or draftee officers or enlisted men; due to wartime priorities and material shortages, even most newly commissioned Regular Army officers did not own one.

The World War II service uniform can be divided between winter and summer, as well as officer and enlisted models. The officers' winter dress consisted of a four-pocket wool service coat (tunic) with "peak lapel-collar" and integral cloth belt, of a dark "chocolate" shade of olive, and pale fawn trousers; this combination was generally referred to as "pinks and greens." Officers had the option of wearing a shirt of the same dark shade as the coat, or khaki; either shirt could be worn with a khaki or dark olive necktie. Late in the war, General Eisenhower popularized yet another type of coat, the M1944 wool field jacket or "Ike jacket." A waist-length garment modeled on the British battledress blouse, this was available for both officers and enlisted men, in "chocolate" or olive-drab wool; it had been intended for field use, but was usually kept for service and walking-out uniform. Officers' summer service uniform consisted of a khaki shirt, trousers, and necktie, with an optional khaki coat (without the cloth belt). Various overcoats, raincoats, and mackinaws were available for bad weather.

The enlisted winter service uniform comprised an olive-drab four-pocket coat with "notched lapel" collar (but without the integral cloth belt), and trousers; these came in both light and dark shades, but both appeared more yellow-brown than the officer's coat. The shirt was either khaki or a light shade of olive-drab, and could be worn with either a khaki or a black necktie. A long, double-breasted wool overcoat and a rubberized raincoat were issued. The enlisted summer uniform was almost identical to the officers' model, and consisted of a khaki shirt, trousers and necktie, but lacked the khaki service coat.

February 1945: Major Charity E. Adams and Captain Abbie N. Campbell (in raincoat) inspect the first unit of African American WACs – 6888th Postal Directory Battalion – to serve in the United Kingdom. All ranks wear the four-pocket service coat, with garrison caps apparently piped in the original WAC branch colors of mixed green and old gold. Note that they all seem to wear ankle socks over their stockings, and field shoes. (NARA)

When the United States entered World War II in December 1941, the service uniform and the combat uniform were basically identical apart from the addition of a steel helmet, leggings, and web gear to the latter. Since the service uniform had not been designed specifically for field use it was impractical in that role: it lacked adequate pockets, was designed to be form-

Support & Service Troops

(1) Chaplain. Each infantry regiment had three chaplains in its table of organization, and African American chaplains had a harder task than their white counterparts. Since they often had to intervene on behalf of their congregants in cases of maltreatment, they did more than simply care for their morale and spiritual wellbeing. With the status but not the authority of an officer, this chaplain wears the "pinks and greens" uniform with a service dress cap; his insignia include the rank bars of captain, and the Christian chaplain's silver cross on the lower lapels. (2) Technician 3rd Grade, 92nd Quartermaster Company. The Tech 3 was equivalent to a staff sergeant for pay purposes, but his grade indicated technical expertise rather than the command authority of "hard stripe" rank. Many African Americans found themselves in units of the Quartermaster Corps, responsible for supplies – a vital but underappreciated specialty. Many quartermaster companies, like this

one, were numbered after the division to which they were assigned; they consisted of a headquarters, three transport platoons, and one service platoon. This GI wears standard M1943 field uniform with insignia of grade and division. (3) Technician 5th Grade, 152nd Coast Artillery Group. Wearing the earlier "Parsons" field jacket with wool pants and leggings, this soldier – earning the pay of a corporal – belongs to a branch of service that saw many redesignations and changes of mission in the latter part of the war. In June 1944 the 54th Coast Artillery Regiment was redesignated 152nd Coast Artillery Group, under XXI Corps – whose shoulder sleeve insignia is illustrated here. However, only a month later the 152nd was disbanded and its men posted away to reinforce other coast artillery units.

(Raffaele Ruggeri © Osprey Publishing)

fitting rather than roomy, was hard to clean, and the necktie was as absurd in combat as the World War I "choker" collar had been. Beginning in 1941, a lined, hip-length, zip-fronted, windproof cotton poplin "Parsons" field jacket began to be issued. Herringbone twill fatigue jackets and trousers were also used for field wear, often in combination with pre-war wool or khaki uniform items. The Army subsequently experimented with a completely new combat uniform, designed on the "layering" principle, that abandoned most of the older conventions. While this sateen cotton M1943 uniform, in the greenish "OD shade No.7," was not adopted in its entirety, parts of it did find their way into general use. The most important item was the crotch-length M1943 field jacket, with four large pockets, epaulettes, and provision for attaching a pile liner and a hood.

April 1943: a platoon of African American US Marine Corps recruits at Montford Point Camp, North Carolina, are addressed by their drill instructor, Sergeant Gilbert H. "Hashmark" Johnson. (NARA)

Special field uniform items were issued for some types of troops, and acquired by others unofficially. The two most significantly different field uniforms were those specially designed for airborne and armored troops – respectively, the loose M1942 paratrooper uniform, with its many capacious pockets; and the heavily lined windcheater jacket with knit collar, cuffs, and waistband, and bib-top overtrousers, produced to protect tank crews in winter.

A wide range of headgear was issued to American soldiers during the war, the most important of these being the service and garrison caps and the steel helmet. The service cap had a large round crown and a brown leather visor. Although it was the standard home service headgear, few wartime soldiers overseas would own one. The higher quality officers' model was popular among AAF flyers, who removed the crown stiffener supposedly for ease while wearing headphones – the consequent dashingly "crushed" appearance

August 19, 1945, in Rouen, France: Chaplain William T. Green, wearing captain's bars, conducts the wedding ceremony for Corporal William A. Johnson, 1696th Labor Supervision Company, and Private First Class Florence A. Collins, 6888th Postal Directory Battalion – note the shoulder patch of European Theater Advanced Base. This couple were the first African Americans to be married in the ETO. (NARA)

was probably of more importance. The garrison cap was modeled on the French calot sidecap of World War I, which could conveniently be folded flat while not in use. The garrison cap was available in khaki or the chocolate-like dark olive for officers, and in khaki or olive-drab for enlisted ranks.

In 1941 most soldiers were still wearing the M1917A1 dishpan-style steel helmet modeled on that used by the British Army in World War I. The new pot-shaped M1 shell-and-liner design had been approved, but few had yet been manufactured; it was general issue by the end of 1942.

At the beginning of the war soldiers were issued the russet leather service shoe, which was roughly similar to a modern lace-up, ankle-length hiking boot. Over these, soldiers wore calf-to-instep cotton canvas leggings that laced through a number of eyelets up the outsides. These were unpopular – they soaked up water, chafed, and took too long to put on. Beginning in 1943 a much more sought-after "two-buckle" boot began to be issued, with a laced foot similar to the service shoe but with an integral leather gaiter-flap at the ankle, fastening with two buckled straps. Various specialist footwear was also available, including the paratroopers' high-lacing "jump" boots, and two types of canvas and rubber protective overboots for extreme winter conditions.

Support & Service Troops

(1) Master sergeant, 6888th Postal Directory Battalion (Colored), Women's Army Corps; UK, 1945. The WACs were a new branch of the US Army, formed in May 1942 in order to relieve men of clerical responsibilities and free them for more physical roles. The original concept had been to recruit 25,000 highly educated, middle-class white women to a Women's Army Auxiliary Corps (WAAC); fully incorporated into the armed forces as the Women's Army Corps (WAC) from July 1943, by the end of the war the Corps numbered nearly 100,000 – including just over 4,000 African American women – fulfilling more than 240 specific roles. This senior NCO is a member of the only African American WAC unit to see overseas service before VE-day. By this date the original and unpopular stiff, visored "Hobby hat" had given place to a garrison cap (by now made without the branch-of-service color piping). The M1944 wool field jacket, based on the British battledress

blouse, was also a popular alternative to the four-pocket service coat for any who could get one. It was not officially authorized for servicewomen before VE-Day, but many in the ETO acquired locally approved examples made in Britain or France. (2) Technician 4th Grade, Corps of Engineers; Italy, 1945. Though enjoying the pay grade of a sergeant, this engineer technician probably has no special training in construction or engineering skills. Many African Americans were assigned to Engineer General Service units, which functioned as stevedores to unload supplies at ports in Europe and the Pacific. (3) Sergeant, Military Police, 92nd Infantry Division; Italy, 1945. MP platoons – part of a division's HQ & HQ Company – were larger than the term implies, with (by this date) 4 officers and 102 enlisted men, many of them NCOs, in a headquarters and two large sections each the size of a conventional platoon. African American MPs found themselves in a dilemma if confronted by white GIs, and tended to turn a blind eye to their misdemeanours while concentrating on men of their own units. Technically they had the right and authority to arrest any soldier breaking military law, but if he tried to arrest or even ticket a white soldier, the black MP might face an angry mob.

(Raffaele Ruggeri © Osprey Publishing)

LIFE OVERSEAS

The American Red Cross created a number of clubs staffed with and exclusively for African Americans. By February 1944 there were 23 African American clubs, but the very existence of the segregated clubs smacked of the "separate, but equal" treatment that so many black Americans were forced to endure in the Southern United States. The American Red Cross and its clubs were independent of the federal government, but the close association between them and the Army overseas did not permit the average enlisted man or officer to notice any clear distinction between the two institutions or their policies.

Of the letters written by white American soldiers who mentioned the issue of race, the majority discuss their surprise at the lack of racial prejudice among the British people. They were shocked that many British women saw no problem in dancing with or even dating African American soldiers (some believed that black Americans somehow convinced the allegedly gullible British that they were Native Americans). Others took consolation from the belief that only the British lower classes were friendly to African Americans. While this issue might seem unimportant (other than to white Americans trying to get a date), some were concerned as to how the friendly treatment African Americans generally received in Britain might affect their postwar expectations when they returned home. While the post–World War I saying had been, "How do you keep them down on the farm after they've seen Paris?", white soldiers now seemed to worry, "How can you keep them in their place now that they've dated a British woman?"

For African American soldiers the color-blindness of the British Isles was an unexpected pleasure, but for white officers, the situation in Britain was complicated. Officers serving with African Americans were both relieved that they did not have to worry about racial animus among their hosts, and concerned as to how white GIs would react to the relaxed British attitudes. White officers serving with white American soldiers tended to share their men's opinions – that this exposure to British calmness over race was simply going to make things more difficult in postwar America.

US NAVY

Prior to World War II, African American sailors were only allowed to serve in Navy kitchens. The US Navy's senior leadership initially resisted extending their role beyond kitchen duties; eventually, however, two warships were crewed exclusively with African American sailors, though they were commanded by white officers. No black officers were available for these ships, because only 13 African Americans were commissioned as line officers in the Navy during World War II. Additionally, the US Navy organized several African American construction battalions, which saw combat in the Pacific.

STEWARD'S MATE DORIS MILLER

Doris Miller, known as "Dorie" to his friends, was born in Waco, Texas, on October 12, 1919. In high school he was a fullback on the football team, and he worked on his father's farm. On September 16, 1939, the 20-year-old Miller enlisted in the US Navy as a mess attendant, third class. He joined the Navy instead of the Army because he wanted to travel, to learn a trade (cooking), and to earn money to help his family. Miller's first assignment was aboard the USS *Pyro* (AE-1), an ammunition ship. On January 2, 1940, he transferred to the battleship USS *West Virginia* (BB-48), where he became the ship's heavyweight boxing champion.

On December 7, 1941, Miller was aboard the *West Virginia* when the Japanese attacked Pearl Harbor. Having risen at 6.00am that morning, Miller was collecting laundry when general quarters was sounded. He headed for his battle station, an antiaircraft battery magazine, only to find it already destroyed by a torpedo strike. Miller then went up to the main deck, where he began carrying wounded sailors to safety. Then an officer ordered him to the bridge of the ship to aid the already wounded captain; and after doing this, Miller

In February 1944, 12 members of the "Golden Thirteen" are pictured soon after their commissioning ceremony as the first black line officers in the US Navy. While African Americans had served as Navy officers before this date, none had been "line" officers – the only category who could command a ship at sea. Left to right, front: Ensigns George Clinton Cooper, Graham Edward Martin, Jesse Walter Arbor, John Walter Reagan, and Reginald Ernest Goodwin; back: Ensigns Dennis D.Nelson II, Phillip George Barnes, Samuel Edward Barnes, Dalton Louis Baugh, James Edward Hare and Frank Ellis Sublett, and Warrant Officer Charles Byrd Lear. Not pictured here is Ensign W. Sylvester White. (NARA)

manned a .50cal AA machine gun, firing on the Japanese aircraft until he ran out of ammunition, and the order was put out to abandon ship.

During the attack, the *West Virginia* was struck by two armor-piercing bombs (both of which penetrated the ship's deck), and five torpedoes in her left side. The explosions from those strikes caused severe flooding below decks, and she slowly sank to the bottom of "Battleship Row." Unlike the most famous battleship in Pearl Harbor that morning, the USS *Arizona* (BB-39), the *West Virginia*'s losses were quite moderate: only 130 killed and 52 wounded out of a crew of 1,541 men. For his bravery that morning, Miller was awarded the Navy Cross, the Navy's second highest award for valor after the Medal of Honor.

Miller was next assigned to the armored cruiser USS *Indianapolis* (CA-35) and, in spring 1943, to the newly constructed escort carrier USS *Liscome Bay* (CVE-56). During Operation *Galvanic* on November 20–23, 1943 – the assault landings on Makin and Tarawa atolls in the Gilbert Islands – the *Liscome Bay*'s aircraft supported operations ashore. At 5.10am on November 24, a torpedo from the Japanese submarine I-175 struck near the stern of the carrier. The aircraft bomb magazine detonated soon afterwards; the carrier sank within minutes, and Dorie Miller was among the 646 sailors who lost their lives. On June 30, 1973, the Navy commissioned the USS *Miller* (FF-1091), a Knox-class frigate, in his honor. For African Americans, Dorie Miller was the first and greatest hero of World War II.

According to this report filed in a Baltimore newspaper, it took over a year before the bravery of Dorie Miller at Pearl Harbor was fully realized by the American public:

Navy Hero Downed 4 Jap Planes

Dorie Miller, who was awarded the Navy Cross for heroism at Pearl Harbor when he manned a machine gun on the battleship [*West Virginia*] after members of the gun crew had been put out of action, is officially credited by the Navy Department this week with having brought down four Jap planes. In addition, "Miller swam to shore and helped in a flying field operation," the department reveals. This is the first official account which credits Miller with actually bringing down any planes. All previous accounts have referred only to his carrying his wounded captain to a place of safety and his manning the gun. For his heroism, Miller received only promotion from second class to first class mess attendant and an increase in pay from $60 to $66 a month.

– *The Afro-American*, Baltimore, Maryland (March 20, 1943)

USS *MASON* (DE 529)

The destroyer escort USS *Mason* was one of only two US Navy vessels whose crews were composed entirely of African Americans. Just as the 99th Fighter Squadron had been an "experiment" for the AAF, so the *Mason* was considered an experiment to find out whether African Americans were capable of performing more than menial tasks in the Navy. The captain of the *Mason*, Lieutenant-Commander William M. Blackford, had previously captained the USS *Phoebe*, a minesweeper working in the Aleutian Islands. Blackford, who came on active duty from the Naval Reserve in January 1941, was only two semesters short of finishing a PhD in chemistry at the University of Virginia. His great-grandmother, Mary Berkeley Minor Blackford, had been noted as an abolitionist, but he himself was no crusader for African American rights; he simply treated his sailors as human beings.

The first real test for the USS *Mason* was her shakedown cruise in April 1944, during which both the machinery of the ship and the crew's ability to work with their new equipment were tested. Exercises, both day and night, included towing, refueling, gunnery, and dropping depth charges. The *Mason* and her crew performed well during the cruise, but the Navy's Bureau of Personnel report included more discussion of the ship's appearance than of her actual performance.

May 27, 1942: Admiral Chester W. Nimitz, Commander-in-Chief Pacific Fleet, pins the Navy Cross – the US Navy's second highest medal for valor after the Medal of Honor – on Steward's Mate Third Class "Dorie" Miller at a ceremony in Pearl Harbor, Hawaii – the scene of Miller's acts of bravery aboard the stricken battleship USS *West Virginia* during the attack of December 7, 1941. (NARA)

The USS *Mason*'s second voyage, to the United Kingdom, would also be her most difficult. As part of Convoy NY-119 the destroyer endured 30 days of near-record wind and waves, which sank three tugs, eight car floats, and five cargo barges. On October 18, 1944, when land was sighted and the month-long ordeal was almost at an end, the weather got even worse: the wind increased to 60 knots and visibility dropped to zero. Unfortunately, this proved to be more than the *Mason*'s structure could endure, and the ship's deck split – two beams in one compartment collapsed, and the seam holding the deck together broke. Nevertheless, within two hours the deck was repaired. The *Mason* then assisted 12 other ships in the convoy, before sailing to the coast of France to salvage barges until the end of that month.

Commander Blackford then recommended his crew for a unit commendation for their efforts during Convoy NY-119, but the commendation never materialized. The convoy's commander also recommended the *Mason* and her captain for decorations; again, they were never awarded. Amazingly, the *Mason*'s crew did not know about these nominations until 50 years later, when a researcher produced a book on the ship.

During their several combat cruises the crew of the USS *Mason* experienced different attitudes regarding their race in the different ports they visited. The reception they received while visiting Belfast, Northern Ireland, was the most positive; from the Ulster point of view the destroyer's crew were simply another bunch of "Yanks." While the English had often referred to them, amiably enough, as "Tan Yankees" (an un-English term they must have learned from Americans), the Northern Irish made no distinction whatever, and they were well treated during their stay. On June 12, 1945, Blackford was abruptly promoted and transferred to the Great Lakes Naval Training Station.

On June 2, 1942, William Baldwin became the first African American US Navy recruit classified for General Service – prior to this date they could only join the Navy as stewards, working in the ships' kitchens. (NARA)

The ship's next captain, Lieutenant-Commander Norman Meyer, had a very different attitude toward the men of the USS *Mason*. He wrongly believed that the majority of his crew were illiterate, and that he had inherited a ship with a poor record. Meyer, a US Naval Academy graduate, was responsible for the most embarrassing incident involving the *Mason* when he accidentally rammed the USS *Spangenburg* while pulling into a North River pier in New York City. After only three months aboard Meyer relinquished command, and the *Mason* was decommissioned a month later, in October 1945.

In 1998 the Secretary of the Navy, John H. Dalton, decided to name an Arleigh Burke-class destroyer the USS *Mason* (DDG 87), to mark the contributions of the sailors of the wartime DE 529.

PC 1264

The patrol craft PC 1264 was the second of the two US Navy vessels whose crews were composed entirely of African Americans. Though she was actually in service longer than the *Mason*, the PC 1264 – a smaller vessel, with a smaller crew (only 300 tons as opposed to the *Mason*'s 1,100, and 63 men against the destroyer's 156) – has sunk into even greater obscurity than her counterpart.

Popularly known as "subchasers," the 369 patrol craft launched during World War II were almost exclusively crewed by reservists and draftees with minimal sea experience. Their duties were wide-ranging, and included escorting convoys, hunting submarines, sinking small enemy vessels, shooting

December 21, 1944: Lieutenant (jg) Harriet Ida Pickens and Ensign Frances Wills became the first African American women to be commissioned in the US Navy's WAVES – Women Accepted for Volunteer Emergency Service. (NARA)

down aircraft, bombarding landing areas, and leading landing craft in to invasion beaches. Designed to be produced easily in small yards, the subchasers were used in all theaters of the war.

The captain of PC 1264, Lieutenant Eric Purdon, was not chosen because of any particular qualities relating to his African American crew. Rather, he seems to have been selected simply because he was available and had served on another subchaser, before briefly – for three months – commanding yet another. Purdon was given the chance to volunteer for the assignment and did so willingly; it brought him two things he wanted – a command, and a challenge. All of the other ship's officers were also volunteers. With one exception (the executive officer, who was a jazz aficionado and had black friends), none of the other officers had any particular feeling for or against African Americans. It is interesting to note that all of them were Northerners or Californians.

PC 1264 was commissioned on April 24, 1944, at the Brooklyn Navy Yard. The ship's 22 months of service proved to be largely uneventful; she spent her career patrolling the east coast of the United States and the Caribbean. The closest she came to combat was during stops in Southern ports, when the officers and crew were threatened with lynchings, for being "race-mixers" or "bothering our women," respectively.

In May 1945 a momentous event occurred on PC 1264 when a new officer reported aboard: Ensign Samuel L. Gravely Jr, who would become, in 1971, the first African American admiral in the US Navy. The ship was preparing for duty in the Pacific when the war ended on August 15, 1945. After VJ-Day many officers and sailors began to be discharged; Lieutenant Purdon turned over command of PC 1264 on October 31. By the time the ship was decommissioned on February 7, 1946, the entire ship's complement was only five officers and 28 sailors.

NAVAL CONSTRUCTION BATTALIONS

In October 1942, the US Navy created the first segregated construction battalions (CBs, better known as "Seabees"). Eventually the Navy established 17 Special and two regular construction battalions with white officers and African American sailors, and more than 14,000 black Americans served in these segregated units during World War II. Men assigned to these construction battalions received instruction in a wide variety of duties, some involving particular skills and others merely requiring physical strength. Additionally, since most of their work took place close to the frontlines, they also received small arms and other combat training.

The construction battalions performed all of the Navy's overseas construction work, including building airfields, roads, housing, defensive positions, docks, wharves, bridges, canals, and storage facilities, and also

The Naval Construction Battalions received much attention in the black press, as this report indicates:

Seabee Units Build Solomon Defenses

Solomon Islands – A battalion of colored Seabees who landed on a jungle-covered island began a few weeks of furious construction work by choosing the site of a prospective airfield, surveying and mapping it, and getting their selection approved – all between sunrise and sunset. Among other things the seabees – navy construction battalions which build a wide variety of works, and when necessary defend them against attack – built a road despite heavy rainfall and installed essential utilities.

In co-operation with a second seabee detachment, which landed shortly afterward, they got the airfield well on its way to completion before giving way to another battalion and moving on to a new job. One of the first things they did on the island was to log and mill their own lumber from native trees since the imported stock was used up quickly. Although a total of fourteen inches of rain fell during the first month, and nine inches during the second, the Seabees went ahead with the construction of a road on the island. They installed lights and telephones, provided a supply of water, and piped it as far as they could with available material. Then they built wood storage reservoirs in which to keep the water. They also installed an air raid warning system which is kept in readiness twenty-four hours a day.

– *The Afro-American*, Baltimore, Maryland (July 3, 1943)

unloaded equipment. Seabees were also frequently called upon to fight alongside ground combat troops or to protect themselves from Japanese attacks. For example, in the Palau Islands, 200 African American Seabees joined an assault against Japanese positions, and half of them became casualties during the first week of combat. The Seabees' efforts made the difference between victory and defeat during a number of Pacific island operations.

THE PORT CHICAGO DISASTER, JULY 17, 1944

As the war in the Pacific expanded, Port Chicago, California, located 35 miles north of San Francisco, became a major munitions facility for the US Navy. By 1944, expansion and improvement of the pier at Port Chicago allowed for the loading of two ships simultaneously. Most of the dangerous work, the loading and unloading of munitions, was done by African American sailors. Unfortunately, neither the sailors nor their white officers had received any special training in the loading and unloading of munitions, though they did receive some instruction in general cargo handling. The majority of their experience came from working with the munitions on a day-to-day basis. The loading of ships went on around the clock, and the different work crews developed a sense of competition regarding who could load the most in an eight-hour shift. Since this race helped to increase the speed of loading, officers encouraged what they saw as healthy rivalry.

On the evening of July 17, 1944, two merchant ships were being loaded at the Port Chicago pier, the SS *Quinault Victory* and the SS *E. A. Bryan*. The munitions being loaded were a combination of high explosive and incendiary bombs, depth charges, and ammunition – more than 4,000 tons in all. In addition, 16 railroad cars were on the pier carrying another 400 tons of munitions. There were 320 cargo handlers, crewmen, and sailors performing the stevedore duties that night.

At 10.18pm an enormous explosion ripped into the night sky; a column of smoke and flames erupted from the pier, and just six seconds later a second massive explosion followed aboard the *E. A. Bryan*. The seismic shock wave was so massive that it was felt as far away as Boulder City, Nevada. The *E. A. Bryan*, the pier, and nearby buildings completely disintegrated; the *Quinault Victory* was spun into the air, its remains crashing back into the bay 500ft from its anchorage. The 320 men on duty that night were killed instantly, while another 390 were wounded, and the blast damaged every building in Port Chicago. The air filled with splinters of glass and other debris, later found as far as 2 miles away. The blast even caused damage 48 miles away across the Bay in San Francisco. Of the 320 men killed in the explosion 202 were African Americans; the disaster at Port Chicago accounted for 15 percent of all African Americans killed in World War II.

Despite the devastation, less than a month after the worst home-front disaster of World War II, Port Chicago was again loading munitions bound for the Pacific. The repercussions of the explosion were both positive and negative. Prior to the disaster, US Coast Guard instructions on safe ship

December 1942: men of the US Navy's 34th Construction Battalion disembark from a landing craft during assault training. While Seabees were specifically tasked with construction work, they were also expected to defend themselves and their sites from Japanese attacks. (NARA)

US Navy & Coast Guard

The Navy possessed a wide variety of uniforms. The enlisted "dungarees" or working uniform consisted of dark-blue bell-bottom denim pants, a light blue cotton shirt and a white "dixie cup" sailors' cap. For wear "on deck" enlisted sailors had two different uniforms for summer and winter, but basically similar in design. Both featured a pullover "jumper" and bell-bottom trousers, in white and very dark-blue respectively. Navy officers' summer dress uniform was a white single-breasted coat with a "choker" collar, matching trousers, and a white service cap. Their winter dress uniform was a navy-blue double-breasted jacket with brass buttons, matching trousers and a blue-topped service cap, worn with a white shirt and black necktie. (1) Signalman third class, US Navy. The enlisted summer dress uniform is worn by this sailor. The white jumper has a plain matching flap collar worn with a black silk neckerchief; apart from his rating patch and the diagonal stripe indicating four years' service,

both in black-on-white, it bears no insignia. Rating badges for the Seamen's branch were worn on the right sleeve, and by all other branches on the left; service stripes appeared only on the left forearm. The jumper is worn with white, pocketless trousers of only slightly bell-bottomed cut, and the white sailor cap. (2) Storekeeper second class, US Coast Guard. The USCG wore uniforms almost identical to the USN; this is the enlisted winter blue dress uniform. For both services the blue jumper had three white trimming tapes on the cuffs and around the blue flap collar, which had a small white star in each corner. Again, the rating badge and service stripes are worn on the left sleeve, but in white and red on dark blue for the winter uniform. The trousers were more widely bell-bottomed for the blue uniform. The flat-topped cap bears the gold tally "US COAST GUARD." (3) Chief machinist's mate, US Navy. This is his rating – his job; his rank is chief petty officer (CPO), and as such he is entitled to a "square rig" dress uniform of similar cut to that of his officers. In peacetime it would take most of a 20-year Navy career to reach this rank, but this CPO has benefited from rapid wartime expansion of the service. The chief's navy-blue double-breasted jacket had two rows of four buttons (instead of an officer's two rows of three), and rating badges and service stripes were displayed on the sleeve as by junior ranks.

(Raffaele Ruggeri © Osprey Publishing)

Enlisted sailors serving on Espiritu Santo Island in the New Hebrides, placing 6in shells in magazines at the Naval Ammunition Depot; they wear working "dungarees." Left to right: Seamen First Class Dodson B. Samples, Raymond Wynn, Edward L. Clavo, and Jesse Davis. (NARA)

loading were often violated, because it was felt that they were either not safe enough or not fast enough; the officers and men on the pier experimented with new procedures which they felt were both safer and faster. After the explosion, the Navy instituted a number of changes in munitions handling procedure, and formalized training with certification was required before a loader was allowed on the docks. The munitions themselves were also redesigned to make them safer while loading.

The explosion had obviously shaken everybody working in the port. For the African Americans, working in a segregated unit under dangerous conditions, discontent soon gave way to open hostility. On August 9, 1944, less than a month after the explosion, African American survivors of the disaster were ordered to begin loading munitions at the Mare Island facility; subsequently 258 black sailors refused to continue to load munitions. Of these, 208 were given summary courts-martial and were sentenced to bad conduct discharges and the forfeit of three months' pay for disobeying orders. The remaining 50 were given general courts-martial on the charge of mutiny. Since the United States was at war, these men were eligible for the death penalty; in the event they each received sentences of between eight and 15 years at hard labor. In January 1946 all of them were given clemency and the remainder of their sentences were remitted. It was not until December 23, 1999, that President Clinton granted them a full and complete pardon.

US MARINE CORPS

The outbreak of World War II found the US Marine Corps without a single African American officer or enlisted man. In fact, the Marine Corps had never allowed African Americans to join, and was the last branch of the US military to admit them when it was ordered to do so by President Roosevelt in June 1942. Under these circumstances it should not be surprising that not a single African American Marine Corps officer was commissioned during World War II. Despite these limitations, many African American units were formed by the Corps, and saw active service in the Pacific.

Although the Marine Corps began to allow African Americans to enlist, few were interested, since the Corps was commonly known as the "white

Brooks E. Gray served in the Marine Corps with the 52nd Defense Battalion in the Marshall and Marianas Islands during World War II, and was called back to active duty during the Korean War. He later recalled:

There was much pride, mixed with bitterness, in all of us at Montford Point during World War II. Real as well as imagined injustices were with us daily in all those segregated units. But on the parade ground ... at the firing ranges ... everywhere, perhaps the most significant thing was the fierce determination to excel. We represented the break-through of the final barrier in the American military by making our mark as a part of the elite Corps ... and we achieved what we set out to do!

– Master Gunnery Sergeant Brooks E. Gray:
http://www.geocities.com/nubiansong/graybio.htm

man's service." In the first month of recruiting only 63 African Americans enlisted, and four months produced only half of the 1,200 that the Marine Corps believed they needed as a minimum cadre for the proper training of the roughly 1,000 African American troops who would enter the Corps each month as a result of the Selective Service system, beginning in January 1943.

The Commandant of the Marine Corps, Lieutenant-General Thomas Holcomb, made it clear that the Corps did not want African Americans even though it was now forced to accept them. In March 1943, Holcomb issued Letter of Instruction 421, which remained classified until after World War II. This document stated that African Americans would never be placed in a situation in which they were superior in rank to any white Marine. The Corps did not want this situation to be obvious to African Americans, so they also had a policy of removing white NCOs from African American units as soon as competent black NCOs were prepared to replace them.

Segregation in the Marine Corps began with the training of African American draftees, which took place at a newly established cantonment in the grounds of Camp Lejeune, North Carolina – Montford Point Camp. The commander of Montford Point Camp was Colonel Samuel A. Woods Jr, a

In September 1944, during the 1st Marine Division's bitterly resisted invasion of Peleliu in the Palau Islands, this group of African American Seabees acted as stretcher bearers for the 7th Marines. (NARA)

Southerner who had graduated from the Military College of South Carolina (better known as the Citadel). He accepted the idea of segregation, but his calmness and fairness nevertheless earned him the respect of his troops. Woods cultivated a paternalistic relationship with his Marines, and there was some wry affection in his nickname of "the Great White Father."

Since the Marine Corps needed competent African American NCOs, they relied upon black recruits who had previous military experience with the Army or Navy. One of the first of these was Gilbert H. "Hashmark" Johnson, who earned his nickname from wearing on his uniform sleeve three of the diagonal "hashmark" stripes indicating previous completed military enlistments. Born in 1905, Johnson joined the US Army in 1923 and served two enlistments with the 25th Infantry Regiment. Starting in 1933, he also served an enlistment as a steward in the Navy; in May 1941 he rejoined the Navy, again as a steward, before being allowed to transfer to the Marine Corps in November 1942.

Since Johnson had infantry experience ranging from company clerk to squad leader, he was ideally suited to serve in the Corps. After completing basic training he was chosen as an assistant drill instructor under a white NCO, and after his subsequent promotion he became a drill instructor. In January 1945, Gunnery Sergeant Johnson became the sergeant-major of the Montford Point Camp. He continued to serve in the USMC after World War II, retiring in 1955. Two years after his death in 1972, the Marine Corps renamed Montford Point Camp as Camp Gilbert H. Johnson.

51ST DEFENSE BATTALION

The first, and for a time the only, African American Marine Corps combat unit was 51st Defense Battalion (Composite). Defense battalions were organized to solve the problems faced by the Marine Corps in placing garrisons on the smaller overseas possessions that the Navy used as bases, and in defending the naval bases that enabled the United States to project its power toward Japan. The most famous of the wartime battalions was a detachment from the 1st Defense Battalion that fought at Wake Island.

By the end of 1942 the nature of the defense battalions' role was changing. Rather than repulsing amphibious landings, they were more likely to be defending against Japanese air strikes. In June 1943 the term "Composite" was removed from the 51st Defense Battalion, and the unit was reorganized. The battalion now contained three groups: a Seacoast Artillery Group, equipped with 155mm guns; an Antiaircraft Artillery Group, with 90mm guns; and a Special Weapons Group, equipped with machine guns, 20mm, and 40mm automatic cannon.

In January 1944, the 51st Defense Battalion began its journey to the Pacific when it moved by rail to San Diego, California; it was assigned to replace the 7th Defense Battalion, already located in the

Ellice Islands, and set sail aboard the merchantman SS *Meteor* on February 11. The 51st remained on Nanoumea and Funafuti in the Ellice Islands for roughly six months, during which it saw almost no enemy action. While in the Ellice Islands, the battalion had reorganized as an AA unit, losing its 155mm guns but adding more 90mm, and exchanging its machine guns and 20mm cannon for more 40mm weapons. On September 8, 1944, the battalion sailed for Eniwetok Atoll in the Marshall Islands, which was under sporadic surveillance and occasional harassment by Japanese aircraft. Duty on Eniwetok was routine and relatively boring, enlivened only by the occasional crash or forced landing of American planes. The battalion sailed back to America in November 1945, and disbanded at Montford Point in January 1946.

Seen here on April 17, 1945, Private First Class Luther Woodward of the US Marine Corps' 4th Ammunition Company was awarded the Bronze Star for "his bravery, initiative and battle-cunning." The award would later be upgraded to the Silver Star. (NARA)

52ND DEFENSE BATTALION

On December 15, 1943, the second African American USMC defense battalion was organized from a cadre of 400 officers and men transferred from 51st Defense Battalion before it left for the Pacific. On August 24, 1944, after more than six months of training, the 52nd moved to Camp

March 1945: three
African American
Marines pause to eat
during the battle of
Iwo Jima. Left to right:
Privates First Class Willie
J. Kanody, Elif Hill, and
John Alexander. (NARA)

Pendleton, California, and on September 21 boarded the transport USS *Winged Arrow* (AP-170). Arriving in the Marshall Islands, it took over the defense of two Marine air groups from other AA units on Majuro and Kwajalein atolls. For six months, from October 1944 to March 1945, the battalion guarded the Marine airstrips against Japanese air attack, and formed reconnaissance parties that searched the smaller islands for Japanese stragglers.

The 52nd deployed to the recaptured island of Guam on May 4, 1945, remaining there for the rest of the war. In November 1945 the 52nd relieved the 51st on Kwajalein and Eniwetok. In May 1946, after returning to Montford Point, the battalion was redesignated the 3rd Antiaircraft Artillery Battalion (Composite).

OTHER MARINE CORPS UNITS

By the spring of 1943, the Marine Corps discovered a need for stevedores to move supplies from the rear areas into combat zones. The Corps organized two kinds of units – depot companies and ammunition companies – to fill this need. Although these companies were envisioned as merely a source of labor, while the two defense battalions were seen as combat units, the reality proved quite the opposite.

US Marine Corps

The Marine full dress uniform consisted of a navy-blue, single-breasted, brass-buttoned coat with a "choker" collar, trimmed with red piping; a white belt, sky-blue trousers, and a white service cap. The winter service ("Alpha") uniform was in the Corps' distinctive forest-green: a four-pocket, open-neck coat with cloth belt, matching trousers, and service cap or garrison cap in the same color. The summer "Bravo" uniform consisted of a khaki shirt, necktie, trousers, and garrison cap. The Marine "utility" uniform was made of greenish-drab herringbone twill and was designed to be worn in combat. It was worn with "boondockers" – rough-side-out brown leather boots similar in height to the Army service shoe. (1) Gunnery Sergeant Gilbert H. Johnson; Montford Point Camp, North Carolina, spring 1945. He is depicted in his forest-green winter service uniform; the garrison cap and both upper lapels bear the blackened USMC eagle-globe-and-anchor

badge. The service coat has blackened buttons, and rank and service sleeve insignia in green-on-scarlet. His medal ribbons reflect his previous hitches in the US Army and US Navy before transferring to the Corps in 1942; below them he wears the Expert Rifleman shooting medal. (2) Sergeant, "utilities." This NCO, drilling at Montford Point, has his sleeve rank badge, and the Corps cypher and badge on the single left chest pocket, stenciled in black on his herringbone twill working and field clothing – the "utility uniform, HBT, sage green, P1941." The matching short-visored utility cap, with its gathered crown, also has the USMC badge stencil. (3) Private first class, full dress uniform. "Dress blues" were not an issue or required purchase item for Marines during wartime, but many African Americans still bought this uniform in order to demonstrate their pride in their branch of service. The buttons and the Corps badges on the service cap and collars are bright gilt, and rank insignia gold-on-red; hidden at this angle are the three-button cuff flaps, trimmed at top, rear, and bottom with red piping. The sky-blue trousers had red "blood stripes" only for NCOs and officers. The cap peak, chinstrap, and boots were polished dark-brown "Cordovan" leather. When worn with a frame-buckle Cordovan garrison belt, instead of this white dress belt with a brass plate, this was termed "undress" uniform.

(Raffaele Ruggeri © Osprey Publishing)

The defense battalions spent most of the war fighting boredom, while the depot and ammunition companies saw combat on Saipan, Tinian, Guam, Peleliu, Iwo Jima, and Okinawa, and suffered most of the African American Marine Corps casualties.

The 1st Marine Depot Company – the first of no fewer than 51 – was activated on March 8, 1943, and the 1st Marine Ammunition Company – the first of 11 – was formed on October 1 that year. In both types of company African American troops carried rifles, carbines or submachine guns, but were not equipped with any heavier weapons. On June 15, 1944, the depot companies saw their first action on Saipan when a squad fought as infantry to reinforce a thinly held line, and the majority of a company helped eliminate Japanese infiltrators. On Saipan, Private Kenneth J. Tibbs became the first African American in the Marine Corps to be killed in combat.

On September 15, 1944, the 1st Marine Division made an assault landing on the island of Peleliu, with the 11th Marine Depot Company and the 7th Marine Ammunition Company in support. The 11th Depot Company paid a price for their part in this battle, with 17 men wounded – the highest casualty rate of any African American USMC company during the war. The prolonged fighting for Okinawa involved approximately 2,000 African Americans, a larger concentration than for any previous battle. Black Marine casualties during the battle amounted to one killed and 18 wounded, one of them twice. By the end of the war 19,168 African Americans had served in the Marine Corps.

OTHER MARITIME SERVICES

US COAST GUARD

The US Coast Guard (USCG) traces its military roots to August 4, 1790, when Secretary of the Treasury Alexander Hamilton established the Revenue Cutter Service. The modern Coast Guard is a combination of five predecessors: the Revenue Cutter Service; the Lifesaving Service (created in 1878 and merged with the Revenue Cutter Service in 1915, the new service taking the name Coast Guard); the Lighthouse Service (created in 1789 and absorbed in 1939); and the Bureau of Navigation and Steamboat Inspection (itself a merger of two agencies organized in 1884 and 1838 respectively, absorbed in 1942).

While African Americans first began to serve in the Revenue Cutter Service in 1831, and First Lieutenant Michael A. Healy became the first African American to command a US government vessel (the Revenue Cutter *Chandler*) in 1877, the Coast Guard itself did not accept African Americans to serve in capacities other than stewards until March 1942. The first group of 150 black volunteers was trained at Manhattan Beach Training Station, New York City; they received instruction in seamanship, knots, lifesaving, and small-boat handling. While classes and other official activities were integrated, the sleeping and mess facilities remained segregated.

The majority of African Americans were assigned to shore duty, including security and labor details, and worked as yeomen, storekeepers, radiomen, pharmacists, coxswains, electricians, carpenters, and boatswains. Other African Americans served on horse and dog patrols on America's beaches, on the watch for enemy infiltration.

Since so many African Americans were assigned to shore duty, the USCG leadership had a legitimate manpower problem: it was nearly impossible to

Two US Coast Guard officers aboard a cutter on the North Atlantic patrol: Ensign J. J. Jenkins (left) and Lieutenant (jg) Clarence Samuels. (NARA)

rotate white Coast Guardsmen to shore duties without transferring African Americans to cutters, which would have integrated the vessels. In June 1943, Lieutenant Carlton Skinner proposed that a group of African Americans be integrated into the crew of a single cutter as an experiment. The Commandant of the USCG, Admiral Russell R. Waesche, agreed, and Skinner was promoted to lieutenant-commander and given command of the weather ship USS *Sea Cloud* (IX-99). The *Sea Cloud* had an integrated crew of 173 officers and men with four African American officers and 50 black Coast Guardsmen.

Although the experiment of integration aboard the *Sea Cloud* lasted a year, no racial incidents occurred, and the integrated crew was just as efficient as any other in the Coast Guard. As a result, the USCG began to integrate other cutters during the remainder of the war. More than 5,000 African Americans served in the Coast Guard during World War II, and about 965 rose to the ranks of petty or warrant officers. The first African American commissioned officer in the Coast Guard was Joseph Jenkins, who was commissioned as an ensign in the Coast Guard Reserve on April 14, 1943 – almost a full year before the first black Americans were commissioned in the Navy. Of necessity, therefore, the Coast Guard became the first branch of the US military to desegregate. In fact, on July 26, 1948, when President Truman ordered the integration of the US military with Executive Order 9981, the Coast Guard was already desegregated.

US MERCHANT MARINE

Merchant shipping has been an integral part of the American economy since before the founding of the United States. In fact, the impressment of American seamen by the British was the immediate cause of the War of 1812.

During World War II the United States produced approximately 2,700 merchant ships, of which 17 were named for African Americans; the first of these, the SS *Booker T. Washington*, was christened in 1942.

Hugh Mulzac became the first African American member of the merchant marine to command an integrated crew during World War II, when for five years he served as the captain of the SS *Booker T. Washington*. Born on March 26, 1886, in the British West Indies, he became a seaman in his youth; he took US citizenship in 1918, and earned his captain's rating in the merchant marine that same year, but racial prejudice prevented his commanding a ship. More than 20 years passed before he was offered command of the *Booker T. Washington*, an integrated vessel whose crew represented 18 different nationalities. During World War II this ship made 22 voyages and carried 18,000 troops to Europe and the Pacific.

The US Maritime Service, the official training organization of the Merchant Marine, had a non-discrimination policy during a time when most of the US military was still segregated. Approximately 24,000 black Americans served as merchant seamen during World War II, which amounts to roughly 10 percent of the total. African Americans served in every capacity aboard these merchant ships, regularly going into combat zones to deliver men and supplies.

February 8, 1943: the captain and some of the crew of the Liberty Ship *SS Booker T. Washington* pose for a picture just after completing their maiden voyage to England. Left to right: Second Mate C. Lastic, Midshipmen T. J. Young and E. B. Hlubik, Radio Operator C. Blackman, Chief Engineer T. A. Smith, Captain Hugh Mulzac, Chief Mate Adolphus Fokes, Lieutenant H. Kruley, Second Engineer E. P. Rutland, and Third Engineer H. E. Larson. (NARA)

CONCLUSION – INTEGRATION DURING THE COLD WAR

In the years following World War II, the struggle for integration within the armed forces gathered momentum. Secretary of the Navy James Forrestal began to experiment with integration during the last months of the war, and finally announced via Circular Letter 48-46 a policy of integration in the US Navy in February 1946. The full application of this new policy would wait for some years while traditional racial attitudes in certain quarters within the Navy vied with its practical desire for efficiency.

Meanwhile, President Harry S. Truman attempted to end military segregation via legislation. In April 1946, the Gillem Board, named after its chairman, General Alvan C. Gillem Jr, produced War Department Circular No. 124, entitled the "Utilization of Negro Manpower in the Postwar Army Policy." This document concluded that the Army should in future "eliminate, at the earliest practicable moment, any special consideration based on race." During October 1947, the President's Committee on Civil Rights issued its landmark report, *To Secure These Rights*, which condemned segregation wherever it existed and specifically criticized segregation in the armed forces. The report recommended legislation and administrative action "to end immediately all discrimination and segregation based on race, color, creed or national origin in ... all branches of the Armed Services." In the meantime, during June 1946 the AAF closed the flight training program at Tuskegee Airfield, Alabama, ending the last segregated officer training in the armed forces. Integrated aviation classes were established at Randolph Field, Texas.

By January 1948, political opposition to integration via legislation, and a need to gain the white liberal and African American votes in the forthcoming presidential election, prompted President Truman to end segregation in the

Sergeant First Class Major Cleveland points out a North Korean position to his integrated machine-gun crew while serving with the 2nd Infantry Division north of the Chongchon River during the Korean War on November 20, 1950. (USAMHI)

armed forces and the civil service via other means. On July 26 of the same year, he signed Executive Order 9981 which stated that it would be the policy of his administration to establish "equality of treatment and opportunity for all persons in the armed services without regard to race, color, religion, or national origin." Faced with continued resistance within the high command of all three branches of military service, Truman established a committee under Charles Fahy to negotiate a full integration policy. As a result, the Air Force made plans to drop many racial barriers before the end of the year, and early in 1949 the first Secretary of the Air Force, Stuart Symington, issued a directive initiating integration throughout. After further opposition, the Army finally agreed on January 16, 1950, to begin integrating all its units via Special Regulations No. 600-629-1.

On June 25, 1950 the Cold War erupted into open conflict when eight divisions of the North Korean People's Army crossed the 38th Parallel to invade the Republic of Korea. Several days later, the United Nations Security Council proclaimed the North Korean action a breach of world peace and requested member nations to assist. On June 29, President Truman authorized the Commander-in-Chief Far East, General Douglas A. MacArthur, to send US ground troops into Korea. Two days later, the first US forces, consisting of the 24th Infantry Division, arrived at Pusan and the Korean War had begun. Additional American forces initially committed to Korea included the 24th Infantry Regiment, as well as other independent black organizations such as the 159th Field Artillery and the 77th Engineer Combat Company. From the end of World War II through 1947, the 24th Infantry had occupied Okinawa, Japan, after which it relocated to Gifu, in central Japan. Under command of Colonel Horton V. White, this regiment reorganized as a permanent component of the 25th Infantry Division on February 1, 1947. The largest regiment in the US occupation force in Japan, the three battalions of the 24th Infantry fought throughout the entire Korean peninsula, from the defense of the Pusan perimeter, the breakout and pursuit of communist forces into North Korea, to the Chinese counter-offensives, and finally to UN counteroffensives that stabilized near the present day Demilitarized Zone in 1953.

On July 21, 1950, a combat team of the 3rd Battalion, 24th Infantry, under Lieutenant Colonel Samuel Pierce Jr, composed of three infantry companies and the 77th Engineer Combat Company, recaptured Yech'on. This action received national attention in the United States, and was considered the first significant successful offensive operation by the US Army in the war. Headlines in the New York *Daily News* the next day read, "Negroes Gain First Korean Victory," while CBS Radio Network news commentator H. V. Kaltenborn announced: "Hooray for the colored troops of the 24th Infantry Regiment!" Captain Charles Bussey, the African American officer commanding the engineer company involved, was awarded the Silver Star for having prevented a flanking attack by a North Korean battalion during

Crew members observe as USS *Wisconsin* (BB-64), flagship of the US Seventh Fleet, shells the North Korean coastline sometime between November 1951 and April 1952. (USAMHI)

the battle. In this same action, his platoon-size unit killed more than 250 enemy soldiers. Bussey's bravery inspired his unit and exemplified the preparedness and leadership capabilities of black soldiers. The 24th Infantry received the Republic of Korea Presidential Unit Citation for its involvement in the action at Pusan. It also had two Medal of Honor recipients. Private First Class William Thompson was killed in action on August 2, 1950, while covering the tactical withdrawal of his platoon in the face of enemy forces advancing in overwhelming strength. Sergeant Cornelius H. Charlton displayed extraordinary heroism in rallying his platoon to continue its assault on a hill near Chipo-ri, just north of the 38th parallel, on June 2, 1951. During several later actions, such as the withdrawal across the Chongchon River in November, 1950, and during the advance across the Han River in March 1951, poor leadership and lack of cooperation between white and black officers led to a less impressive performance by the 3rd and 1st Battalions respectively. Regimental morale was revived in August 1951 after the appointment of Colonel Thomas D. Gillis as the new commanding officer, and Company F conducted a valiant bayonet and grenade charge on September 15 of that year. Unfortunately, this was largely ignored by higher command and the news media on this occasion.

Other African American servicemen distinguished themselves during the air war in Korean skies. By 1950, the US Air Force had 25 black pilots in integrated fighter squadrons led by Captain Daniel "Chappie" James Jr,

An African American gunner keeps a watchful eye for "bandits," or enemy fighters, as his US Air Force B-29 Superfortress of the 98th Bomb Wing flies a combat mission over North Korea. (USAMHI)

assigned to the 36th Squadron, Fifth Air Force. James was an exceptional fighter pilot who often flew his F-86 Sabre jet on dangerous, unarmed reconnaissance missions behind enemy lines. He flew a total of 101 combat missions in Korea and earned the Distinguished Flying Cross (DFC) before being reassigned stateside. In July 1951, he became the first African American in the USAF to command an integrated fighter squadron. The first black Marine Corps pilot, Second Lieutenant Frank E. Peterson Jr, flew 64 combat missions and earned the DFC and six Air Medals in the final months of the Korean War. Ensign Jesse L. Brown, the US Navy's first African American fighter pilot to die in combat, was shot down while providing close-air support for units of the 7th Marines during the Chosin Reservoir breakout in December 1950. Brown was posthumously awarded the DFC for performing dangerous combat actions that resulted in his death. His white shipmate, Lieutenant (jg) Thomas Jerome Hudner, Jr, was also awarded the Medal of Honor for attempting to save Brown after his plane crashed.

The Korean War began to change the face of the American military. Already initiated by a high command under pressure from Washington DC, integration was accelerated during August 1950 as a growing surplus of black replacements were assigned to previously all-white US Army units. During September 1950, the 1st Marine Division also began to receive numerous African American Marines. By early 1951, 9.4 percent of all black troops in the Korean theater of war were serving in about 41 newly and unofficially integrated units. A further 9.3 percent were in integrated, but predominantly black, units. Segregation began to disappear, not so much via legislation or executive order, but as a result of strategic necessity. By demonstrating that large numbers of blacks and whites could work and live together, American servicemen did much to destroy a fundamental argument of the opponents of integration and made further civilian reforms possible.

During April 1951, General Matthew B. Ridgway, head of the United Nations Command in Korea, requested that the Army allow him to integrate all African Americans within his command. On July 26 of the same year, the Army announced that the integration of all its units in Korea, Japan, and Okinawa, would be completed within six months. By May 1952, the whole of the Eighth Army was integrated. On October 30, 1954, General George C. Marshall, the US Secretary of Defence, announced that the last racially segregated unit in the armed forces had been abolished.

BIBLIOGRAPHY

Abdul-Jabbar, Kareem, & Anthony Walton, *Brothers in Arms: The Epic Story of the 761st Tank Battalion, WWII's Forgotten Heroes* (New York; Broadway Books, 2004)

Alt, William E., & Betty L. Alt, *African-American Soldiers, European-American Wars: African-American Warriors from Antiquity to the Present* (Westport, CT; Praeger Publishers, 2002)

Army & Navy Journal (New York; 1863–1919)

Arnold, Thomas S., *Buffalo Soldiers: The 92nd Infantry Division and Reinforcements in World War II, 1942–1945* (Manhattan, KS; Sunflower University Press, 1991)

Astor, Gerald, *Right to Fight: A History of African-Americans in the Military* (Novato, CA; Presidio Press, 1998)

Berlin, Ira (ed.), *Freedom: A Documentary History of Emancipation, 1861–1867, Series II, The Black Military Experience* (Cambridge; Cambridge University Press, 1982)

Biggs, Bradley, *Triple Nickles: America's First All-African-American Paratroop Unit* (Hamden, CT; Archon Books, 1986)

Billington, Monroe Lee, *New Mexico's Buffalo Soldiers* (Niwot, CO; University Press of Colorado, 1991)

Blackford, Mansel G. (ed.), *Board the USS Mason: The World War II Diary of James A. Dunn* (Columbus, OH; Ohio State University Press, 1996)

Brandt, Nat, *Harlem at War: The African-American Experience in WWII* (Syracuse, NY; Syracuse University Press, 1996)

Buckley, Gail L., *American Patriots: The Story of African-Americans in the Military from the Revolution to Desert Storm* (New York; Random House, 2001)

Canfield, Bruce N., *US Infantry Weapons of World War II* (Lincoln, RI; Andrew Mowbray Publishers, 1994)

Carter, Allene G., & Robert L. Allen, *Honoring Sergeant Carter: Redeeming an African-American World War II Hero's Legacy* (New York; Amistad Press, 2003)

Cashin, Herschel V., *Under Fire with the Tenth US Cavalry* (New York, 1899)

Cimprich, John, *Fort Pillow, a Civil War Massacre, and Public Memory* (Baton Rouge, LA; Louisiana State University Press, 2005)

Colley, David P., *Blood for Dignity: The Story of the First Integrated Combat Unit in the US Army* (New York; St Martin's Press, 2003)

Colley, David P., *Road to Victory: The Untold Story of World War II's Red Ball Express* (Washington DC; Brassey's Inc, 2000)

Cornish, Dudley Taylor, *The Sable Arm: Black Troops in the Union Army, 1861–1865* (New York; Longmans, Green, 1956)

Dabbs, Henry E., *African-American Brass: African-American Generals and Admirals in the Armed Forces of the United States* (Charlottesville, VA; Howell Press, 1997)

Davis, Benjamin O., Jr, *Benjamin O. Davis, Jr.: American* (Washington DC; Smithsonian Institution Press, 1991)

De Clouet, Fred, *First African-American Marines: Vanguard of a Legacy* (Nashville, TN; James C. Winston Publishing Company, 1995)

Edgerton, Robert B., *Hidden Heroism: African-American Soldiers in America's Wars* (Boulder, CO; Westview Press, 2001)

Field, Ron, *Civil Rights in America, 1865–1980* (Cambridge; Cambridge University Press, 2002)

Fischer, Perry E., & Brooks E. Gray, *African-Americans and European-Americans – Together Through Hell: US Marines In World War II* (Turlock, CA; Millsmont Publishing, 1994)

Fletcher, Marvin E., *America's First African-American General: Benjamin O. Davis, Sr, 1880–1970* (Lawrence, KS; University Press of Kansas, 1989)

Francis, Charles E., *Tuskegee Airmen: The Men Who Changed a Nation* (Boston; Branden Publishing Company, 1997)

Gatewood, Willard B., Jr, *Black Americans and the White Man's Burden, 1898–1903* (Urbana, Chicago, & London; University of Illinois Press, 1975)

Gatewood, Willard B., Jr, *Smoked Yankees & the Struggle for Empire: Letters from Negro Soldiers 1898–1902* (Urbana, Chicago, & London; University of Illinois Press, 1971)

Gibran, Daniel K., *92nd Infantry Division and the Italian Campaign in World War II* (Jefferson, NC; McFarland & Company, 2001)

Glass, E. L. N. (ed.), *The History of the Tenth Cavalry, 1866–1921* (Fort Collins, CO; Old Army Press, 1972)

Goodman, Paul, *Fragment of Victory in Italy: The 92nd Infantry Division in World War II* (Nashville, TN; Battery Press, 1993)

Greene, Robert E., *Pictorial Tribute to the Tuskegee Airmen of World War II* (Fort Washington, MD; R. E. Green Publisher, 1992)

Griggs, William E., *World War II African-American Regiment That Built the Alaska Military Highway: A Photographic History* (Jackson, MS; University Press of Mississippi, 2002)

Gropman, Alan L., *Air Force Integrates, 1945–1964* (Washington DC; Office of Air Force History, 1978)

Hargrove, Hondon B., *Buffalo Soldiers in Italy: African-Americans in World War II* (Jefferson, NC; McFarland & Company, 1985)

Hawkins, Walter L., *African American Generals and Flag Officers: Biographies of Over 120 African-Americans in the United States Military* (Jefferson, NC; McFarland, 1993)

Holway, John B., *Red Tails, African-American Wings: The Men of America's African-American Air Force* (Las Cruces, NM; Yucca Tree Press, 1997)

Homan, Lynn M., & Thomas Reilly, *African-American Knights: The Story of the Tuskegee Airmen* (Gretna, LA; Pelican Publishing Company, 2001)

Homan, Lynn M., & Thomas Reilly, *Tuskegee Airmen* (Charleston, SC; Arcadia Publishing, 1998)

Jakeman, Robert J., *Divided Skies: Establishing Segregated Flight Training at Tuskegee, Alabama, 1934–1942* (Tuscaloosa, AL; University of Alabama Press, 1992)

Johnson, Jesse J., *Pictorial History of African-American Soldiers in the United States: In War and Peace (1619–1969)* (Hampton, VA: published by Alex Bielakowski, 1970)

Kelly, Mary P., *Proudly We Served: The Men of the USS Mason* (Annapolis, MD; Naval Institute Press, 1995)

Kenner, Charles L., *Buffalo Soldiers & Officers of the Ninth Cavalry 1867–1898* (Norman, OK; Black & White Together, 1999)

King, W. Nephew, *The Story of the Spanish-American War and the Revolt in the Philippines* (New York; P. F. Collier, 1900)

Knapp, George E., *Buffalo Soldiers at Fort Leavenworth in the 1930s and Early 1940s* (Fort Leavenworth, KS; Combat Studies Institute of the US Army Command & General Staff College, 1991)

Kohn, Richard H., et al, *Exclusion of African-American Soldiers from the Medal of Honor in World War II: The Study Commissioned by the United States Army to Investigate Racial Bias in the Awarding of the Nation's Highest Military Decoration* (Jefferson, NC; McFarland & Company, 1997)

Kryder, Daniel, *Divided Arsenal: Race and the American State During World War II* (New York; Cambridge University Press, 2000)

Lanning, Michael L., *African American Soldier: From Crispus Attucks to Colin Powell* (Secaucus, NJ; Carroll Publishing, 1997)

Leckie, William H., *The Buffalo Soldiers* (Norman, OK; University of Oklahoma Press, 1967)

Lee, Ulysses, *United States Army in World War II: Special Studies – Employment of African-American Troops* (Washington DC; Government Printing Office, 1966)

Lynk, Miles, *The Black Troopers, or the Daring Heroism of the Negro Soldiers in the Spanish-American War* (New York; AMC Press, 1971)

MacGregor, Morris J., Jr, *Integration of the Armed Forces, 1940–1965* (Washington DC; US Army Center for Military History, 1989)

McGee-Smith, Charlene E., *Tuskegee Airman: The Biography of Charles E. McGee – Air Force Fighter Combat Record Holder* (Boston; Branden Publishing Company, 1999)

McGovern, James R., *African-American Eagle: General Daniel "Chappie" James, Jr* (Tuscaloosa, AL; University of Alabama Press, 1985)

McGuire, Phillip (ed.), *Taps for a Jim Crow Army: Letters from African-American Soldiers in World War II* (Lexington, KY; University Press of Kentucky, 1993)

Moore, Brenda L., *To Serve My Country, To Serve My Race: The Story of the Only African American WACs Stationed Overseas During World War II* (New York; New York University Press, 1996)

Morehouse, Maggi M., *Fighting in the Jim Crow Army: African-American Men and Women Remember World War II* (Lanham, MD; Rowman & Littlefield, 2000)

Nalty, Bernard C., *Right to Fight: African-American Marines in World War II* (Washington DC; Marine Corps Historical Center, 1995)

Nalty, Bernard C., *Strength for the Fight: A History of African-American Americans in the Military* (New York; Free Press, 1986)

Nankivell, John H., *Buffalo Soldier Regiment* (Lincoln & London; University of Nebraska Press: Bison Books, 2001: reprint of 1927 edition)

National Park Service, *Port Chicago Naval Magazine* (Washington DC; Government Printing Office, 2005)

Newton, Adolph W., *Better Than Good: An African-American Sailor's War, 1943–1945* (Annapolis, MD; United States Naval Institute Press, 1999)

Nichols, Lee, *Breakthrough on the Color Front* (Colorado Springs, CO; Three Continents Press, 1993)

Osur, Alan M., *Separate and Unequal: Race Relations in the Army Air Forces During World War II* (Washington DC; Air Force History & Museums Program, 2000)

Osur, Alan M., *African-Americans in the Army Air Forces During World War II: The Problem of Race Relations* (Washington DC; Office of Air Force History, 1977)

Phelps, J. Alfred, *Chappie: America's First African-American Four-Star General – The Life and Times of Daniel James, Jr* (Novato, CA; Presidio Press, 1991)

Purdon, Eric, *African-American Company: The Story of Subchaser 1264* (Annapolis, MD; United States Naval Institute Press, 2000)

Putney, Martha S., *When the Nation Was in Need: African-Americans in the Women's Army Corps During World War II* (Lanham, MD; Scarecrow Press, 2001)

Records of the Union and Confederate Armies (Washington DC; Washington Government Printing Office, 1880–1901)

Rollins, Richard (ed.), *Black Southerners in Gray: Essays on Afro-Americans in Confederate Armies* (Rendondo Beach, CA; Rank & File, 1994)

Rutledge, Lee A., *Campaign Clothing: Field Uniforms of the Indian War Army 1866–1871* (Tustin, CA; North Cape Publications, 1998)

Rutledge, Lee A., *Campaign Clothing: Field Uniforms of the Indian War Army 1872–1886* (Tustin, CA; North Cape Publications, 1997)

Sandler, Stanley, *Segregated Skies: All-African-American Combat Squadrons of World War II* (Washington DC; Smithsonian Institute Press, 1998)

Sasser, Charles W., *Patton's Panthers: The African-American 761st Tank Battalion in World War II* (New York; Pocket Books, 2004)

Schubert, Frank N., *Voices of the Buffalo Soldiers* (Albuquerque, NM; University of New Mexico Press, 2003)

Schubert, Frank N., *On the Trail of the Buffalo Soldier: Biographies of African Americans in the US Army, 1866–1917* (Wilmington, DE; Scholarly Resources, 1995)

Scipio, L. Albert, *Last of the Black Regulars: A History of the 24th Infantry Regiment 1869–1951* (Silver Springs, MD; Roman Publications, 1983)

Scott, Emmett J., *The American Negro in the World War* (Washington DC; 1919)

Scott, Robert R. (compiler), *War of the Rebellion: A Compilation of the Official Series II, The Black Military Experience* (Cambridge; Cambridge University Press, 1982)

Shaw, Henry I., & Ralph W. Donnelly, *African-Americans in the Marine Corps* (Washington DC; History and Museums Division, Headquarters Marine Corps, 1975)

Stanton, Shelby L., *US Army Uniforms of World War II* (Mechanicsburg, PA; Stackpole Books, 1991)

Stillwell, Paul (ed.), *Golden Thirteen: Recollections of the First African-American Naval Officers* (Annapolis, MD; Naval Institute Press, 1993)

Tucker, Phillip Thomas, *Cathy Williams: From Slave to Female Buffalo Soldier* (Mechanicsburg, PA; Stackpole Books, 2002)

Warren, James C., *Freeman Field Mutiny* (San Rafael, CA; Donna Ewald Publishers, 1995)

Wright, Kai, *Soldiers of Freedom: An Illustrated History of African Americans in the Armed Forces* (New York; African-American Dog & Leventhal Publishers, 2002)

Wright, Lowry G. et. al., "Letters from African-American Soldiers during World War II," in Robert D. Marcus and David Burner (eds), *America Firsthand, Volume II: From Reconstruction to the Present* (New York, St Martin's Press, 1995) pp.220–38

INDEX

References to illustration captions are shown in **bold**. All military units and ranks are US Army unless otherwise stated.

A

Abrams Jr, Creighton W. 162
Adair, Lt Henry R. "Hank" 127, 129
Adams, Maj Charity E. **189**
"African Brigade" 9
Afro-American, The (Baltimore) 139, 166, 175, 197, 201
Agua Chiquita Canyon (1880) 16, 70
Agua Prieta (1914) 17, 123
Aguas Calientes (1916) 17, 92, 124–125, **125**
Aguinaldo, Emilio 113, 119
Ahearn, Lt George 109–110
aircraft **159**, **219**, 220
Alamo 98
Alexander, Lt John H. 27, 28
Allin, Erskine S. 86
Almond, Maj-Gen Edward M. 177
American Expeditionary Force (AEF) 134–144, **146**, **151**
Anadarko, Battle of (1874) 15, 49–51, 88
Andrews, Col George 76, 77
Andrews, C/Sgt J. E. 106, **107**
Andrews, Lt William **147**
antiaircraft artillery 173, 175
Antiaircraft Artillery Battalion (Air Warning), 477th, S-3 (Operations) **172**
Antiaircraft Balloon Battalion, 320th 186
"Apache Kid, The" 73
Apaches 28, **39**, 43, 44, 46, 59–60, 70, 71, 73
  see also Chiricahua Apaches; Lipan Apaches; Mescalero Apaches; San Carlos Apache scouts; Warm Springs Apaches
Arapaho tribe 39
Arayat, Mt (1899) 16, 115–116
Arbor, Ens Jesse Walter, USN **196**
Ardeuil (1918) 17, 140, 141
Arickaree Fork of the Republican River (1868) 14, 37, 38
Arizona 15–16, 22, **60**, 72–75; Geronimo Campaign in (1885–86) 16, 72–73
Arizona, USS **196**
Armes, Capt George A. 34–36
Armored Division, 12th 170
armored force **167**, **168**, 168–173, **171**
arms 86–88
  bayonet, M1896 **110**, **118**
  bazooka, M9A1 **178**
  carbines **43**, 86, **107**, 149, **183**; Springfield **29**, **51**, **58**, **67**, **81**, **85**, 86–87, **87**, 149
  howitzer, 155mm M1 **169**
  machine guns, World War I 150
  mortar, 81mm **179**
  pistol, M1911 Colt .45cal **127**, 149
  pre-World War I 149–150
  revolvers **58**, **67**, **81**, **83**, 87, **110**, **132**, 149
  rifle muskets **29**, **43**
  rifles **137**, **140**, **141**, 149, **182**, **183**; Krag-Jorgensen 95, **97**, **110**, **118**, **132**, 149; Springfield **20**, **29**, **58**, 87, **88**, **127**, **132**, **134**, **137**, **141**, 149

sabers **29**, **43**, **50**, **51**, **85**, **132**, **149**, 150
  sword, M1913 cavalry trooper's ("Patton") 150
  World War I 149–150
Army & Navy Journal 22–23, 26, 27, 40, 82, 94, 95, 97, 101, 105, 108, 112, 119, 130, 145, 150
Army Reorganization Act (1920) 17, 152
Arnold, Gen Henry H. "Hap" 164, 165
Arrington, Pvte George 74
Arsart, Chief 45
artillery in WWII **169**, **171**, **172**, 173, 175–176, **190**
Ash, Sgt John W. 120
Askew, Cpl Preston 120
Ayres, Capt Charles G. 106
Aztec 119

B

Back, Col William H. 119
Bacon, Capt John M. 45
Bailey, Isaac 109
Baker Jr, Sgt-Maj Edward L. 104
Baker, 1Lt Vernon J. **183**
Baker & McKinney 84
Baldwin, Lt-Col T. A. 55, 100
Baldwin, William **199**
Ballou, Maj-Gen Charles C. 133
Barnes, Ens Phillip George, USN **196**
Barnes, Ens Samuel Edward, USN **196**
Barnum, Adj 1Lt Malvern Hill 105
Bates, Lt 116
Baugh, Dalton Louis, USN **196**
Beaver Creek (1868) 14, 38–40
Beck, Lt William 85
Beecher Island, Battle of (1868) 37, 38
Beecher Island Annual… 38
Belfast, Northern Ireland 198
Bell, Pvte Dennis 109–110
Benjamin, Steward's Mate Eli **202**
Berry, C/Sgt George 106, **107**
Beyer, Capt Charles D. 64
bicycle trials **94**, 95
Big Bow, Chief 41, 46
Big Foot 79
"Big Nims" (366th Infantry, 3rd Bn) **143**
Big Red Food, Chief 48–49, 50, 51, 52
Big Sandy Creek, Colorado (1867) 14, 36
Big Tree, Chief 41
Bigelow Jr, Capt John 105
Bigstaff, Sgt Peter 129
"Billy the Kid" (William Bonney) 61, 62
Binarsville (1918) 17, 143
Black Horse 52
Black-Seminole Indian Scouts 55, 57
Blackford, Mary Berkeley Minor 197
Blackford, Lt-Cdr William M., USN 197, 198
Blackman, Radio Operator C. **215**
Blunt, Lt-Col M. M. 76
Boland, Wagoner John 106
Bonney, William ("Billy the Kid") 61, 62
Booker T. Washington, SS **215**, 215
"Boomers" 77, **79**
Booth, Maj Lionel F. 13
Bostic, Pvte B. 112

Boston, Pvte Willie 141
Bougainville, Solomon Islands 19, **177**, 177, **180**, **182**
Boyd, Capt Charles T. 127, 128
Boyer, Pvte Eli 44
Boyne, Sgt Thomas 64
Bradford, Maj William F. 13
Bradley, M/Sgt Frank **159**
Bradley, Gen Omar N. 181–182
Branch, Pvte William 50, 88
"brave conduct of Lieutenant Clark, of the Tenth (Colored) Cavalry…" **72**
Braxton, 2Lt George W. 111
brigadier-general **174**
British Expeditionary Force (BEF) 134
Brown, Sgt Benjamin 74, 75
Brown, Sgt D. T. 104
Brown, Ens Jesse L., USN 220
Brown, Col William C. 121, 122, 125
Buck, John 109
Buell, Lt-Col George P. 51–52
"buffalo soldiers" name first used 22, 36
Bulge, Battle of the (1944) 6, 19, 169, 179–180, 182
Bullis, Lt John L. 57
Bureau of Colored Troops 10, 14
Burge, Pvte Benjamin 74
Burley, Sgt Robert **65**
Burnett, Pvte Chester **155**
Burnett, Lt George 72
Bush, President George 140
Bussey, Capt Charles 218–219
Butler, Maj-Gen Benjamin 8
Butler, Pvte Charlie 141
Butler, Pvte T. C. 102
Butte de Mesnil (1918) 17, 136

C

Cailloux, Andre 12
Caldwell, Lt Vernon A. 102
Camansi (1900) 16, 117
Camp Barkeley, Texas 184
Camp Furlong, New Mexico 152
Camp Little, Arizona 131
Camp Mackall, N. Carolina 179
Camp Pendleton, California 209–210
Camp Stephen D. Little, Arizona 152
Camp Stuart, Virginia 133
"Camp Thomas", Chickamauga Park, Georgia 96, 97
Camp Wichita, Indian Territory 40
Camp Wikoff, Long Island **101**
Campbell, Capt Abbie N. **189**
"Captain Dodge's colored troopers to the rescue" **25**
captains **137**, **163**, **189**
Carney, Sgt William H. 12
Carolinas Campaign (1865) **9**
Carpenter, Capt Louis H. 36, 37, 38–39, 50, 69
Carpenter, Cpl W. S. 112
Carr, Maj Eugene 38
Carranza, Venustiano, and his forces 121, 125, 126–127, **127**, **129**
Carrizal (1916) 17, 126–130, **127**, **129**

Carrizo Canyon (1881) 16, 70, 72
Carroll, Lt-Col Henry 59, 66, 67, 108
Casey, Sgt John F. 49, 84–85
"Cathay, William" 31, 82
Cavalry, 1st 31, 78, 94, 99, 102
Cavalry, 2nd 78, 173
Cavalry, 3rd 102, 106, **107**
Cavalry, 5th 38, 63, 78
Cavalry, 6th 59–60, 66, 67, 78, 102, 105; Company M 53
Cavalry, 7th **32**, 32, 79, **81**, 124, 125; Companies G and I 33; Troops D, F, I and K 81
Cavalry, 8th 78
Cavalry, 9th: 1866–91 22–23, 24, 25, 26, **30**, 34, 42, 46–47, 48, 51–52, 54, 59, 60, **61**, 61, 64, 66–67, 70, 72, 76–77, **79**, 79, **81**, 81, 85, 87, 88; 1892–1941 18, 93, 96, 98, **101**, 102–103, 104, 106, 108, 112, 119–120, 121–122, 131, **148**, 150, 153, 154; Band **39**, **45**, 64, 98, **146**; Company A 34, 42, 46, 64–65, 66, 78; Company B 34, **62**, **63**, 64–65, 66, **110**; Company C 44–45, 59, 64, 65, 66; Company D **25**, 42, **43**, 62–64, 66, 78, 84; Company E 34, 42, 64, 66; Company F 42–45, 46, 59, 61, 66; Company G 45, 65–66, 70, 78; Company H **47**, 47, 61, 66; Company I 64, 66, 71, 72, 79; Company K 30–31, 34, 42, 44–45, 66, **67**, 68, 72; Company L 45, 46, 60, 66, 86, **89**; Company M 45, 46, 61, 66; insignia **89**, **146**; NCOs **65**, **83**; Troop C **50**, **104**; Troop D **146**; Troop E 106; Troop F 78; Troop G **155**; Troop H **89**; Troop I 78, **80**, 80; Troop K 78; Troop L **132**; Troop M 28; troopers **58**, **100**
Cavalry, 10th: 1866–91 14, 22, 24, **26**, 26, 30, 31, 34, **35**, 36, **37**, 38, 40–41, **48**, 48, 49–50, **51**, 51–52, 55, 57–58, **60**, 64, 66, 68, **69**, 69–70, **70**, **72**, 72, 73–74, 86–87, 88; 1892–1941 93, 94–95, 96, 97, 98, 99, 100, 102, 104, **107**, 107–108, 108, 112, 120, 121–122, **122**, 123, 124, 125, 126–127, **129**, 129–130, 131, 147–148, **148**, 149, 150, 153–154; 1st Squadron 98–99, 154; 2nd Squadron 99, 125, 148, 154; 3rd Squadron 154; 50th anniversary 130; Band 54, 84, 105; Company A 27, 55–56, 88–89; Company B 69; Company C 50, 69, 85; Company D 41, 52, 53, 54; Company E 50; Company F 34–36; Company G 57, 69, 86, **110**; Company H "Carpenter's Brunette's" 36–37, 38–40, 50, 69, 84–85; Company I 34, 36, 38–40, 72; Company K 34, 73; Company L 34, 50; Company M 34, **51**, 52, 53–54; insignia 36, **89**; Machine Gun Troop 124, **125**, 125, **126**, 148, 150, 154; sergeants **41**, **58**; squadrons separated 17, 153–154; Troop A 95, 99, 103, 104, 105, 109; Troop B 99, 104, 105; Troop C 99, 104, 106, **127**, 127–129, **154**; Troop D 99, 104–105, **132**; Troop E 95, 99, 104, 105, 106; Troop F 99, 104, 105, **116**, 123, **146**, **150**; Troop G 99, 104, 106, **107**; Troop H 73, 99, 109; Troop I 99, 104, 105; Troop K 95, **127**, 127–128, 129, 123; Troop M 99, 109; trooper **85**; trumpeter **29**
Cavalry, 13th 124, 125
Cavalry Brigade, 2nd 124, 125

Cavalry Brigade, 8th 124, 125, 126
Cavalry Division 96, 99, 100, 102
Cavalry Division, 1st 153
Cavalry Division, 2nd 18, 173, **174**; 3rd Brigade 153; 4th Brigade 153, 154, 161
Cavalry Division, 3rd 153
Cavalry Reconnaissance Troop, 93rd 177–178
Cedar Springs, ambush near (1889) 16, 73–75
Central Plains Campaign (1867–73) 14, 32–41
Chambers, Sgt William **115**
chaplains 24, **190**, **192**
Charleston Harbor, Battery Wagner, attack on (1863) 6, 12, 14
Charlton, Sgt Cornelius H. 219
Chemical Decontamination Company, 1st 18, 155
Cheyenne tribe 22, **32**, 32, 33, 34–36, 37, 39, 52–53
Cheyenne Agency (1875) 15, 52–54
Chickamauga, Georgia 96, 97
China-Burma-India theater **185**, 185, **188**
Chiricahua Apaches 59, 72
Christy, Sgt William 35
Cimarron 60
City of Washington 98
Civil War, American (1861–65) **6**, 6, 8–13, **9**, 9, 14
Clark Jr, Steward's Mate Harold **202**
Clark, Sgt John C. 182
Clark, Pvte Lig J. 117
Clarke, Lt Powhattan **72**, 73, 130
Clavo, Seaman 1st Class Edward L. **205**
Cleveland, Sgt 1st Class Major **217**
Clinton, President Bill 28, 205
Clous, Capt J. W. 48
Coast Artillery Group, 152nd **190**
Colfax County War, New Mexico (1876–78) 15, 60–61
Collins, PFC Florence A. **192**
Colorado 15–16, 62–64; Ute Campaign (1879) 15, 62–64
Colored Citizen, The 114
Columbus, New Mexico 124
Comancheros 14, 41, 48
Comanches 22, 36, 48, 41, 49–51, **51**, 52 *see also* Kwahada Comanches 55
Concho 98
Confederate forces, African-Americans in 13, 14
Congress, Act of (1866) 14, 22, 24
Conn, Cpl John R. 104
Connecticut, regiments raised in 8, 10
Connecticut Infantry, 29th 10
Connecticut Militia, Signal Corps bicycle unit 95
"contrabands" 8
Convoy NY-119: 198
Cooney, James C. 68
Cooney, Capt Michael 47, 68
Cooper, Capt Charles L. 73
Cooper, Ens George Clinton, USN **196**
Cooper, Trumpeter James H. 106
Copeland, Steward's Mate Jonell **202**
Cordin, Pvte C.W. 115–116
Cork, Pvte Adam 50
Corps, V 96
Corps d'Afrique 9
Coxey, Jacob Sechler, and "Coxey's Army" 93–94
Coxey's Rebellion (1894) 16, 93–94

Cranshaw, Sgt Tennie 115
Cree Indians 94
Creek, Pvte Charles 79
Creelman, James **99**, 102
Croix de Guerre **92**, 92, **136**, 138, 139, 141, 142, 143, **144**, 144, **146**, **170**, 187
Crump, Pvte Jeremiah 65
Cuba, invasion of (1898) 6, 96–112, **99**, **100**, **104**, **105**, **107**; casualties and recognition 108–109 *see also* Spanish-American War
Curtis, Richard 109
Cusack, Lt Patrick 44–45, 78
Custer, Lt Bethel M. 47–48
Custer, Libby 33

D

Daggett, Lt-Col Aaron S. 101
Dakota Territory (1880–91) 16, 22, 76–81
Dalton, John H. 199
Dart, 1Lt Clarence A. **162**
Davidson, Lt-Col John W. "Black Jack" 41, 49, 50, 52
Davis Jr, Lt-Col Benjamin O. **161**, 162–163, **163**, 165, 166, 167
Davis Sr, Brig-Gen Benjamin O. 18, **150**, 153, 160–161, 163, **174**
Davis, Seaman 1st Class Jesse **205**
Davis, Sgt S. 34
Davis, Pvte William J. 106
Day, 2Lt Matthias W. 65
decorations 108–109, 168, 187 *see also* Croix de Guerre; Distinguished Flying Cross ; Distinguished Service Cross/Medal; Légion d'Honneur; Medal of Honor, Congressional; Navy Cross; Silver Star
Delaney, Maj Martin R. 10
Denison, Col Franklin A. 138
Denny, Sgt John **62**, 65
Denver, Colorado 64
Dimmick, Capt Eugene D. 106
discrimination, 1866–91 29–31
Distinguished Flying Cross 220
Distinguished Service Cross **92**, 92, 138, 139, 141, 142, 143, **183**
Distinguished Service Medal 104–105
Dockery, Steward's Mate James E. **202**
Dodd, Col George A. 124, 125
Dodge, Capt Francis **25**, **43**, 62, 63–64
Double Lakes 56, 57
Douglass, Frederick, sons of 12
Drake, Pvte Alonzo 70
Drexel Mission (1890) 16, 79, **81**, 81
Driscoll, George 109
DuBois, Dr W. E. B. 133
Ducat, Capt Arthur C. 106
Dudley, Lt-Col N. A. M. 61, 62, 64, 66
Duffield, Gen H. 100
Dumas, Maj Francis E. 10
Duvall, Robert L. 109

E

E. A. Bryan, SS 202–203
Eagelson, 1Lt Wilson D. **162**
Eagle Heart, Chief 41
Eagle Springs (1867) 14, 42–44
Eisenhower, Gen Dwight D. 180, 181, 189

"Ejecting an Oklahoma Boomer" **79**
El Caney (1898) 16, 100–102
El Viso fort **99**
Elk Creek, skirmish at (1874) **51**, 51–52
Ellice Islands 209
Emancipation Proclamation (1863) 6, 8, 14
Emmet, 2Lt Robert T. 65–66
Engineer Battalion, 317th 176
Engineer Battalion, 318th 177
Engineer Combat Company, 77th 218–219
Engineers, Corps of **193**
Eniwetok Atoll, Marshall Islands 209
enlistment, 1866–91 25–26
ensigns **196**, **200**, **214**
equipment 88–89, **89**; pre-World War I **146**,
    151; saddles **51**, **81**, 88, **110**, **122**, **125**;
    USAAF **163**; World War I **137**, **141**, **143**;
    World War II infantry **183**; *see also* uniform
Evans, Lt George 57
Ewers, Lt-Col E. P. 102
Executive Order 8802 18, 159
Executive Order 9981 19, 182, 214, 217

F

Fanita 109, 111
Far East Command 19
Faustino, Papa 120
Field Artillery **171**
Field Artillery, 159th 218
Field Artillery Battalion, 333rd **169**
Field Artillery Battalions, 593rd through 596th
    177
Field Artillery Battalions, 597th through 600th
    176
Filipino insurgents 113, 115, 116–117, 118, 119
Filipino nationalist forces 92
Fitz Gerald, Dr. J. A. 30
Fletcher, Sgt Nathan **65**
Flipper, 2Lt Henry O. 27–28, **28**
Florida 99, 109, 110–111
Florida Mountains (1877) 15, 59–60
Fokes, Chief Mate Adolphus **215**
"Forgotten Heroes" **104**
Forrest, Gen Nathan Bedford 13
Forrestal, James 216
Forsyth, Maj George A. 36–37, 38
Forsyth, Lt-Col James W. 79, **81**, 81
Forsyth's Scouts, rescue of (1868) 36–38
Fort Assinniboine, Montana 93, 95
Fort Bayard, New Mexico 33, 59, 66, **88**, 93
Fort Benning, Georgia 152, 179
Fort Bragg, N. Carolina 179
Fort Buford, North Dakota 93
Fort Clark, Texas 46
Fort Concho, Texas 31, 54, 55, 57
Fort Cummings, New Mexico 31
Fort Custer, Montana 31
Fort Davis, Texas 28, 34, 45, 77
Fort Des Moines, Iowa 17, 133
Fort Dodge, Kansas 86
Fort Douglas, Utah 93, 112
Fort Ethan Allen, Vermont 121
Fort Gibson, Indian Territory 36, 41
Fort Huachuca, Arizona 121, 130, 131,
    152–153, 177
Fort Keogh, Montana **75**, 93, 95
Fort Knox, Tennessee 155
Fort Leavenworth, Kansas 24, 26, 29–30, 154

Fort Lincoln, Washington DC **9**
Fort Logan, Colorado 112
Fort McClellan, Alabama 176
Fort McKinney, Wyoming **61**
Fort Missoula, Montana **90**, 93
Fort Pillow, Tennessee, massacre at (1864) 13, 14
Fort Riley, Kansas 30, 34, 153, 154
Fort Robinson, Nebraska 78, 93, 150
Fort Selden, New Mexico 33, 59
Fort Sill, Oklahoma 27–28, **37**, 40, 49
Fort Snelling, Minnesota **78**
Fort Stanton, New Mexico 61
Fort Verde, Arizona **70**
Fort Wallace, Kansas **32**, 30, 38
Frank Leslie's Illustrated Newspaper 6
Frapelle (1918) 17, 143
Freeland, Pvte Alfred 65
Freemont, L/Cpl 57
French Army 134, 135; Army, Fourth 135;
    Division, 16th 136; Division, 36th 138;
    Division, 37th 143; Division, 59th 138;
    Division, 157th "Red Hand" 140–143,
    146; Division, 161st 138; Infantry, 232nd
    138; Infantry, 325th 138
Frohock, Capt William 44
Funston, Maj-Gen Frederick 124

G

G-3 (Operations) 165–166
Galveston Daily News 57
Gant, Steward's Mate Que **202**
Gardner, Alexander **33**
Garrard, Capt 78
Garretson, Brig-Gen Henry 111, 112
garrison life: 1873–80 **29**; 1882–91 **85**;
    1902–14 **132**
Gazette, The (Cleveland, Ohio) 98
Garrison, Lindley M. 122
General Orders 25, **41**, 84, **85**, 142
General Service Engineer Regiment, 41st 155
Geronimo, Chief 59, **70**, 72, 73
Geronimo Campaign in Arizona and Mexico
    (1885–86) 16, 72–73
Gibbon, W. F. 74
Gibbs, PFC Zacariah **186**
Gibson, Sgt E. D. **41**
Gillem Board 216
Gillis, Col Thomas D. 219
Gilmer, Lt 119
Gilmore, Cpl 57
Glackens, William **99**
Glass, Maj E. L. N. 121, 122
Gomez, Gen Felix 130
Gomez, Gen Maximo 99, 111
Goode, Pvte Benjamin H. 117
Goodwin, Ens Reginald Ernest, USN **196**
Goybet, Gen 142
Graham, Capt George Washington 36, 39
Graham, Sgt John 106–107, 108
Grassa, Roberto 119
Gravely Jr, Adm Samuel L., USN **200**
Graves, John Temple 129
Gray, Master Gunnery Sgt Brooks E. **206**
Gray, Pvte Conny 102
Great War see World War I
Greaves, Cpl Clinton 59, 60
Green, Com Sgt D. P. **115**

Green, Chaplain William T. **192**
Greenville, Louisiana 33, 82
Grierson, Col Benjamin H. 24, 29–30, 31,
    36, 41, 66, 68–69
Griffin, Lt Seth 42
Griffith, Sgt Thomas 106
Guadalcanal 19, 177
Guilfoyle, Col John Francis 121

H

Hamilton, Alexander 213
Hamilton, Col John M. 102–103, 108
Hams, Pvte Thornton 74
Hancock, Gen Winfield Scott 32
Hare, Ens James Edward, USN **196**
Harper's Weekly **11**, **72**, **79**, **104**, 106, **148**
Harris, 1st Sgt Morris O. **168**
Harris, Farrier Sherman 105–106
Harrison, Pvte Julius 74
Hatch, Col Edward 24, **30**, 48, 61, **65**, 66, 68, 70
Hawkins, Gen 102
Hayman, Cpl Perry 53–54
Haynes, T/Sgt Charles **159**
Hayward, Col William 139
Hazen, Col William B. 24
Healy, 1st Lt Michael A., USCG 213
Helena 110–111
Hembrillo Canyon (1880) 15, **65**, 66–67
Henry, Brig-Gen Guy V. 79, **81**, 81, 95, 111
Heyden, Lt J. L. 79
Heyl, Capt Edward 42, 46
Hill, Gen Benjamin 122
Hill 188, Champagne Marne Sector (1918)
    17, 140–141
Hindenburg Line 138–139
Hlubik, Midshipman E. B. **215**
Hoag, Pvte Jonathan **170**
Hodge, Capt W. G. 82
Hoffman, Gen Roy 133
Hoffmann, Col William 29–30
Holcomb, Lt-Gen Thomas 207
Holliday, Presly 109
Holmes, Pvte Burton 141
Hooker, Capt Ambrose 66
Horse Head Hills (1868) 14, 45
Houston, 1st Sgt Adam 107–108
Houston, Cpl H. C. 128
Howard University 133
Howard's Well (1872) 15, 46–47, **47**
Hudner Jr, Lt(jg) Thomas Jerome 220
Hughes, Tech 5 Sherman **186**
Humfreville, Capt J. Lee 30–31
Hunter, Lt Alexander 13
Hunter, Maj-Gen David 8

I

Iba (1900) 16, 118
Illinois, 6th 111
Illinois Record 103
"Immune Regiments" 96
Indian Territory 22, 36, 48–51
    see also Oklahoma Territory
Indianapolis, USS 196
Infantry, 2nd 102
Infantry, 4th 62–63, 98
Infantry, 5th 30

Infantry, 6th 102, 125, 126

Infantry, 8th 78

Infantry, 9th & 10th 102

Infantry, 11th 52

Infantry, 12th **99**, 101, 102

Infantry, 13th 102

Infantry, 15th 66

Infantry, 16th 31, 66, 102

Infantry, 21st 102

Infantry, 24th 162, 217, 218; 1866–91 25, 26, **29**, 55, 57–58, 73–74, **74**, 77, 84, 89; 1892–1941 93, 94, 96, **97**, 98, 102, 106, 108, 112, 115, 119, 120, 124, 131, 149, 152; 1st & 2nd Battalions 152; 3rd Battalion 152, 218–219; Company B **53**; Company E 26, 48; Company F **88**, 219; Company G **110**, **132**; Company H 69, 104, 117; Company I 48; Company K **43**; corporals **20**, **85**; insignia **89**; prepares for overseas deployment 18, 178; resurrected 17, 152; sergeants **53**, **84**, **132**

Infantry, 25th **177**, 177, **180**; 1866–91 25, 26, 31, 48, 55, 57–58, **58**, **75**, 76, 77, 84, 88, 89; 1892–1941 93, 94, 96, 97, 98, **99**, 100, 101, 102, **105**, 112, **113**, 115, 116, 120, 131, 149, 152–153; bandsman **85**; bicycle company **94**, 95; on Bougainville 19, **177**, 177, **180**, **182**; Company A 76; Company B 76, **78**, 115–116, 117; Company C 76; Company D 76, 101; Company E 76, 101, 116, **182**; Company F 76, 93, **118**, 118; Company G 76, **90**, 93, 101; Company H 76, 93, 101, **118**; Company I 49, 50, 51, 76, **118**; Company K 76, 116–117; Company M 117, **118**; enlisted man **29**; Provisional Battalion 152; sergeants **115**; shoulder knots **89**

Infantry, 38th 22, 24–25, 30, 32, **33**, 33, 34, 47–48, 82; Company A 31; Company K **32**, 32–33

Infantry, 39th 22, 25, 33, 82

Infantry, 40th & 41st 22, 25, 33

Infantry, 56th 144

Infantry, 365th 133, 176

Infantry, 366th 18, 133, 155; 3rd Battalion **143**

Infantry, 367th 133; 1st Battalion 144; Company C **137**

Infantry, 368th 133, 143, 177

Infantry, 369th "Harlem Hell Fighters" 133, 136–138, 139, **140**, **141**, **144**, **153**, 177; Company B **137**; Company C **136**; Company L **92**; flag **146**; see also US Army National Guard: New York, 15th

Infantry, 370th "Black Devils" 133, **137**, 138–139, **146**, 176, **183**; Company F 138; Company H **146**

Infantry, 371st 134, 140–143, **146**, **151**, 176; Company B 141–142; Company C 140

Infantry, 372nd 133–134, 140, 142–143, **146**

Infantry Brigades, 185th and 186th 134

Infantry Division, 1st 100; 1st & 3rd Brigades 102

Infantry Division, 2nd 96, 99, 100, **217**

Infantry Division, 24th 217

Infantry Division, 92nd "The Buffaloes" 17, 92, 133, 143, 144, **170**, 173, **176**, **178**, **183**; formation of (all-black) 17, 133; insignia **146**; Military Police sergeant **193**; mortar platoon **179**; reactivated 18, 176–177

Infantry Division, 93rd 92, 133, 134, 135, 153, 173; deploys to Guadalcanal 19, 177; insignia **146**; reactivated 18, 177–178

insignia **89**; buttons **10**, **23**, **63**; cap **29**, **45**, **53**, **58**, **89**, **110**, **132**, **146**; Cavalry, 10th, regimental crest 36; collar **132**, **146**; flags **89**, **146**; guidon, 1885-pattern **89**; hat, 8th Army Corps **118**; helmet plates **89**; pre-World War I **146**, **147**, 147; sharpshooter's cross, post 1885-pattern **50**; shoulder **89**, **146**; skirmisher's medallion **50**; swordsmanship device **50**; US Navy **204**; US Marine Corps **211**; World War I **137**, **146**, **147**, 147; World War II **171**, **174**, **183**

integration in armed forces begins 19, 216–217

Isa-tai (medicine man) 48–49

Island Mound, Missouri, action at (1862) 6, 8, 11, 14

Italian campaign, WWII **176**, 176, **178**, **179**, **183**

J

Jackson, 2Lt Elisha 108

Jackson, M/Sgt Walter C. **176**

Jackson, 1Lt William H. 111

James Jr, Capt Daniel "Chappie", USAF 219–220

Jefferson Barracks, Missouri 24–25, 30

Jenkins, Ens Joseph. J., USCG **214**, 214

Jenkins, Sgt Matthew 138

Jennis, Capt George 35

Johnson, Lt Carter P. 99, 109, 110

Johnson, Gunnery Sgt Gilbert H. "Hashmark" **191**, 208, **211**

Johnson, Sgt Henry **63**, **136**

Johnson, Cpl John H. 117

Johnson, Col W.T. 133

Johnson, Cpl William A. **192**

Jones, Sgt David D. **176**

Jones, Pvte Elise 106

Jones, Sgt Eugene W. 175

Jones, Pvte T. C. 102

Jordan, Sgt George **67**, 68

Juh, Chief 59

Juin, Gen Alphonse **170**

K

Kaltenborg, H.V. 218

Kansas 22, **32**, 32–33, **33**, 34

Kansas Colored Infantry, 1st 8, 11

Kansas Volunteer Cavalry, 18th 35–36

Kettle Hill (1898) 16, 92, 101, 102, **104**, 104, 106, **107**, 108

Keyes, Capt A. S. B. 53

Kickapoo Springs (1870) 14, 46

Kickapoo tribe 42, 44, 57–58

Kiowa tribe 14, 36, 40–41, 46–47, 49, 50–51

Knox, Frank 108

Korean War (1950–53) 6, 19, **217**, 217–220, **218**, **219**

Kruley, Lt H. **215**

Kwahada Comanches 55

L

Labor Supervision Company, 1696th **192**

Lakota tribe 37

Lane, Senator James H. 8

Larson, 3rd Engineer H. E. **215**

Las Animas Canyon (1879) 15, **62**, 64–66

Las Guásimas (1898) 16, 99–100

Lastic, 2nd Mate C. **215**

Lawson, Capt Gaines 49, 50, 51

Lawton, Brig-Gen Henry W. 99

Lear, W/O Charles Byrd, USN **196**

Lebo, Capt Thomas C. 73

Lee, Pvte Fitz 109–110

Lee, Capt P. L. 57

Lee, Gen Robert E. 13

Légion d'Honneur 142

Leona 98

Leonhauser, Capt Harry A. 116, 117

Leslie's Illustrated Newspaper 111

Lewis, Pvte Hamilton 74

Lewis, Cpl John E. 105

lieutenants **47**, **140**, **147**, 162, 164; first **150**, 183; junior grade **200**, **214**; second **28**

Lightfoot, Sgt James R. 117

Lincoln (1878) 15, 61–62

Lincoln, President Abraham, and his Administration 6, 8, 12–13

Lincoln County War, New Mexico (1877–78) 15, 61–62

Lipan Apaches 44, 45, 57–58

Liscome Bay, USS 196

Liscum, Lt-Col E. H. 108

Little, Capt 50

Little Bear, Chief 94

Little Rock, Arkansas, muster in **11**

Little Wound, Chief **81**, 81

Livermore, Lt Richard L. 105

Llano River, South Fork (1869) 46

Lone Wolf, Chief 49, 50

Loud, Capt John S. 46–47, 81; wife of 46–47

Louisiana, regiments raised in 9, 10

Louisiana Heavy Artillery (African Descent), 1st 8

Louisiana Infantries (African Descent), 6th and 7th 10

Louisiana Native Guard, 1st **6**, 8, 11–12

Louisiana Native Guard, 2nd (later 74th USCT) 8, 10

Louisiana Native Guard, 3rd **6**, 8, 12

Luzon, campaigning in 115–119

Lyon, Lt Henry G. 106

M

MacArthur, Gen Arthur 114

MacArthur, Gen Douglas A. 217

McBryar, J. William 123

McClellan, Capt Curwen B. 66, 67

McClellan Creek (1874) 15, 52

McClures Magazine **99**

McCown, 2Lt Peter 108

McCoy, Lt Frank R. 105

Mackenzie, Col Ranald S. 25, 45, 48, 52

McKinley, President William 96

McMurdo, Dr Charles D. 147–148

McSween, Alexander 61, 62

Mack, Sgt Lewis 50

Maine, USS 96

Maison-en-Champagne (1918) 17, **141**

majors **171**, **189**

Manacling (1900) 16, 119

Mangus 73

Manila 113–114, 115
Mare Island 205
Marshall, Lt Andrew D. **164**
Marshall, Gen George C. 165, 167, 181, 182, 220
Marshall Islands 210
Martin, Lt A. C. 117
Martin, Ens Graham Edward, USN **196**
Mason, USS (DDG 87) 199
Mason, USS (DE 529) 19, 197–199
Massachusetts, regiments raised in 8, 10
Massachusetts Cavalry, 5th 10
Massachusetts Infantry, 54th 10, 12
Massachusetts Infantry, 55th 10
Massachusetts Volunteer Infantry, 6th 111, 112; Companies L & M 111–112
Massachusetts Volunteers, 2nd 98
Maxwell Land Grant & Railway Company 60
Mays, Cpl Isaiah **74**, 74–75
Maytorena, Gen 122
Meade, Marshall W. K. 75
Medal of Honor, Congressional 22, 123; 1866–91 37, 46, 48, 60, **62**, 63, 64, 65, 68, 70, 71, 72, 73, 75, 79, 80; 1898 104, 106–107, 111; in Civil War 10–11, 12; first awards 12, 46; in Korea 219, 220; World War I 137–138, 140; World War II **183**
Medical Battalion, 317th 176
Medical Battalion, 318th 177
Medical Officer **147**
Medical Training Battalion, 66th, Company A 184
Medicine Lodge Creek **35**
Merritt, Col Wesley 63–64
Mescalero Apaches 45
Meteor, SS 209
Mexican 2nd Cavalry Regiment 128
Mexicans 44, 46
Mexico 22
    border operations 17, 92, 121–130, 152; Punitive Expedition (1916) 17, **122**, 124–130, **127**, 147–148, 150 expeditions into (1876–77) 57–58 Geronimo Campaign in (1885–86) 16, 72–73
Meyer, Lt-Cdr Norman, USN 199
Miami 98
Miles, Gen Nelson A. 25, 52, 95, 111, 112
Military Police **193**
Milk Creek Canyon (1879) 15, **25**, 62–64
Milk River 84
Miller, Steward's Mate Doris "Dorie" 195–197, **198**
Miller, Sgt Richard 120
Miller, USS 196
Mississippi, regiments raised in 9, 10
Mitchell, Lt 119
Mizner, Brig-Gen J. K. 95
Mont des Singes ("Monkey Mountain") 138
Montana & Pacific Railroad 93–94
Montford Point Camp, N. Carolina, USMC **191**, 207–208
Monthois (1918) 17, 142
Moore, Capt France 60
Morey, Capt Lewis S. 127, 129
Moro warriors 92, 149
Moros people 120
Morris Island, Charleston Harbor, capture of (1863) 12

Morrow, Sgt-Maj A. A. **115**
Morrow, Maj Albert P. 66, 67
Moss, Col James A. **94**, 95, 101, 144
Mow-way, Chief 48
Mower, Col Joseph A. 25
Muller, Lt José 101
Mulzac, Capt Hugh **215**, 215
Munez, Gen 99, 109
Murphy, Tech 5 Hudson **186**
Murphy-Dolan faction 61
musicians 39, **45**, 54, **78**, 84, **85**, 105, **146**

N

Naco (1914–15) 17, 121–124
Naile (wagon-master) 44
Nana 71, 72
Nashville, Tennessee 98
Navajo scouts 59, 60, 64
Naval Ammunition Depot **205**
Navy Cross 196, 197, **198**, **202**
NCOs, 9th Cavalry **65**
Neill, Lt-Col Thomas H. 53
Nelson II, Ens Dennis D., USN **196**
New Mexico 15–16, 22, 33, 59–68, 70–72; Colfax County War (1876–78) 15, 60–61; Lincoln County War (1877–78) 15, 61–62; Victorio Campaign (1879–81) 15–16, 64–72, **65**
New York City, Union League Club 153
Nimitz, Adm Chester W. **198**
Nolan, Capt Nicholas 27, 55–56, 57, 69–70; "lost patrol" (1877) 15, 55–57
Norman, Pvte Willie 123
Normandy 19, 186, 187
North Carolina Colored Volunteers, 1st 9
Norvell, Maj S. T. 53, 54, 99, 104

O

O'Donnell (1899) 16, 116–117
officers, African American, first appointment of 10
officers, black, 1866–91 27–28
officers, black, begin training at Fort Des Moines 17, 133
officers, white, 1866–91 26
Ojo Caliente 64
Okinawa, battle for (1945) 19, 212
Oklahoma Territory 77
    see also Indian Territory
Old Fort Lancaster (1867) 14, 44–45
Old Fort Tularosa (1880) 15, **67**, 67–68
Olsbrook, 2Lt William N. **162**
O'Neil, Capt Joseph P. **118**, 118
Operation *Galvanic* 196
Ord, Gen E. O. C. 57
Ordnance Ammunition Company, 57th 186–187
organization, 1866–91 24–31
Otis, Maj-Gen Ewell S. ("Colonel Blimp") 114

P

Pacific Theater, WWII **177**, 177–178, **180**, 185, 186, 196, 201, 202, **205**, **207**, 209, 210, 212
"Packing up in a Hurry" **105**

Palmer, Lt George 89
Parachute Infantry Battalion, 555th 18, 179, **181**, **183**
Paris, Treaty of (1898) 113
Parker, Lt John H. 106–107, 108
patrol craft (PC) 1264 199–200
Patton, George S. 150
Payne, Capt J. Scott 62
Peace Commission (1869) 40–41
Pearl Harbor (1941) 195–197, **198**
Pecos River, scouting near **43**
Pecos River, Texas (1869) 45–46
Pegram, Maj James W. 13
Peleliu, Palau Islands 19, **207**, 212
Pendergrass, Sgt J. C. 103
Peninah 76
Pennsylvania 113
Peoria 99, 109, 110–111
Peppin, Sheriff George 61, 62
Peronne, France 186–187
Perry, Pvte Howard P., USMC **208**
Pershing, Brig-Gen John J. "Black Jack" 94, 124, 125, 126, 127, 130, 134, 135
Peterson, Cpl Arthur E. 114
Peterson Jr, 2Lt Frank E., USMC 220
Philippine Insurrection (1899–1902) 16–17, 92, **113**, 113–120, **115**, **116**, **118**, 146–147
Philippines, Stotsenberg Camp, Luzon 131
Phillips, Capt Albert E. 124, 150
Phoebe, USS 197
Phoenix, Sgt John W. **176**
Pickens, Lt(jg) Harriet Ida, USN **200**
Pierce Jr, Lt-Col Samuel 218
Pine Ridge Agency 78, 79, 80, **83**
Pinkston, Pvte Alfred **51**
Pipton, Samuel **50**
Pocahontas, USS 134
Pond Creek 37
Pope, Pvte Malachi G. 30
Port Chicago, California, disaster (1944) 202–203, 205
Port Hudson, Louisiana, Siege of (1863) **6**, 6, 12, 14
Port Tampa, Florida 98, 99
Postal Directory Battalion, 6888th, WAC **189**, **192**, **193**
Prairie Dog Creek (1867) 14, 35–36
Pratt, Lt Richard H. 41
Prioleau, Chaplain George W. 98
privates **110**, **132**, **136**, **155**, **156**, **183**, **208**; first class **137**, **183**, **186**, **192**, **209**, **211**
Progress 27
Puerto Rico, 6th Massachusetts, Company L in 111–112
Pulajanes 120
Purdon, Lt Eric, USN 200
Pusan, Korea 6
Pyro, USS 195

Q

Quakers (Society of Friends) 40
Quartermaster Company, 92nd **190**
Quartermaster Regiments, 47th and 48th 17, 155
Quartermaster Truck Company, 666th **186**
Quillet, Col 142
Quinault Victory, SS 202–203

R

Rafferty, Capt William 53
Rankin, J. P. 62
Ransom, Fletcher R. **104**
Rattlesnake Canyon (1880) 16, 68–70
Reagan, Ens John Walter, USN **196**
"Red Ball Express" **186**, 187
Red Cross clubs, American 194
Red River, North Fork (1872) 15, 47–48
Red River War (1874–75) 15, 48–52
Remington, Frederic **25**, **26**, **32**, **48**, **60**, **69**
Republican River, Arickaree Fork (1868) 14, 37, 38
Reynolds, Pvte William A. **187**
Rhode Island, permission to raise regiments in 8
Rice, Col Frank 112
Richardson, Sgt Curtis A. **176**
Richmond–Petersburg Campaign (1864) **9**
Ridgway, Gen Matthew B. 220
Rio Grande River 33
Robb, 1Lt George S. 136–138
Roberts, Brevet Capt Charles H. 82
Roberts, Pvte Needham **136**
Roberts, Lt T. A. 106
Robinson, Pvte Berry 61
Robinson, 2Lt Jack Roosevelt **174**
Robinson, Sgt James 70
Rodney, Capt George B. 126
Rodocker, D. **62**, **63**
Rogers, Lt H. A. **147**
Roman Nose, Chief 33, 35
Roosevelt, President Franklin D. 159, 206
Roosevelt, Lt-Col Theodore "Teddy" **6**, 92, 99, 103
Rosebud Agency 78
"Rough Riders" (1st US Volunteer Cavalry) **6**, 92, 99, 102, 103, 104, 106, 108
Royall, Maj William B. 38, 39
Rucker, M/O Lt J. N. **147**
Rudisal, S/Sgt Columbus **155**
Rutland, 2nd Engineer E. P. **215**

S

Saline River (1867) 14, 34–35
Samples, Seaman 1st class Dodson B. **205**
Samuels, Lt(jg) Clarence, USCG **214**
San Angelo, Texas **26**, 31
San Carlos Apache scouts 66
San Elizario (1877) 15, 61
San Juan Heights (1898) **6**, 16, 100, **101**, 101, 102–108, **104**, **107**, 112
San Pedro Springs protest (1867) 42
Sanborn, Capt W. T. 93
Sanders, Capt Chester 138–139
Santa Cruz de Villegas (1916) 17, 125–126
Santa Fe Railroad 94
Sante Fe Plaza, New Mexico **39**
Santiago de Cuba 99, 100, **104**
Saragossa, Mexico 57–58
Satank, Chief 41
Satanta, Chief 35
Satchell, James **50**
Schenck, Lt William T. 117
Schofield, Maj George W. **51**, 87
Schofield, Gen John W. 87

Scott, Cpl Edward **72**, 73
Scott, T/Sgt Gordon A. **176**
Sea Cloud, USS 214
seamen first class, US Navy **205**
Sechault (1918) 17, 142
Second Confiscation and Militia Act (1862) 8, 14
Selective Service Act (1917) 17, 131
Selective Training and Service Act (1940) 18, 154–155, 158
sergeants **29**, **193**; first **53**, **84**, **174**, **217**; cavalry **41**, **58**, **62**, **65**, **67**; infantry **23**, **33**, **92**, **115**, **118**, **132**, **140**, **141**, **176**; staff **155**, **171**; US Army Air Force **159**, **163**US Marine Corps **191**, **211**
Shafter, Maj-Gen William 55, 57, 58, 96, 100, 101
Sharpe, Pvte William 44
Shaw, S/Sgt Ford M. 182
Shaw, Col Robert Gould 12
Shaw, Sgt Thomas 72
Shellman, Sgt James **176**
Sheppard, S/Sgt James A. **159**
Sheridan, Gen Philip 24, 37, 38, 40, 66
Sierra Bonitos, Arizona **48**
Sierra Piñito (1886) 16, 73
signalman 3rd class, US Navy **204**
Silver Star **101**, 108–109, 168, 187, **209**, 218
Sioux tribe 39; uprising (1890–91) 77
Sitting Bull, Chief 78
Skinner, Lt-Cdr Carlton, USCG 214
Smith, Lt Fred 42
Smith, Sgt J. P. 97
Smith, Cpl Luchious 104–105
Smith, Chief Engineer T. A. **215**
Smith, Lt W. E. 105
Smither, Lt R. G. 57
Smoky Hill River 32–33, 34
Solomon Islands 201 *see also* Bougainville
Soule, Will **35**
South Carolina Infantry (African Descent), 1st 8
Southern Plains Campaign (1867–75) 14–15, 42–54
Spaatz, Lt-Gen Carl 165
Spangenburg, USS 199
Spanish-American War (1898) 16, 92, 96–112, **99**, **100**, **104**, **105**, **107**, 113, 145, 146, **148**; casualties and recognition 108–109
Spanish troops 100, 101, 102, 103, 104, 106, 109, 112
Spillsbury, Lemuel H. 130
Springarn, Dr Joel E. 133
Staked Plains, Texas Panhandle 41, 48, **51**, 51–52; 1875–77 campaign 15, 55–57
Stance, Sgt Emanuel 46
Stanford, Ted **168**
Stanton, Edwin M. 9, 10
Stevens, 1st Sgt Jacob W. 115
Stewart, Ollie 175
Stillwell, Jack 38
Stockholm **144**
Stokes, Pvte Earnest 117
Stoney, Pvte Bruce 141
Stowers, Cpl Freddie 140
Stuckey, Pvte Amos 117
Sublett, Ens Frank Ellis, USN **196**
Swann, Steward's Mate Alonzo A. **202**
Symington, Stuart 217

T

Tabon-Tabon (1900) 17, 120
Tafoya, José 56
Tagbac (1900) 16, 120
Tampa, Florida 97, 98
Tampa Morning Tribune 97
tanks **167**, **177**
Tank Battalion, 758th (formerly 78th) 18, 155
Tank Battalion, 761st 19, **167**, 168–169, **171**; Company B 168
Tank Battalion, 784th **168**
Tank Destroyer Battalion, 827th 169–172
tank destroyers 168, 169–173, **171**
Tayabacoa, rescue at (1898) 16, 109–111
Taylor, Lt Harvey 138
Taylor, Pvte Lloyd A. **156**
technician 3rd Grade **190**
technician 4th grade **193**
technicans 5th Grade **186**, **190**
Tennessee Cavalry (Unionist), 13th 13
Tennessee Infantry (African Descent), 3rd 10
Terrazas, Gen Joaquin 70
Terry, Sgt Gilbert A. **176**
Texas 22, 25, 34, 42, 68–70, 76, 77
Texas, West, campaign in (1875–81) 15, 55–58
Texas "Panhandle" **51**, 51–52; 1875–77 campaign 15, 55–57
Thomas, Adj-Gen Lorenzo 9, 10
Thompkins, Pvte William H. 109–110
Thompson, Maj J. M. 115
Thompson, PFC William 219
Thornburgh, Maj Thomas T. **25**, 62
Tibbs, Pvte Kenneth J., USMC 212
Tinaja de los Palmos 68
Titus, Tpr Joseph 58
To Secure These Rights 19, 216
Tompkins, Maj Frank 125, 126
Tongue River Indian Agency 95
Trimble, Pvte Andrew 44
Trippe, Capt P. E. **116**
troopers, cavalry **56**, **58**, **63**, **85**, **100**, 149
Troxel, Capt O. C. 148
Truck companies, Port and Amphibious 186–187
Truman, President Harry S. 19, 176, 182, 214, 216, 217
trumpeter **29**
Tucker, W/O Carlyle M. **176**
Turner, Cpl David 32
Turner, Maj Thomas P. 13
Tuskegee Airmen *see* US Army Air Force: Pursuit Squadron, 99th
Tuskegee Army Air Field, Alabama 19, **161**, 163, 164–165, 216; officers' club 164
Tuskegee Normal and Industrial Institute 133
Two-Strike, Chief 79, **81**, 81

U

Ullmann, Gen Daniel 9
Ulna **147**
Umbles, Sgt William 56, 57
uniform
    1866–91 82–85
    1872-pattern **20**, **29**, **51**, **53**, **56**, **58**, 83, 84
    1882-pattern **58**, **81**, **85**, 145
    1898-pattern **110**, **116**, 145–146

1902-pattern **116**, **132**, **146**, 146–147, 148, **149**, **150**

armor and artillery units **171**

infantry, WWII **183**

pre–World War I 145–149

US Army Air Force **163**

US Marine Corps **211**

World War I 145–149

World War II **163**, **174**, 188–192, **190**, **193**, **211**

Zouave 82

see also equipment

Union forces, African-Americans in 8–13, 14

United States declares war on Germany (1917) 17, 131

US Air Force 219–220; Bomb Wing, 98th **219**

US Army Air Force (formerly US Army Air Corps) **156**, 161–168, **163**

Bombardment Group (Medium), 477th **163**, 166–167, 168

Bombardment Squadrons, 616th through 619th 166

cadets **161**

equipment **163**

Fighter Group, 33rd 165

Fighter Group, 332nd 18, **159**, **162**, **164**, 164, 165, 166; officers' club **162**

Fighter (formerly Pursuit) Squadron, 99th ("Tuskegee Airmen") 18, 161–162, **163**, 163, 164, 165–166, 197

Fighter Squadrons, 100th & 101st 164

Fighter Squadrons, 301st & 302nd 164

Freeman Field, Indiana, and officers' club 167

Godman Field, Kentucky 167

Selfridge Field, Michigan 166–167

Tuskegee Army Airfield *see* Tuskegee Army Air Field, Alabama

uniform **163**

US Army begins integration via Special Regulations No. 600-629-1 19, 217

US Army National Guard 131, 133

Columbia, District of, 1st Separate Bn 131

Connecticut, 1st Separate Company 131

Illinois, 8th 131, 133

Maryland, 1st Separate Company 131

Massachusetts, Company L 131

New York, 15th 131, 133, 134, 136; color guard **134** *see also* Infantry, 369th

Ohio, 9th Bn 131

Tennessee, Company G 133

US Cavalry Journal 148

US Coast Guard 203, 205, 213–214; African Americans integrated into crew of single cutter 18, 214; officers **214**; uniforms, WWII **204**

US Colored Heavy Artillery, 6th 13

US Colored Light Artillery, 2nd 13

US Colored Troops (USCT) 10–11

US Colored Troops, 4th **9**

US Colored Troops, 116th 25

US Marine Corps 206–212; ammunition companies 210, 212; Ammunition Company, 4th **209**; Defense Battalion, 1st 209; Defense Battalion, 51st 208–209; Defense Battalion, 52nd 206, 209–210; depot companies 210, 212; in Korean War

220; Letter of Instruction 421: 207; Marine Ammunition Companies, 1st & 11th 212; Marine Depot Companies, 1st & 11th 212; Marine Division, 1st 19, **207**, 212, 220; Marines, 7th **207**; ordered to admit African Americans into its ranks 18, 206; recruits **191**; uniform, WWII **211**

US Merchant Marine 214–215, **215**

US Military Academy, West Point 27, 154, 162

US Navy: begins integration via Circular Letter 48–46: 19, 216; Construction Battalion, 34th **203**; construction battalions (CBs or "Seabees") 18, 201–202, **207**; first ship (USS *Mason*) crewed entirely by African Americans 19, 197–199; "Golden Thirteen" officers 195, **196**; gun crew **202**; in Korean War 220; PC (patrol craft) 1264 199–200; Port Chicago disaster (1944) 202–203, 205; Seventh Fleet **218**; Steward's Mate "Dorie" Miller 195–197, **198**; USS *Mason* (DE 529) 19, 197–199; WAVES (Women Accepted for Volunteer Emergency Service) **200**; in WWII 195–205, **204**

US Signal Corps 95, 102

US Volunteer Cavalry, 1st ("Rough Riders") 6, 92, 99, 102, 103, 104, 106, 108

US Volunteer Infantry (USVI) 108

US Volunteer Infantry, 48th 108, 114, 115

US Volunteer Infantry, 49th 115, 119

Ute Campaign, Colorado (1879) 15, 62–64

V

Valencia 115

Vara de Rey, Gen Joaquin 100

Victorio, Chief 28, 64, 66, **67**, 67–68, 69, 70

Victorio Campaign, New Mexico (1879–81) 15–16, 64–72, **65**

Viele, Capt Charles D. 50, 52, 69

Villa, Francisco "Pancho", and his forces 92, 121, **122**, 122, 124, 125, 130

Vincent, 1Lt Frederick R. **47**, 47

W

Waesche, Adm Russell R. 214

Walker, Cpl John 104–105

Waller, Pvte Reuben 37, 38

Walley, Pvte Augustus 71, 72, **101**, 109

Wanton, Pvte George 109–110, 130

War Department Circular No. 124: 216

Ward, Capt R. G. 11

Warm Springs Apaches 64, 65–66, **67**, 67–68, 69–70; campaign (1880) 28

Washington, Cpl M. 117

Washington, Pvte Frank 141–142

Watkins, Pvte William 31

Webster, Pvte Tillman 141

West Virginia, USS 195–196, 197, **198**

Westmoreland, William C. 162

Wham, Maj Joseph W. 73–74, 75

Wheeler, Pvte James 74

Wheeler, Maj-Gen Joseph 96, 99, 100

White, Col Horton V. 218

Whitehead, Lt H. C. 105

Wichita Agency 49, 50–51

Wickoff, Col 102

Wilberforce University, Xenia, Ohio 28

Wilks, Sgt Jacob B. 42, 43–44, 85

Willard, Lt H. O. 105

Williams, Cathay 31, 82

Williams, Pvte Jerry 30

Williams, Sgt Moses 71, 72

Williams, Pvte Squire 74

Williams, Capt William J. 111

Wills, Ens Frances, USN **200**

Wilson, Cpl William O. 79, **80**, 80

Winged Arrow, USS 210

Wint, Maj Theodore J. 99, 104, 105

Wisconsin, USS **218**

Wolley, Elbert 109

Woman's Heart 50

Women's Army Corps (WAC) **189**, **192**, **193**

see also female buffalo soldier

Wood, Col Leonard 99

Wood, Sgt Leslie B. **176**

Woods, Sgt Brent 72

Woods Jr, Col Samuel A. 207–208

Woodward, Col Charles F. 111, 112

Woodward, PFC Luther **209**

World War I (1917–18) 6, 17, 92, 131–144; formations 133–134; French Army, integration into 135, 136; officers 133; service in Europe 134–144, **135**, **137**, **140**, **141**, **143**, **151**

World War II (1941–45) 6, 18–19, 154, 156–212, 213–214, 215

US Army in 160–194; armored force 168–173, **171**; artillery **169**, **171**, **172**, 173, 175–176, **190**; cavalry 173, **174**; infantry **176**, 176–182, **177**, **178**, **179**, **180**, **181**, **182**, **183**; life overseas 194; support & service troops 184–188, **185**, **186**, **187**, **190**, **193**; tank destroyers 168, 169–173, **171**; uniforms **174**, 188–192, **190**, **193**; volunteer replacements, infantry 179–182;

see also US Army Air Force

US Marine Corps in 206–212

see also US Marine Corps

US Navy in 195–205, **204**

see also US Navy

Wounded Knee Campaign (1890–91) 16, 78–81

Wright, Capt Henry 81

Wright, Lt Henry H. 64

Wright, Lt Henry J. 59

Wright, Lowry G. 184

Wynn, Seaman 1st class Raymond **205**

Y

Yankton 76

Yarborough, William P. 162

Yauco (1898) 16, 111–112

Yech'on, recapture of (1950) 218–219

Young, Col Charles 27, 28, **124**, 125, 126, 130, 133, 161, 162

Young, Midshipman T. J. **215**

Z

Zealandia 115